My Times
in the Hudson Valley

The Insider's Guide to Historic Homes, Scenic Drives,
Restaurants, Museums, Farm Produce & Points of Interest

By Harold Faber
Former Correspondent for
The New York Times

Most of the following articles were originally published
in *The New York Times* and are reprinted here with the
permission of *The New York Times*.

BLACK·DOME
Black Dome Press
RR 1, Box 42
Hensonville, NY 12439
(518) 734-6357
fax (518) 734-5802
e-mail: BlackDomeP@aol.com

Black Dome Press Corp.
RR1, Box 422
Hensonville, NY 12439
Tel: (518) 734-6357
Fax: (518) 734-5802

First Edition

Most of the articles in this book first appeared in *The New York Times* and are reprinted here with the permission of *The New York Times*.

Library of Congress Cataloging-in-Publication Data

Faber, Harold.
    My times in the Hudson Valley : the insider's guide to historic homes, scenic drives, restaurants, museums, fresh farm produce & points of interest / by Harold Faber.--1st ed.
        p. cm.
    "Most of the following articles were originally published in the New York times."
    ISBN 1-883789-14-1
    1. Hudson River Valley (N.Y. and N.J.)--Description and travel.
    2. Hudson River Valley (N.Y. and N.J.)--Guidebooks. I. Title.
    F127.H8F32   1997
    917.47'3--dc21   97-33995
                                                                          CIP

Design by Carol Clement, Artemisia, Inc.
Cover art by Carol Clement

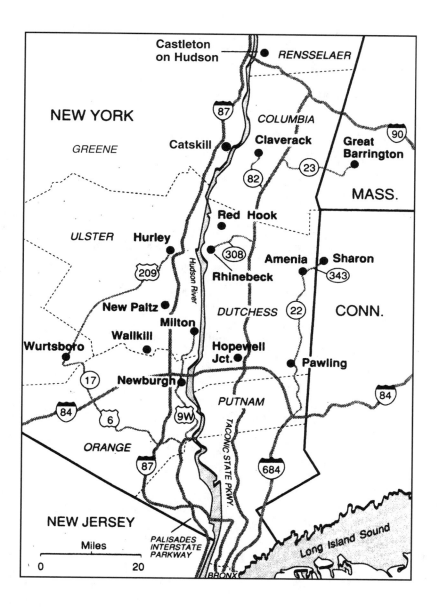

BOOKS BY HAROLD FABER

George Marshall: Soldier and Statesman, 1963
From Sea to Sea: The Growth of the United States, 1967
The Book of Laws, 1979
The Discoverers of America, 1992

WRITTEN WITH DORIS FABER

American Heroes of the 20th Century, 1967
The Assassination of Martin Luther King, 1978
Martin Luther King, 1986
Mahatma Ghandi, 1986
We, the People: The Story of the United States Constitution, 1987
Great Lives: American Government, 1988
The Birth of a Nation: The Early Years of the United States, 1989
Great Lives: Nature and the Environment, 1991
Great Lives: American Literature, 1995

BOOKS EDITED

The Kennedy Years, 1964
The New York Times Election Handbook, 1964
The Road to the White House, 1965
The New York Times Election Handbook, 1968
The New York Times Guide for New Voters, 1972
Luftwaffe: A History, 1977
The Mill on the Roeliff Jansen Kill, 1993

CONTENTS

INTRODUCTION

After more than fifty years of reporting and editing for *The New York Times*, I retired in 1995. For the last twenty-five years of that time, I wrote news of the Hudson Valley, working from my home in Ancram in Columbia County, in the middle of a lovely dairy farm area.

In that time, my stories covered a wide range—apples and cherries, farms and farm economics, corn and cows, flowers and weeds, historic houses and museums, trains and roads, tourist attractions and restaurants, and, above all, the Hudson River—its beauties, its fish, and its pollution.

Together, these stories present a changing picture of the Hudson Valley, from essentially a rural farm area to a rural residential area. In the years that I have lived and worked there, the most striking fact has been the decline in farming; the number of farms dropped precipitously, especially dairy farms. The once familiar sight of black and white Holstein cows grazing in pastures is now largely a memory, and empty barns stand forlornly on once-busy farms.

Among the other trends I've observed are an increase in the number of people moving up to second and vacation homes in the rural areas of the valley; a rising tide of concern about the environment, especially about the Hudson River and its banks; a rapid expansion in the number of art galleries, antique shops and little theaters; and a phenomenal explosion of restaurants and cafes. Sometimes it seems that new restaurants and cafes spring up as fast as the dandelions in spring—and many, of course, die. It is part, no doubt, of the national preoccupation with the dubious concept that tourism will bring economic prosperity.

Every town and city along the river, and inland, too, is trying to attract tourists and their dollars, leading me to wonder: If everybody becomes a tourist, who will be left to serve them? But that interest in tourism gave me the opportunity to visit wonderful places in the Hudson Valley and to describe them to residents of the metropolitan New York area, as you will see in the following pages.

But before I present those pictures of the beautiful Hudson Valley, let me tell you something about me and how I got to write them. Following is an article I wrote a while back for the *Silurian News*, the newspaper of the Silurians, an organization of old-time newspaper reporters and editors (and now, media journalists and public relations people), that describes how I got that glorious opportunity.

(May 9, 1990)

Back in September, 1939, two important things happened—World War II broke out and I wrote my first story for *The New York Times*.

Fifty years later, that war and a couple of others are long since over, but here I am, after a series of ups and downs as a reporter, war correspondent and editor, still writing for *The Times*.

In 1939, at the age of 19 while a student, I was hired as the City College correspondent on the recommendation of Irving Rosenthal, professor of journalism. I was managing editor of the *Campus*, the college newspaper, and somehow impressed him.

I became part of a long and distinguished line of City College kids who made it at *The Times* (like Abe Raskin before me and Abe Rosenthal after). The salary: $12 a week, but remember those were the days of five-cent subway fares.

My beat included the Board of Higher Education, the governing body for the four city colleges as well as the college itself. My first story was one paragraph about the enrollment for the year at City College, but things got more exciting after that. There were two running stories: The Rapp-Coudert investigation of communism at the city colleges and the furor about the appointment of Bertrand Russell as a professor at City College. Even though I attended classes as a senior that year, they couldn't compare with the excitement of the old city room and writing a story.

David H. Joseph, the city editor, sat with his back to the windows on 43rd Street, next to his assistant, Walter Fenton, to whom I usually reported.

In those days, the city room was less than half the size it is today, torrid in the summer before the days of air-conditioning, with old wooden desks and standard Royal and Underwood typewriters (before electric typewriters or computers). Reporters typed on paper with carbons for extra copies and even cried "copy" for boys (no girls) to come and take it to the desk.

I sat at a desk next to Bill Carney, who had just returned from covering the Spanish Civil War. My colleagues were Lester Bernstein, the Columbia correspondent, and Murray Ilson, the N.Y.U. correspondent, all of us working our tails off to get a real job as a full-time reporter. (We all succeeded.)

Around me in the later afternoons and evenings were the stars of the city staff: Ray Daniell, "Old Jim" Hagerty, Warren Moscow, Frank Adams, Russell Porter, Barney Darnton, Craig Thompson, Kathleen McLaughlin, "Young Jim" Hagerty, Milton Bracker and the incomparable, gentle Mike Berger, the friend of all the copy boys and kids on the staff.

In that simple world, Joseph believed in covering everything. Four or more reporters covered politics, two labor, every ship coming into New York

Harbor was met to interview passengers about the state of affairs abroad, and a dozen or so covered police news.

He also believed in keeping a large staff on hand in case something happened. So, every evening between about 7 p.m. and 10 p.m., one, two or even three bridge games got under way while reporters waited for a "good night" or a disaster.

I remember my first major fast-breaking story very well: the night the Board of Higher Education met to decide whether to retain Bertrand Russell. I was disappointed that Joseph assigned Frank Adams, his top general news reporter, to cover, not me, but he asked me to assist Frank. I was devastated, but Frank was very understanding.

It was an exciting night. In those days, before TV and radio news reporters, a dozen or more print reporters turned up from the *Herald Tribune*, *News*, *Mirror*, *World-Telegram*, *Journal-American*, *City News*, *Standard News*, the AP, *Brooklyn Eagle*, *Post* and out of town papers.

I was one of the only reporters there who had covered the board before. But Ken Bilby of the *Trib* knew how to operate. In advance, he arranged to have a board member meet him with the result in the men's room after the vote was taken, but before it was announced.

But I had some friends, too. I watched one of them slip a document to Ordway Tead, chairman of the Board. Then he handed me a copy. It was a lawsuit challenging the appointment. I gave it to Frank. The *Trib* beat us by one edition on the verdict but we had an exclusive on the lawsuit.

I didn't get put on the staff as a reporter until a few months after I graduated. Starting salary: $25 a week.

After four years of interruption in the Army in World War II, I returned to the city staff in 1946, doing all kinds of stories. A short about the death of a giraffe in the Central Park Zoo was selected later for "A Treasury of Great Reporting." Here it is:

The New York Times, October 23, 1946

Leo the giraffe, one of the favorite attractions at the Central Park Zoo, died suddenly on Monday. He was sixteen years old.

He was born in Kenya, Africa, a member of the family Giraffe camelopardalis, which became well known in Tertiary times and spread all over southern Europe and India. In recent years, however, the family has restricted its activities to Africa, south of the Sahara.

Leo came to this country on July 14, 1937, when he was seven, with his first wife, Pauline. They immediately settled in the Manhattan Zoo and began to earn their living as attractions for crowds of humans.

Pauline died in 1943.

"Leo, was everybody's favorite," one of the keepers recalled. "They came from all over to see Leo."

The giraffe was discovered ill at eight o'clock Sunday morning. A veterinary was called, but before definitive medical treatment could be supplied he died. The cause of death was believed to be tuberculosis, with pneumonia complications.

Surviving are his widow, Pauline II, and two cousins at the Bronx Park Zoo, Jack and Jill. He had no children.

Interment was private, following cremation by the Department of Sanitation.

In 1950, I went off to Korea as a war correspondent along with Bill Lawrence (Political Bill, to differentiate him from Atomic Bill Laurence) and Dick Johnston, but didn't last very long. I got shot in the leg along the Naktong River in September, 1950, then injured in a plane crash.

When I got out of Walter Reed Army Hospital in Washington, I married the reporter who had sat at the next desk to mine in the city room, Doris Greenberg (who had been an N.Y.U. correspondent before she became a full time reporter).

Shortly after I returned to the paper in 1951, I became day national news editor, making assignments for the national staff and master-minding political elections.

Those were the days when the paper was divided into day and night staffs: The day staff covered the news, the night staff got it into the paper. Integration came later in the regime of Turner Catledge as managing editor.

I was on the desk for the three major stories of 1950s and 1960s, working with several superb reporters: the black revolution in the South, with Johnny Popham and Claude Sitton; man's venture into space, with Dick Witkin and Walter Sullivan; and the assassination of President Kennedy, with Tom Wicker.

In that period, I also started to edit books, the first being *The Kennedy Years*, with members of *The Times* staff, and to write some of my own, among them *George Marshall*, a biography of the World War II commander in chief, and *From Sea to Sea*, a U.S. history.

When *The Times* expanded into other fields, I went upstairs as editorial director of a new Book and Education Division, where we started the "Large Type Weekly," which continues; several school-oriented newspapers, which have disappeared; and many ill-fated books.

When that venture collapsed, my wife and I moved to our farm in upstate New York where we write books together and where I became the Hudson Valley correspondent for *The Times*.

<hr>

As I said at the beginning of this introduction, my writing for *The Times* ended in 1995.

CHAPTER 1

A Hudson Valley Tour

A good place to start is with a tour of the Hudson Valley that I knew and wrote about. My Hudson Valley was defined by the internal bureaucracy of *The New York Times*, which had a large suburban staff covering Westchester and Rockland Counties. So my area of coverage began at the northern ends of those counties and extended north to Albany and Troy, and even as far north as the river ran, to its origin on the southern slopes of Mount Marcy in the Adirondack Mountains.

A word of caution as you read the following articles, which date back to 1972—I have eliminated prices for restaurants and hotels, as well as admission fees, which have escalated rapidly in recent years.

SHUNPIKING IN THE VALLEY
(April 30, 1978)

I am continually astonished by friends from the New York City area who have never visited the major attractions at their doorstep in the Mid-Hudson Valley. They seem to be obeying an iron law of tourism that says that natural beauty is enhanced by its distance from home, a premise I disagree with. They speed up the Taconic State Parkway or the Thruway to the Adirondacks or Vermont or someplace else—if they're not off to Greece or Spain or the Riviera.

If they'd stayed closer to home, they would have discovered that on a number of fascinating back roads only hours from Times Square are some of the most splendid vistas of incomparable beauty along the Hudson River, baronial homes rivaling the chateaus of the Loire, small museums that are miniature gems of American history. All are particularly appealing in apple blossom time, now through mid-May.

Recently I put together a shunpike Baedeker of the Mid-Hudson Valley for people with a weekend or more to spend on an automobile tour. My wife and I went over the entire 200 miles in about eight hours, stopping only for lunch and to collect information, but I do not recommend so speedy a tour for other travelers. Since it's impossible to see everything on a one-day trip, I suggest selecting one area for leisurely day-tripping, or staying overnight once or twice.

A few additional words of caution: Some country roads have as many potholes as New York City streets, so drive carefully. There's no way to avoid short stretches through crowded shopping strips, so be prepared for interludes of traffic jams. It's sometimes difficult to get down to the river's edge because of railroad tracks (some with unguarded crossings), riverfront mansions and industrial development, so expect an occasional frustration.

THE EAST BANK

A good place to start is the eastern end of the Bear Mountain Bridge. Instead of crossing the bridge, take State Route 9D north along the Hudson River (7.5 miles) to Garrison, where the Boscobel Restoration overlooks the river opposite West Point. It takes 45 minutes to complete a guided tour of the elegantly furnished Federal style mansion, completed in 1808, but there's no time limit for enjoying the grounds and the river view. Tip from the management: Low broad-heeled shoes are required for walking through the building.

From Boscobel it's four miles along 9D to Cold Spring. Just before entering the village, about 200 yards south of the Grand Union, is the usually uncrowded Foundry School Museum, operated by the Putnam County Historical Society. It displays tools, paintings, old photographs and diagrams of the foundry that made cannon for the Army in the early 1800s.

Left on State Route 301 in Cold Spring and over the railroad tracks at the end of Main Street is a small but pleasant picnic area that juts into the Hudson. On the left is a view of West Point, on the right Storm King Mountain and in the center river boats. It's a good place to watch boat launchings, to picnic on benches or just sit.

Back on 9D, the road is as close to the river as it ever gets, with changing views of the Hudson. Seven miles north in Beacon, turn right on Teller Avenue and continue to the corner of Van Nydeck Street. There you'll find the Madam Brett Homestead, a little throwback in American history operated by the Daughters of the American Revolution.

Catharyna Brett (1687-1764), the daughter of Francis Rombout, a Mayor of New York, was a feminist. A widow, she operated a grist mill, a Hudson River sloop and a trading post and, in an uncharacteristic move for her era, created small plots from the 85,000 acres she had inherited and sold them to settlers. The home, built in 1714 and occupied by the family until 1955, contains furniture, dishes, clothing and other things that she and her family used.

HYDE PARK

From the Brett Homestead, the easiest way to continue is to retrace some city streets back to 9D. I haven't found any good way to avoid the traffic mess on 9D and U.S. 9 through Wappinger's Falls and Poughkeepsie (about 27 miles), but it's not as bad on Sunday as it is on weekdays. After that is one of the best-known, and deservedly so, tourist attractions in the entire state, the Franklin D. Roosevelt Home and Museum at Hyde Park.

Perhaps because it is so close, many New Yorkers have never entered the F.D.R. complex. For foreign visitors, it is at the head of the list of things they must see. For those of us who lived through the Roosevelt years and served in the armed forces in World War II, it is still a goosebump experience.

The home, built in 1826 and rehabilitated in 1915, is a large rambling country house. The 32nd President was reared there, and when he and his wife, Eleanor, were not in the White House they spent much of their time there with his mother, Sara Delano Roosevelt. (On cassette, Eleanor Roosevelt, in her unmistakable high-pitched voice, describes life there.) The museum is crammed with pictures, gifts, maps, papers and other memorabilia of the Roosevelt Presidency and World War II.

Storm King Mountain from Cold Spring.
Photograph by Klara B. Sauer. Courtesy of Scenic Hudson.

Two miles north of the F.D.R. Home, on U.S. 9, which is crowded with motels and restaurants, is the less well-known Vanderbilt Mansion.

The Italian Renaissance mansion, built in 1898 for Fredrick Vanderbilt, grandson of the commodore, is a breathtaking permanent memorial to the baronial life of the American magnates of the turn of the century.

As a counterpart to the opulence of the mansion, the grounds are simpler but well tended by the National Park Service. There are views of the Hudson and a place to picnic at Bard Rock at the northern end of the estate.

Another baronial estate open to the public, 1.5 miles north on U.S. 9, is the Ogden and Ruth Livingston Mills Mansion in Staatsburg, now a state park. It is an imposing 65-room structure, with palatial art, tapestries, furnishings and exciting river views.

MCINTOSH COUNTRY

From Staatsburg it's 6.5 miles north on U. S. 9 to Rhinebeck, an interesting village with bookstores, country stores, a movie house showing old films, an arts center, a crafts fair in June, the Dutchess County Fair in August and some good eating establishments, one of which, the Beekman Arms, contends that it is the oldest inn in continuous operation in America.

A little north of Rhinebeck, turn left on State Route 9G. Six miles from the intersection, turn left again—to Clermont, the ancestral home of the Livingston family, now operated as a state park.

The grounds, overlooking the Hudson, are among the most beautiful of any along the river that are open to the public for picnics and just looking.

Clermont is at the southwestern tip of Columbia County, which is one of the major apple-producing areas of the nation. Between 9G and U.S. 9 are many country roads that afford leisurely driving between trees snow white with apple blossoms in May and later with McIntosh apples, the premier apple of New York and still one of the best. They will not be ready for pick-it-yourselfers, however, until October.

Coming out of Clermont, continue on the country road to the left until it joins 9G in Germantown. From there, it's seven miles farther north to Olana, the Persian castle built by Frederic Edwin Church, a painter of the Hudson River, with sweeping views of the river and of the Catskill Mountains.

The city of Hudson, about four miles north of Olana on 9G, has three attractions: a revitalized Warren Street, which resembles a miniature Georgetown; a Parade Walk overlooking the river, dating from 1785, and the American Museum of Fire Fighting on Harry Howard Avenue across from the Hudson Middle School at the northern end of the city.

THE WEST BANK

Back near Olana, the Rip Van Winkle Bridge crosses the Hudson River into Catskill, which has numerous motels for a midpoint overnight halt. When you resume the journey, take U.S. 9W—one of the worst roads in the state because of cement plants and trucks and 90-degree turns—south 14 miles to Saugerties. Seaman Park there is noted for its chrysanthemums that bloom in the fall. From Saugerties it's 10.5 miles on Route 212 to Woodstock, a hide-out for artists since the late 1800's. Now it is a "with-it" small village, with art galleries, boutiques and highly individualistic homes—well worth a stop.

Out of Woodstock, State Route 375 and then State Route 28 lead into Kingston, where in 1777 George Clinton took the oath of office as the first Governor of New York and where the first Senate sat, giving the city the title of "first capital of New York." The stone house where the Senate met has been restored and is operated by the State Historic Trust. To get there take Washington Avenue, turning left at the second traffic light, then right on Fair Street.

The Senate House is the anchor to Kingston's former Stockade Area, where Peter Stuyvesant built a wall to protect the Dutch settlement from the Indians in the 1630's. The area has been rebuilt into pleasant shopping and walking streets, flanked by old Dutch stone houses.

From Kingston, State Route 213 runs west along the Rondout Creek, then south 10.5 miles to Perrine's Bridge, built in 1860 and said to be the oldest covered bridge in the state. For photographers, the wooden bridge across the Wallkill provides a fascinating contrast to the ultra-modern Thruway bridge a few yards to the west.

Seven miles farther south on 213, which loops a little north before turning west, is High Falls, which was a key point on the old Delaware & Hudson Canal, chartered in 1825 to carry anthracite coal over the mountain from the mines of northern Pennsylvania. Several locks of the canal are maintained as a tourist attraction. Nearby on Mohonk Street is the Delaware & Hudson Canal Museum, with numerous exhibits of canal lore.

THE SHAWANGUNKS

Mohonk Road climbs slowly up the Shawangunk (pronounced Shongum) Mountains for fives miles to the gates of the Mohonk Mountain House, an improbable structure with red-roof turrets and sprawling wings in the wilderness. One of the last of the huge old-time Victorian chateaus that once were the ultimate in luxury for Catskill vacationers, it has the atmosphere of a medieval castle and manor and was the locale for *The Stone Bull*, the thriller by Phyllis A. Whitney.

As one example of Mohonk's scope, it is two miles by private road to the hotel, which sits at an elevation of 1,253 feet. It has 305 rooms, is open all year and offers what its brochure accurately describes as spectacular views. Its Skytop Tower, across Mohonk Lake at 1,546 feet, provides equally spectacular views.

Mohonk (914-255-1000 or 212-253-2244) operates on the American plan but also welcomes day visitors. But a few words of warning: No liquor is served except at the table, no smoking is the rule, and do not go for a quick tour. It takes time to appreciate Mohonk's extensive gardens, trails and views.

If you pass by Mohonk, it's six miles on the same mountain road and then by way of State Route 299 to New Paltz, which will celebrate its 300th anniversary this June (1978). Immediately after the road crosses the bridge over the Wallkill, take the first left turn into Huguenot Street, which New Paltz calls "the oldest street in America with its original houses"—stone houses, some dating to 1692.

BACK TO THE HUDSON

Out of New Paltz, State Route 32 winds through some of Ulster County's extensive apple orchards to Newburgh, a depressed city with gorgeous panoramic views of the Hudson River and of Mount Beacon on the east bank. One interesting way to see them contrapuntally is to turn left (east) on State Route 17K, a Broadway that is much wider than New York's Broadway, into downtown Newburgh. The river is framed between rows of buildings.

A right turn on Liberty Street leads to Washington's Headquarters, probably the best-known of all the places where he slept during the Revolutionary War. It's operated by the State Historic Trust. Even its parking lot has a magnificent river view.

Washington and his wife, Martha, lived in Newburgh for almost a year and a half between the time Cornwallis surrendered at Yorktown in 1781 and the signing of the Treaty of Paris, which ended the war in 1783. In addition to the stone house in which they slept, the complex includes a museum with portraits, artifacts and documents of the Revolutionary era in the Hudson Valley.

Newburgh is attempting to refurbish its riverfront, with parking lots overlooking the river and a small park with picnic benches. But the river vistas remain scarred by the sight of rotting boats and docks and cranes loading scrap iron on railroad cars.

Out of Newburgh, U.S. 9W leads south four miles into State Route 218, the spectacular Storm King Highway, which hugs the side of Storm King Mountain until Cornwall-on-Hudson. One stop especially attractive for children is the Museum of the Hudson Highlands. It is a nature museum with live animals, many of them under signs marked "Please touch."

Five miles farther south, the Storm King Highway enters the grounds of the United States Military Academy at West Point, where roads are open to the public every day. If I had to choose just one spot on the west bank of the Hudson for out-of-town visitors to see, it would be West Point,

West Point is not a place to hurry through. In addition to offering splendid views of the river, it affords an opportunity to observe the cadets in action, with numerous sports events (some of them open to the public without charge), parades and daily drills. A map and a printed guide are available at the entrance gate.

The grounds also house the West Point Museum, with displays of banners, flags, medals and dioramas of military campaigns and other military history. If there's time, stop at the Hotel Thayer which offers meals and lodging and, once again, splendid views of the Hudson.

About a mile south of West Point, 218 meets U.S. 9W again. From there it's about three miles to the Bear Mountain Bridge and the end of this springtime tour.

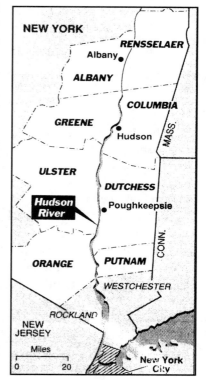

CHAPTER 2

A Trip Up the River

The Hudson River has its source in Lake Tear in the Clouds on the slopes of Mount Marcy, the highest peak in the Adirondack Mountains. It flows through sparsely settled areas for a while and is, therefore, relatively clean until it reaches Glens Falls, where it starts picking up industrial wastes from a more highly concentrated population.

Farther downstream, the Mohawk River joins the Hudson, bringing with it water and pollution from Schenectady, Amsterdam and farther west. Just south of the confluence is Albany, the capital of New York State. The Hudson River then flows south to New York City and the Atlantic Ocean, about 315 miles from its crystal clear source in the Adirondacks.

Following is an article I wrote for the magazine section of *The Times*, which was never printed, but which remains a detailed picture of a trip up the river from the ocean on a freighter bringing cargo to the port of Albany in 1973. The number of ocean-going ships using the river has dropped since then, but the trip remains the same.

(AUGUST 1, 1973)

The Hudson River is not as long as the Mississippi, but it is wider. It does not meander as much, but it is deeper. Like the Mississippi, the Hudson has had its showboats and its paddlewheel steamboat races, but, unlike the Mississippi, it has had no Huck Finn or "Old Man River" to make it part of the national heritage. Even though there have been scores of books written about the Hudson, none can compare with Mark Twain's *Life on the Mississippi*, let alone the adventures of Huck and Tom.

Like the Mississippi, though, the Hudson is a remarkable river and, to borrow a phrase from Mark Twain, well worth reading about. In its scant 315 mile course, it is an estuary, a sewer, a trout stream, a swimming hole, a source of drinking water, a dumping ground for industrial wastes, a spawning ground for shad and striped bass, a coolant for power plants, a carrier of tugs and barges, a gateway to the Great Lakes and the St. Lawrence River and a channel for freighters, tankers, sail and power boats.

Unlike the rampaging Mississippi, the Hudson flows gently to sea. But life on the Hudson these days is one damned controversy after another.

One dark and rainy night recently, a small Swedish freighter, the Maria Gorthon, *headed up the Hudson River on the evening tide toward Albany. I had boarded the ship the day before at the State Pier in New London, Connecticut, where part of her cargo of wood pulp had been unloaded.*

With the lights of the tall buildings of Manhattan twinkling in the rain, the Maria Gorthon *sailed past the old, empty, dark and decrepit piers and sheds of the once-flourishing waterfront of the West Side, her course steady, with only a lonely tug ruffling the calm waters of the river. The ship glided through the murky waters between the light-ed apartment houses on both sides of the river, cleaving through some of the most polluted water in the United States—220 million gallons of raw sewage a day, every day, are deposited in the Hudson by the residents and industries of Manhattan, an astonishing 200 gallons a day per person.*

"Half ahead," the pilot ordered as the ship approached the abandoned 125th Street pier of the Hudson River Day Line. "Half ahead," the quartermaster replied. As the ship slowed to a speed of about seven knots, the pilot explained: "You've got to slow down as you

pass the barges working there. Otherwise they bounce up and down on the waves."

A forest of red and black cranes, illuminated by floodlights, towers above the barges and men at work on the North River Sewage Treatment Plant under construction just north of the Day Line pier. When completed sometime between 1978 and 1980, the plant will cover a 32-acre platform above the Hudson, converting sewage into concentrated sludge, which will be dumped at sea, and cleansed water, to be returned to the Hudson. Even now, while under construction, the North River project is a compendium of superlatives—it is believed to be the largest construction job of its type anywhere; it will take the longest time to be completed; and it is the most expensive. The cost, $770 million, just half of all the money it will take to clean up the Hudson.

"The day the North River plant is finished we're going to be able to say the Hudson is clean," Henry L. Diamond, the State Commissioner of Environmental Conservation, says. But that day is five to seven years off.

Near Yonkers, a small boat chugged alongside the Maria Gorthon. *As both vessels moved ahead at the same speed, two men, a Hudson River pilot and an apprentice pilot, climbed up a flimsy ladder dropped from the side of the* Maria Gorthon. *His work done, a harbor pilot climbed down. As the lights of Yonkers fell behind, on the bridge of the* Maria Gorthon *were her skipper, Captain Ragmar Annersten, a Viking-looking man in his fifties from Helsingford, where the Gorthon Lines has its home base; the pilot, Captain James Maloney, in his late fifties, with 15 years of experience on the river; the apprentice, Colin McCluney, 31, with 10 years of experience on tug boats; a quartermaster at the wheel steering the ship; a mate keeping the log and signaling changes of speed to the engine room; and me.*

Maloney asked the captain about the ship's maximum speed (15 knots) and its draft (lightly loaded, it was 15 feet deep in the water). After some calculation, he said, "We ought to be in Albany at seven o'clock, captain." It was then 9:25 p.m. "Would you like to take it, Colin?" he asked. The apprentice nodded.

"Half ahead," McCluney ordered. The senior pilot, Maloney, explained: "We're slowing down because there's an oil barge dis-

charging at Hastings. If we went too fast, we could bounce it, break-
ing lines and causing an oil spill." Oil spills are one of the river's
major problems, I had found out earlier from the Coast Guard com-
mander in Albany, who said he spent most of his time directing
cleanups of oil on the water.

As the ship sailed under the Tappan Zee Bridge, outlined by a
necklace of lights, Maloney pointed to Ossining on the right: "It's a
funny thing, with all the wonderful sights on the river, the mountains,
West Point, Hyde Park, the only thing that almost all the foreign crews
ask to see is Sing Sing."

Rounding Croton Point, the ship entered Haverstraw Bay, the
widest part of the river, three miles wide and six miles long.

Haverstraw Bay ends near Verplanck Point, one of the few places
where the tracks of the Penn Central Railroad do not block access to the
river. In 1782, Verplanck was the scene of a great military parade, with
George Washington reviewing the French troops who had helped defeat
Lord Cornwallis at Yorktown. Today, it is one of the unspoiled settle-
ments on the river, with wide streets, several old brick houses dating back
to Colonial days, and only a few standardized suburban-type houses. It is
also the home of Ace Lent, one of the most knowledgeable fishermen on
the river.

I had found him in his fish and bait shop on the point a few weeks earlier, ready as usual to talk about fish and the river: "There are more fish than
people ever dreamed of. Stripers up to 30 pounds are common. Sturgeon? You
won't believe it, but there are sturgeon in that river bigger than me." He is six
feet tall and weighs 250 pounds. "All those fish in the river going to waste, all
those millions of dollars going to Russians for caviar, and we have it right
here," he said, shaking his head.

"At one time, I could look out of my window and see 30 boats with drift
nets for shad passing by," he recalled. "Now there are none." What he sees
these days is a great increase in commercial traffic, tankers, freighters, barges,
about one ship every 20 minutes by his count. "Is the river getting cleaner?"
I asked. "What do you mean by that?" he replied. "As far as fish there are as
many as there ever were. A lot of people think there aren't any fish because
they don't know how to catch them. They don't realize that fish don't bite all
the time. Spills? The oil spill situation is getting better. Swimming? There are
some places where you can swim right now. Sure, I'd say the river is getting
better."

On the bridge of the Maria Gorthon, *just north of Stony Point, McCluney was too intent on the river ahead to talk. Wearing a black raincoat but no hat, he paced back and forth on the enclosed bridge, sometimes stepping out to the rain-swept open bridge, using field glasses at times to inspect a blur on the river, preparing to take some sort of action if he saw another ship. Maloney seemed relaxed, but he lighted one cigarette after another. "You know, Colin's riding on my license," he said. "It's still my responsibility." Maloney looked out into the night at some lights on the river when McCluney called out, "Half ahead." As the ship slowed, Maloney said: "If a tug shows three lights on its mast like that, it's pulling a load. If there are only two lights, it's pushing. You can tell by the lights even if you can't see the barges." The* Maria Gorthon *picked up speed, rounding a bend in the river in front of Indian Point, once a picnic ground for New Yorkers on excursion boats, but now one of the most controversial areas on the river.*

When I visited Consolidated Edison's nuclear power facility at Indian Point later, I was greeted by an executive vice president, a public relations man, the directors of its two research laboratories and several scientists eager to tell me "the facts" which they feel somehow have not got across to the public. Obviously on the defensive because of criticism from conservationists and the courts, along with newspaper articles about fish kills, thermal pollution and desecration of the landscape, they are baffled by the intransigence of environmental organizations, what they see as a boycott of their research and the refusal of their critics even to visit the plant.

Harry G. Woodbury Jr., Executive Vice President for Environmental Affairs, conducted me through the site, pointing out Indian Point 1, Con Edison's first nuclear plant, in operation since 1962 but now down for refueling; Indian Point 2, which has just gone "critical," producing its first power on a test basis; and Indian Point 3, under construction. On the riverfront, we visited a laboratory conducting experiments on larvae and tiny fish that get sucked up into the plant with water used for cooling despite a curtain of air bubbles and one-quarter inch metal mesh barriers. The fish killed at the barrier are counted and reported to the State Department of Environmental Conservation, they said. Some of the tiny organisms are also killed, with a mortality rate of between 7 and 39 per cent, according to Dr. Gerald Lauer, a research professor at the New York University School of Experimental Medicine, who is director of the laboratory.

The second Con Edison laboratory, operated by Texas Instruments, is located about a mile south of Indian Point, on the waterfront at Verplanck. Its objective is to study the impact of the nuclear plants on fish and other aquatic life in the river. Among the experiments under way are tagging fish to check their migratory habits, running tank tests to learn the effects of temperature and pressure on the fish, and raising fish in hatcheries. "They said we couldn't raise striped bass that way, but we are," Dr. Victor Kaczynski, technical director of the laboratory, said.

Woodbury said that Con Edison had offered to mitigate any damage it had caused, citing these alternatives under study: air curtains to prevent fish from impinging on intake screens; different sized mesh screens; noise (which he said was not very successful); pervious dikes which permit water but not fish to go through; cooling towers (recommended by the staff of the Atomic Energy Commission, but which he said were monstrously large, about half the size of a football field and perhaps 500 feet high, an intrusion on the landscape and of unknown efficiency); and fish hatcheries to replace killed fish.

"The A.E.C. staff says the striped bass kill from Indian Point 1 and 2 will be 30 to 50 per cent in the Hudson and 24 to 40 per cent in the Mid-Atlantic," he said. "But we say it's 3 per cent a year and could result in a 5 to 10 per cent loss of the total population in a 10-year period. If the damage to fish is what is postulated by the A.E.C. staff, we will put up the cooling towers and have them in operation by 1978. But before you impose a $20 million a year bill on consumers, we ought to get the facts, whether or not we are doing that kind of damage. That's why we are asking for a delay, so we can get the facts."

"Port five," McCluney ordered. The Maria Gorthon *turned five degrees to the left following the river channel north of Peekskill. "Midships," he called out. The quartermaster steered with the rudder straight, and the ship was on a steady course through the Highlands, a stretch of about 15 miles from Haverstraw Bay almost to Newburgh where the river cuts through the Appalachian Mountains.*

The hills on both sides were dark as the ship passed the Bear Mountain pier, where an occasional excursion boat still docks on a Sunday, and under the Bear Mountain Bridge. McCluney sounded the ship's whistle as she approached a blind curve at West Point, one of the few times during the entire trip that it was used. The lights of the Military Academy gleamed in the darkness as the ship turned 95 degrees to port. The channel here, more than 150 feet deep, is called "World's End" because it is so deep.

"Watch it," Maloney said. "He'll turn when you see that four-second flashing light on Magazine Point on the tip of Constitution Island." The island, named after a British fort built during the Revolutionary War, is now an Audubon reservation. As the light on the east bank of the river came into view, the ship veered to the right and continued upstream.

A storefront on Main Street in Cold Spring is the office of the Hudson River Sloop Restoration, operators of the *Clearwater*, a replica of one of the sloops that were the main form of transportation on the river in the 1800s. The *Clearwater* is now in its fifth year of duplicating those sloop voyages, this time to alert people to the problems of the river and its potential. Cold Spring is the focus of several other environmental societies that act on the theory that eternal vigilance is needed to keep "the interests" from making the Hudson an industrial sewer. They believe that Con Edison is the chief villain, that it lies about the number of fish it kills, that the State Department of Environmental Conservation is not doing its job and that not enough research is being done about the river and its problems.

I asked David Seymour, president of the Hudson River Fisherman's Association, which is an organization more of conservationists than fishermen, if the river was getting cleaner. "On the one hand we have had a gain, but on more refined analysis, we may have had a net loss," he said. He conceded that there was less sewage pollution than before, but warned against chemical pollution from heavy metals such as lead, mercury and cadmium being dumped into the river as industrial wastes.

His concerns were echoed by John J. Burns III, president of the Sloop Restoration, and several of the young men and women who have made the *Clearwater* a symbol of their struggle to keep the Hudson alive. Burns described himself as cautiously optimistic about the future of the river: "I am stopped by the feeling that we are adopting the wrong technology on municipal sewage disposal just at the time when new things are coming up. We ought to take a good hard look at the new system of reverse osmosis before we get locked into those big centralized sewage disposal plants." He thinks we may have taken a step backward with the 1972 Water Pollution Control Act, which cuts Federal spending for sewage treatment plants. In his opinion, it also undercuts the 1899 Refuse Act, which prohibits industrial discharges into the nation's waterways. Pete Seeger, the folksinger, father of the *Clearwater* and probably the person who has done the most in recent years to alert the public to the endangered Hudson, sings in one of his newest songs:

If you'd like to swim in our Hudson
And if you think pollution's a crime
Then sing it with me one more time:
Bring back, bring back,
These waters are yours and mine
Bring back, bring back
Bring back old Eighteen Ninety-nine.

Seeger thinks the river is clearer than it was last year. "Keep in mind, though," he added when I talked to him, "that the river could look clearer, but be more full of poisonous metals." This year (1973) Seeger, who lives in Beacon overlooking the Hudson, has curtailed his travel to concentrate on the river. "The world will be saved, if it is saved at all, by people fighting for their homes, wherever they are," he said.

"When will we be able to swim in the Hudson?" I asked. "I'd say that within five years, we'll have swimming on beaches in the mid-Hudson," he said. When I asked Seymour the same question, he said people were already swimming at Little Stony Point, Garrison, Cold Spring and just above Beacon.

The Maria Gorthon *was almost through the Highlands, considered by all the pilots and almost everybody else to be the most beautiful stretch of the Hudson by day. As we passed in the night, all we could see were dark masses of hills. "I took a trip up the Rhine once and it can't compare," Captain John Hamilton, one of the senior pilots, had told me when I talked to him in Albany. His family settled on the Hudson in 1702, and his father, grandfather and great-grandfather had all been rivermen before him. "If I were younger," Hamilton, who once skippered a Hudson River Day Liner and who is now in his late fifties, said, "I'd try to organize a passenger business on the river."*

On the Maria Gorthon, *Maloney stared ahead into the darkness, broken by a few navigational lights and an occasional light on the shore: "It's not so bad, fog and snow are worse. You know, radar is useless when there's ice. The ice on the surface breaks it up and you can't see the shore." The pilots, who know every inch of the river, its channel and the shorelines, say they really don't need navigational aids like buoys or radar, although they are helpful. "I've gone through the Highlands in a fog without seeing a thing," one of them had told me. "You sort of develop a feel; you can feel it."*

At the northern end of the Highlands, Storm King Mountain is the center of what is perhaps the longest and most intense fight between a power company and the conservationists. Ten years ago Con Edison proposed to build a two million kilowatt pumped storage power plant near Storm King, about 40 miles north of New York City, and the controversy is not yet resolved. The plan seemed simple enough. Pump water out of the river in offhours, store it in a high reservoir, then use it at peak periods to generate electricity by letting it flow down back to the river. Irreparable damage to the scenic beauty of the river, the conservationists argued. They won a major initial victory in the courts, which ruled that the Federal Power Commission had to consider scenic and historic resources as well as power needs in approving a projected plant. The F.P.C. did and approved the plant again. The Scenic Hudson Preservation Conference then took another tack; it challenged a state decision that the plant would not endanger water quality standards. But the courts overruled that. Now the plant, whose estimated costs have risen from $234 million to $400 million, is again being challenged—environmentalists say it's uneconomical, its intake screens will kill fish, and it will endanger a New York City aqueduct.

Con Edison officials cite F.P.C. and court decisions in their favor, and insist on their responsibility to provide power for people. They argue vehemently that the project would not detract from the beauty of Storm King. They say that the reservoir would be a mile from the mountain, at a lower elevation; that the power plant would be underground and hidden from view except for a channel where the water would enter and leave the river; that they will build a mile-long riverfront park there; that there will be no thermal pollution of water since it will not be used to cool a power plant; and that there will be no adverse effect on striped bass or shad.

One thing was obvious as I listened to the arguments—that the long fight was symbolic, based on ideology, with compromise apparently impossible. Despite Con Edison's moves to meet the objections, the opponents are firm in their opposition to any plant at all at that site. Yet Con Edison has announced that it will start construction in November; the opponents are girding for another round of battle.

North of the Highlands, the Maria Gorthon *ran through the cleanest part of the Hudson. From Peekskill north the river is categorized by the state as "Class B," meaning that it is approved for swimming, although one state engineer warned me to stay away from the few open sewer lines that still exist. From Beacon north to Coxsackie, the river is classified as "Grade A," meaning that it can be used for drinking water if it is chemically treated to remove or neutralize any sewer effluents, as well as swimming.*

But there are threats to the river in this largely rural stretch of the valley, threats from the ever-expanding needs of New York City. Behind Newburgh, where George Washington made his headquarters for much of the Revolution, the proposal to enlarge Stewart Airport into a jetport has split the countryside into a jobs versus environment argument. Near the village of Catskill, residents are banding together to stop the State Power Authority from building a power plant to supply the New York Metropolitan Transportation Authority, whose trains run nowhere near this quiet county seat.

In the rural area of the Hudson Valley, interspersed among the villages, hills and trees, are some of the worst industrial polluters of the river, monitored constantly by environmental groups. Some of the manufacturing plants—copper, chemicals, paper—have been dragged into court and fined for pollution; others have voluntarily cooperated in planning or building pollution control facilities; a few have been forced by the State to post bonds to insure compliance. The State outlook on the status of industrial pollution control is optimistic, holding that the program outside of New York City will be complete by 1976.

Between New York City and Albany, there are 28 major industrial polluters with a total waste flow of 33 million gallons a day into the river, according to the State tabulation. Of them, 11 have completed their pollution control facilities, eight more should be completed next year, four in 1975 and the last five in 1976. The situation in New York City is not that sanguine; industrial waste pours into the sewer system and, therefore, it will not be neutralized until the North River plant is finished.

As we sailed under the Rip Van Winkle Bridge, the Catskill Mountains to the west were invisible. The darkness also blocked sight of Olana, the Persian-type home of Frederic Edwin Church, one of the best known painters of the Hudson River School, built in the 1870s just south of the city of Hudson on the east bank. On a clear day Olana, now a museum open to the public, provides what is, to me, the most beautiful view of the Hudson and the Catskills.

Before boarding ship, Maloney had been informed that a cement ship would be sailing during the night from Hudson, a thriving whaling port in the early 1800s but now, like most river towns, a bit seedy,

29

with a decaying waterfront. He picked up his walkie-talkie: "This is the Maria Gorthon *approaching Hudson," Maloney said. "We'll pass on one whistle." "One whistle it is," the voice said.*

Maloney explained that the phrase, dating back to the days when ships signaled to each other by whistles, still meant that they would pass port (left) to port, while two whistles meant starboard (right) to starboard. In a few minutes the two ships passed quietly in the night, but no whistles sounded. "Before we had walkie-talkies, there was a lot of guesswork, heartache and grey hairs, " Maloney said. "Now you can talk and agree on how to pass. It's the cheapest form of insurance."

As the day began to break, it was a relatively easy run to Albany, a growing inland port 150 miles upriver from the Battery, up the 400-foot wide channel dredged to a depth of 32 feet to handle ocean-going vessels. It was raining hard in the early morning hours as McCluney took the ship into dock, in front of two ships waiting to load grain for the Soviet Union. It was 6:15 a.m. The average run from Yonkers to Albany takes about 10 hours, but we had made it in a little less because of tide waters pushing most of the way.

Is the Hudson beautiful but damned—damned by cement plants, power plants, oil tank farms and other artifacts of modern industry that pollute air, water and scenery? After months of traveling up and down the river, I found almost unanimous agreement that pollution was being successfully attacked and that the river was improved but that new dangers were being recognized—for example, pollution by heavy metals, which is now beginning to be confronted, and by run-off of pesticides and fertilizers, which is not. Also, at a time when almost everyone recognizes power and energy shortages, where can new power plants be built if residents oppose use of river water for coolants and if people everywhere oppose atomic plants?

Are we moving fast enough to clean up the Hudson? No, say the environmentalists, who seem sometimes to be fighting yesterday's battle. Too fast, say the power people, who still regard the Hudson (and other rivers) as a proper industrial resource. "Maybe we are doing something right since we are being attacked by both sides," Commissioner Henry Diamond said when I interviewed him in his Albany office. "We have spent $1.4 billion since 1965 in cleaning up the Hudson and we are now beginning to get the payoff."

Diamond's engineers have maps and figures to show that 17 municipal sewage treatment plants have been completed and are in operation, 12 (including North River) are under construction and 33 more are in the design stage. The statistics are encouraging because they show a slow and steady progress toward the goal of cleaner waters, but they are deceptive because they indicate a greater achievement than is real. For example, the 17 plants that are completed are small, treating only 43 million gallons of the 657 million gallons of sewage generated every day by residents of the Hudson Valley. The 12 plants under construction are much larger and will handle 398 million gallons a day when finished. But that leaves 216 million gallons a day for the 33 plants that are under design. Thus a scorecard today would show 614 million gallons of raw sewage a day still being poured into the Hudson.

An encouraging word is behind the figures, though. Everyone understands that it takes a long time and a lot of money to build sewage treatment plants—but they are being built. For example, the plant in Albany, an area second only to New York City in the amount of river pollution, will be open in October, removing another 30 million gallons of sewage a day from the river. And month after month, plant after plant will become operational. The best estimates are that most of them will be in use by the time the North River plant is completed. Perhaps we could have started earlier, perhaps we could have moved faster, but the fact is that we have moved. The Hudson is not going down the drain, as many predicted only five years ago. It is costing more to clean up the river than the early estimates (one expert said $400 million and another $1 billion), but, then, what doesn't? It is taking a little longer (back in 1965, one official guessed seven to ten years, while others said longer than that) but, then, what construction projects don't? By every available measure, the Hudson is cleaner and getting cleaner day by day—by crabs, fish in the river, dissolved oxygen, smell, and sight.

But there are still some problems. On that day when New York harbor becomes clean enough to swim in, the water won't look it. It won't be crystal clear; its color may be muddy brown, or tinged with brown or green because of the presence of tiny organisms. The heavy metals will still be in the river bottom sediments, an unknown threat. Some fish still will be killed at the intake gates of power plants. And, ironically, the teredo, or marine borer, once a victim of polluted water, is returning to chew away at the wooden underpinning of New York's piers as the water gets cleaner.

Who gets the credit for the renaissance of the Hudson? It's clear that the climate of public opinion has changed, that citizens have certified their willingness to pay to clean up the rivers of the state by passing two multi-billion dollar bond issues at a time when other propositions on the ballot, like that for transportation, were defeated. Federal, state and city officials, despite some reluctance to increase local taxes, are cooperating. But behind them all, behind the change in public opinion, behind the governmental action, there is a dedicated band of local lovers of the river, who belligerently and steadfastly refused to be put off by the "experts" from industry and government who said it couldn't be done or that it was too expensive. Now that their battle is almost won, they still believe that eternal vigilance is the price citizens must pay to protect their environment. If plaques are ever put up to mark the historic battle to save the Hudson, they should not be for President Johnson or Governor Rockefeller, under whose administration some of the key legislation was passed, but for Pete Seeger, the Hudson River Fisherman's Association, the Hudson River Sloop Restoration, the Scenic Hudson Preservation Conference and a host of anonymous men and women.

In an industrial society, the Hudson cannot be restored to the pristine quality it had when Henry Hudson sailed up the river in 1609 and frightened the Indians. But it can be and is becoming an ever-flowing source of recreation and pleasure, for boaters, water skiers, swimmers and just ordinary citizens who want to gaze upon its beauties, as well as a channel for tankers and freighters.

"When will you go swimming in the Hudson?" I asked Commissioner Diamond.

"When the North River plant goes into operation," he replied.

———•———

The North River plant did go into operation but Diamond never got to swim in the Hudson because the very next year PCBs were discovered in the river and everything changed. (see chapter 14)

Chapter 3

The Beautiful Hudson Valley: West Point

When friendly tourists come to the area and ask where they should go, the answer is easy: West Point, Hyde Park, and Olana. Following is a sampling of the dozens of stories I have written about them.

WEST POINT
(August 19, 1988)

Because of its beauty, historic importance and training missions, the United State Military Academy at West Point—on the west bank of the Hudson River about 45 miles north of New York City—attracts hundreds of thousands of visitors a year, including an increasing number of foreign tourists. Military officers estimate the visitors at 2.5 million to 3 million a year, although some tourism officials put the number at perhaps half that.

Either way, it's a lot of tourists, and a major problem. Any visitor can see traffic jams there almost any day of the year. Built in horse-and-buggy days, the roads are narrow and winding, unable to support a growing number of Army vehicles, supply trucks, the cars of military personnel and the cars of thousands of visitors, as well as marching cadets in training or attending classes.

As a result of the crowding, a new traffic control system went into effect in June, restricting tourist access to the central core of the Academy where the cadets live, study, and receive their training.

"From the superintendent's point of view, our mission to train and educate the corps of cadets at the same time as providing for the best possible visit for the public came into conflict," said the Academy's public affairs officer, Col. James N. Hawthorne.

The solution: A system of shuttle buses for the military and civilian staff and of commercial tour buses for the public, with parking for both on the periphery of the grounds.

"Our interest is not to prevent people from visiting," Colonel Hawthorne said. "On the contrary, we want people to come to West Point, but in an orderly and systematic way. After all, it is a National Historic Site."

Instead of do-it-yourself walking or driving tours of the Academy grounds, visitors are now encouraged to take an organized bus tour, with guides giving the history of the Academy, its buildings, its traditions and above all, its cadets over the years and their contributions to their country.

HISTORY
Standing on the promontory overlooking the Hudson River, you don't have to be a soldier to understand West Point's commanding strategic importance in American history. Below, the river curves in a beautiful S-shape, putting any vessels that pass in peril from cannon shot from above.

Cadets in review at the United States Military Academy at West Point.
U.S. Army photograph.

Back in 1775, Gen. George Washington and other revolutionaries decided that a fort was needed at West Point to protect the heartland of New York from the British fleet. But it was not until 1778 that Col. Thaddeus Kosciusko, a French-trained Polish military engineer, arrived to supervise construction of fortifications there.

Two years later, West Point faced its most serious threat when the commandant, Gen. Benedict Arnold, the hero of the Battles of Quebec, Valcour Island and Saratoga, turned traitor and attempted to sell it to the British. The plot was thwarted by the capture of Maj. John André, a British officer. Arnold escaped, and became an officer in the British Army.

After the war, it became obvious that the nation needed professional officers to lead its army. Under President Thomas Jefferson, the Military Academy was created at West Point in 1802. Its first class consisted of 10 men; last month 1,325 men and women were enrolled as new cadets.

Everywhere the new cadets march, they see reminders of Col. Sylvanus Thayer, "the father of the Military Academy," who was superintendent from 1817 to 1833: there is a Thayer Gate, Thayer Road, the Thayer Hotel and a statue as well.

Equally enduring is the system of education that he installed to produce leaders of personal integrity and academic excellence by fostering mental and physical discipline, regular habits of study and classroom sections limited to under 15 students. Since it opened, West Point has produced more than 40,000 graduates, including famous generals who have commanded armies: Ulysses S. Grant, Robert E. Lee, John J. Pershing, Douglas MacArthur and Dwight D. Eisenhower.

VISITORS CENTER

As its name implies, the Visitors Center is a good place to start. It contains a model cadet room (these rooms cannot be seen in the barracks, which are closed to the public), a theater with movies covering a cadet's four years, restrooms and a gift shop. And the Center provides maps for tours of the grounds. It is open every day of the year except Thanksgiving, Christmas and New Year's Day. The grounds of the Academy are open to the public from 8 A.M. to sunset, though. There is no admission fee for either the Center or the grounds and parking is free at the adjoining Buffalo Soldiers Field. Information: (914) 938 2638.

The chapel at West Point, with Michie Stadium and
Fort Putnam in the background.
U.S. Army photograph.

THE WEST POINT MUSEUM
(September 10, 1989)

It would be a hard heart indeed that did not beat a little faster at the sight of the Army's Corps of Cadets, 4,361 strong, in their dress uniforms, marching in precision on the plain at the core of the United States Military Academy at West Point. It is a site that reverberates in American history. In 1778, during the Revolutionary War, Col. Thaddeus Kosciusko supervised construction of fortifications on the strategic bluff overlooking the Hudson River. A year later Baron Frederick von Steuben began to train infantrymen of the Continental Army there. Shortly after, its commander, Gen. Benedict Arnold, the hero of the battles of Quebec and Saratoga, turned traitor and tried to betray West Point to the British.

From its beginning, West Point played a key role in early American history. After the American Revolution it became even more important as the home of the United States Military Academy, founded in 1802, and has trained the officers who have commanded American armies in war and peace since then. The history of the Academy, of the United States Army, and indeed of warfare, is told in capsule form in West Point's museum. The museum, established in 1854, has been remodeled, and reopened Sept. 1 as part of a visitors' complex in the Academy's new South Post.

Although the museum, with an ever-growing collection of weapons, uniforms, maps, pictures, paintings, dioramas and flags, serves mainly as a teaching tool for cadets, it is also open to the public. It is one of the key points of interest for visitors to West Point, which itself is a major tourist attraction. Of the more than two million people who visit West Point each year, more than 300,000 take time to tour the museum.

It will be a little easier now because the Visitors Center in the village of Highland Falls, about 50 miles north of New York, has ample parking. The center is a few hundred yards south of the main gate to West Point on what was formerly the campus of Ladycliff College. Sitting on the floor of what used to be the college's gymnasium is a World War II jeep, a World War I tank and a replica of the first atomic bomb.

After an expenditure of about $10 million, the college's Gothic-style Rosary Hall, which was built in 1934, has become Olmsted Hall, named for Maj. Gen. George H. Olmsted, class of 1922, who contributed almost half of the cost. Many of its interior walls were torn down to make additional open space for the new museum's galleries. The building overlooks the Hudson River, but many of its windows are boarded up to prevent sunlight damaging the fragile uniforms and papers on display. As another precautionary step, the museum will rotate historic flags, uniforms, maps and other paper every three years.

The museum director, Michael E. Moss, and his staff oversee a collection of about 15,000 artifacts, including 7,800 weapons, but only about 5 percent are on display at any one time. The earliest examples include an Egyptian battle-ax from about 900 B.C. and Persian swords, axes, daggers and spearheads of the same period. The first item from American history is a 12-pound cannon, part of the booty captured from the British at the Battle of Saratoga in 1777 and sent to West Point for storage and distribution to the Continental Army.

"There has to be some magic in the displays, something that will bring people into the past and make it living for them," Mr. Moss said, explaining that the museum tries to achieve this by showing personal articles of famous generals and other leaders. Among them are a pair of George Washington's flintlock pistols, Adolf Hitler's pistol, Hermann Goering's marshal's baton, Napoleon Bonaparte's First Consul Sword, which was presented by France to Gen. Dwight D. Eisenhower after World War II, and the bathrobe worn by Gen. Douglas MacArthur when he was a cadet (not now on exhibition).

The museum is divided into six major galleries: the history of West Point, the history of warfare, American wars, the history of the United States Army, small weapons and large weapons. In addition, the museum displays artifacts in many places on the grounds. At Trophy Point, for example, where a shaft of pink marble juts into the sky as a memorial to the 2,230 officers and men of the regular Army (contrasted to volunteers) who died in the Civil War, 131 cannon, from the Revolutionary War through the Korean War, are on display. There is also a segment of the great chain stretched across the Hudson River in the Revolutionary War to prevent the British from sailing up it. At the entrance to the West Point gallery is a fine painting of the S-shaped bend in the river (which is why it was a strategic fortification in the Revolutionary War) as seen from Trophy Point by Robert Weir, who was a professor of drawing at the academy for 42 years. There are paintings, drawings and uniforms of famous graduates throughout the museum.

But there are no portraits, because none are available, of West Point's first two graduates, Joseph Swift and Simon Levy, who entered on July 4, 1802, and graduated in the same year. Among the other exhibits in the West Point gallery are paintings of graduates who made their mark in the Mexican War and the Civil War, among them Jefferson Davis, Robert E. Lee and Ulysses S. Grant. Much attention is devoted to Col. Sylvanus Thayer, who is often called "the father of the military academy" because he transformed it into a first-class engineering school when he took command in 1817.

His sword and chess set are on display, and that chess set unintentionally symbolizes the academic approach of most military historians, with their emphasis on strategy and tactics.

But inscribed on the bottom of a large mural depicting the history of weapons from the slings and javelins of ancient man to the mushroom cloud of the atom bomb is this quotation from Gen. George S. Patton: "Weapons change, but the man who uses them changes not at all."

Below the mural is a display of cannon, including the first gun, a French 75-millimeter cannon, fired by American soldiers in World War I, an ornate bronze Chinese cannon captured by Americans during the Boxer Rebellion, and many artillery pieces of other wars. Prominent in the center of the mural is an ordinary stirrup. "It was very important, because it changed mounted warfare," Mr. Moss explained. "It meant that riders on horseback had something to use as a base for their legs as they rode and could use their weapons more efficiently."

The emphasis on weapons of the past and how they were used is illustrated graphically in two large dioramas of decisive battles. One depicts the Battle of Cynoscephalace in 197 B.C., when a Roman legion, using short swords, spears and elephants defeated a Macedonian phalanx in northern Greece, establishing the supremacy of the Roman army in that part of the ancient world. Another diorama shows a Roman army under the command of Julius Caesar laying siege to Avricum in southern France in 52 B.C., with details of the towers, ramps, catapults and ballistas, the large-scale crossbows that fired flaming projectiles.

It seemed to me, as I toured the galleries, that the distant past was treated more graphically than more recent developments, certainly more so than Korea or Vietnam.

As a World War II veteran and a former war correspondent in Korea, I was especially interested in the museum's treatment of those two conflicts. Given that the museum is relatively small, I thought the World War II displays in various galleries were substantial. Particularly interesting were two large murals by Linzee Prescott. One showed the invasion of Omaha Beach on D-Day, June 6, 1944, in impressive detail. In the other, Mr. Prescott, himself a paratrooper, depicts the air drop of Americans into Normandy at the same time.

But the treatment of Korea was scant. It is mentioned in one of three panels on limited war (in the gallery on the history of warfare) along with the Vietnam War and the Arab-Israeli conflicts. It is also included in one other panel (in the gallery on the history of the Army) showing troops in Vietnam, the Dominican Republic and Vietnam and as occupying forces in Germany, Japan, and Korea.

"We have very little on Korea in our collection," Mr. Moss conceded, noting, however, a rising interest in that war, possibly as a result of pressure from Korean veterans after the recent emphasis on Vietnam memorials. "But we have put out an appeal for things brought back from Korea because we want to put together a display on military equipment and arms used in that conflict."

Although the exhibit on the Vietnam War seemed to be sparse too, Mr. Moss said that, like other American wars, it was represented proportionately, although its artifacts were scattered among several sections of the museum.

"No matter how much we have on display a veteran of some war is going to come in and say that we should have more," he said. "It is a concern to us. Our answer is that we will rotate our exhibits."

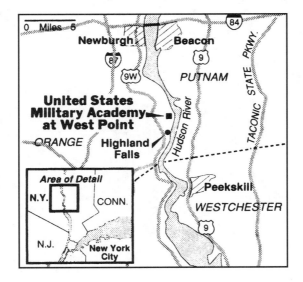

CHAPTER 4

The Beautiful Hudson Valley:
Hyde Park

It was always a delight to cover stories at the Franklin D. Roosevelt Home and Museum at Hyde Park—except on weekends when it could get crowded. But there is more to Hyde Park than the FDR and Eleanor Roosevelt memorials, as you will see in the following articles.

HYDE PARK
(April 13, 1976)

"Another Millionaire in Dutchess"—that was the headline in the Poughkeepsie *Sunday Courier* of May 12, 1895, over a story reporting that Frederick William Vanderbilt, the grandson of Commodore Vanderbilt, had bought an estate overlooking the Hudson River at Hyde Park in Dutchess County. The influx of men of great wealth joining the landed gentry already in residence along the river had an unpredictable side effect: Their drive to build grandiose part-time mansions with extensive grounds, gardens and farms served to preserve and protect the scenic beauty of the Hudson Valley from commercial and residential development.

Their legacy—a magnificent stretch of riverfront estates ranging from the baronial Vanderbilt mansion to the large, comfortable home of the Roosevelts—is now a major tourist attraction in the northeast, close enough to the New York metropolitan region for a one-day visit or a more leisurely two-day weekend trip.

Only 80 miles from Manhattan, a two-hour drive, Hyde Park is desperately trying to retain its small town rural character while at the same time catering to hundreds of thousands of tourists each year. Local residents, who have organized a Hyde Park Visual Environment Committee, are worried about congestion along Route 9, the two-lane major north-south traffic artery, although they recognize the necessity for motels and restaurants.

For the visitor, however, Hyde Park is still a modest town with many of the amenities of smallness. There are few lines at the major attractions and parking is free and relatively easy.

In an eight-mile stretch along Route 9, there are ample opportunities to enjoy—without pushing or crowding—the same river sites that drew President Roosevelt back to Hyde Park each summer, to wonder at the extravagances of the Gilded Age and to learn something about the role of the Hudson River in the history of the state and the nation.

From south to north, all between Route 9 and the river with magnificent views of the Hudson, there are three major attractions, each worth a leisurely tour—the Franklin D. Roosevelt Home and Museum, the Vanderbilt Mansion and the Mills Mansion—as well as an art museum and a theater.

The house where Franklin D. Roosevelt was born (in 1882) and raised has a lived-in, family look, unlike the more formal atmosphere of the Vanderbilt Mansion. It was here that Roosevelt brought his bride, Eleanor, in 1905, it was

Franklin D. Roosevelt's home in Hyde Park.
Courtesy of New York State Department of Economic Development.

here that they raised their five children, it was here that he returned after his political campaigns, and it was here that he was buried in the family rose garden in 1945. It was also here that his wife never felt at home; she regarded it as the domain of her mother-in-law, Sara Delano Roosevelt, and felt the atmosphere to be oppressive.

That feeling is conveyed to visitors through the second floor of the house, where Eleanor's tiny bedroom is squeezed in between the larger and more commodious rooms of her husband and his mother.

But most visitors are impressed by the intimate quality of the house, although it served as the summer White House for many years. Before that it was the home of the Roosevelt family, and the visitor can see portraits, for example, of Isaac Roosevelt, the President's great-great-grandfather, who was active in the Revolutionary War, and his great-grandfather James, who in 1819 was the first of the family to settle in Dutchess County.

Of interest also are Franklin Roosevelt's tiny boyhood bedroom, the leash and blanket of his dog, Fala, in the master bedroom, the Dresden chandelier in a room near the dining room, and the birds he collected when he was a boy.

The home, a national historic site administered by the National Park Service, is open seven days a week. Admission is free for those under sixteen years of age and those over 62.

In addition, a cassette description of the house in the words and voice of Eleanor Roosevelt is available. Outside the house, there are nature trails leading down toward the Hudson River, with a printed guide available, showing how Roosevelt adapted some of his conservation ideas on his own property.

F.D.R. LIBRARY

The first of the six presidential libraries now in existence, the F.D.R. Library and Museum, all in one flagstone building, was opened to the public in 1941. The library section is open only to researchers and scholars, but the museum is open daily to all (except Christmas Day).

In the museum, among the displays that attract special attention are Roosevelt's White House desk, his ship models, his homemade wheelchair, gifts from heads-of-state, pictures from various stages of his career, public papers showing corrections in his own handwriting, and, of course, the numerous cartoons of him, his tilted cigarette holder, and of Fala.

The newest edition to the museum, the Eleanor Roosevelt Wing, was opened in 1972. It contains items from her wardrobe, the White House china and pictures of the children, as well as mementos of her work in the United Nations.

The opening of the display is marked by a crystal, engraved with her hands, bearing the words of Adlai Stevenson: "She would rather light a candle than curse the darkness, and her glow has warmed the world."

A group of Mrs. Roosevelt's admirers has organized a committee to try to purchase Val-Kill, her retreat from the Roosevelt home, several miles inland. It was there that she and some friends organized a furniture factory in the late 1920s, and it was there that she felt at home herself.

VANDERBILT MANSION

A visit to the Vanderbilt Mansion and estate offers a journey into the opulence of the Gilded Age. Once the country home of Frederick W. Vanderbilt and his wife, Louise, the three-story mansion, built of Indiana limestone in Italian Renaissance style, was completed in 1898. The total cost of all construction and improvements for the property has been estimated at $2.2 million, at a time when a man worked all day for $1.

The 54-room lavishly furnished mansion was the scene of many gala parties, but it was occupied only part of the time. The Vanderbilts went to New York for the opera and social season, to Palm Beach for March and April, to Hyde Park for the early summer, then to Newport until Labor Day, sometimes to their "cottage" in the Adirondacks, and sometimes on their yacht to Europe.

At one time, there were more than 60 full-time employees on the estate—17 in the house and 44 on the grounds and farm, with additional help hired when there were guests.

The estate was given to the nation in 1940 by Margaret Van Alen, a Vanderbilt niece. It is a national historic site, administered by the National Park Service. The mansion is open to the public. There is no charge for parking.

One of the great delights of a Vanderbilt visit is walking over the 211 acres that overlook the Hudson River and inspecting the specimen trees.

ULRICH MANSION

As a change of pace, the Edwin A. Ulrich Museum, about two miles north of Hyde Park center and about a mile north of the Vanderbilt Mansion exit on Route 9, is a small, private, unpretentious building owned and operated by Mr. Ulrich. Now 79 years old, Mr. Ulrich, a former oil distributor in Poughkeepsie, devotes full time to his collection of paintings of the Waugh family.

The walls of his home, Wavecrest, are filled with seascapes and other paintings of Samuel Bell Waugh (1814-1884), his son, Frederick Judd Waugh (1861-1940), and his grandson, Coulton Waugh (1896-1973). Also available are biographies of the painters, slides, and how-to books by the youngest Waugh and others.

Mr. Ulrich cares for his collection himself and is delighted to stop and explain how he became interested in the Waughs (he was a classmate of Coulton's), why he is collecting them (because they're good and he likes them), how he maintains the museum (with his own funds, no foundation grants), and how he started the Edwin A. Ulrich Museum of Art on the campus of Wichita State University in Kansas.

The Ulrich Museum at Hyde Park is open Fridays through Mondays, and at other times by appointment (914) 229-7107.

NORRIE STATE PARK

Four miles north of Hyde Park center, the Margaret Lewis Norrie State Park offers a marina for yacht-watching, camping facilities and picnic grounds on the Hudson River. There is no charge for visitors (except for yachts), and it is open daily (914) 889-4646.

Under the supervision of the Taconic State Park and Recreation Commission, it has just been consolidated with the Mills complex farther north for administration. There is a hiking trail along the river that connects both facilities. (Note: The Norrie Point Inn listed in some guide books is not open.)

MILLS MANSION

Lack of funds has closed the upper floors of the Mills Mansion just off Route 9 in Staatsburg, which is part of the town of Hyde Park. However, there still are guided tours every half hour of the building (which is sometimes called the Mills Museum).

The official name of the complex was, until recently, the Ogden and Ruth Livingston Mills Memorial State Park. Now it is part of the Mills-Norrie State Park, operated by the Taconic State Park Commission. No admission charge, except on the two nine-hole golf courses.

The story of the Mills establishment started in 1792 when Morgan Lewis, a Revolutionary War general who later became the third governor of New York State, bought the property. The house that he built burned in 1832, but he and his wife, Gertrude, rebuilt it. In 1888, their great-granddaughter, Ruth Livingston Mills, inherited it, and she and her husband, Ogen Mills, enlarged it considerably.

Two large wings were added and the exterior decorated with balustrades, pilaster and floral swags. The interior, consisting of 65 rooms, was decorated in the style of Louis XV and Louis XVI.

But the ornate building, not quite as elaborate as the Vanderbilt Mansion, was used only in the autumn. At other times, the family was at different homes, in Paris, New York, Newport or California.

Mrs. Mills died in 1920 and her husband in 1929. Their son, Ogden Livingston Mills, was Secretary of the Treasury under President Hoover. Following his death, his sister, Mrs. Henry Carnegie Phipps, gave the estate to New York in memory of her parents.

The mansion is open for free guided tours, Wednesday through Sunday. Just opened is a hiking trail along the Hudson, south to the Norrie State Park.

VAL-KILL
(October 12, 1984)

HYDE PARK, N.Y.—The centennial of the birth of Eleanor Roosevelt was celebrated here today with the dedication of her home, Val-Kill, as a National Historic Site, the only one in the United States to honor a First Lady.

But the dedication was, as several speakers pointed out, in memory of her not merely as an active First Lady and the wife of President Franklin D. Roosevelt, but also a historic figure in her own right.

"If we had a process of secular canonization there would be no candidate surer of success than she," Governor Cuomo, the keynote speaker, said. "She worked tirelessly on behalf of people all over this planet, committing herself with a passion and eloquence that two decades after her death are still important, still vibrant, still new."

The ceremonies, attended by 500 friends and admirers, were held on a cool, crisp afternoon on the lawn at Val-Kill, framed by a background of crimson maple, yellow hickory and bronze oak leaves turning in the autumn sun.

A symbolic long, white ribbon was jointly cut by her three surviving sons, Franklin D. Jr., Elliott and James, Mr. Cuomo, and Trude W. Lash, chairman of the Eleanor Roosevelt Institute and the National Centennial Commission. Speeches recalled Mrs. Roosevelt as head of the Human Rights Commission of the United Nations, a leader of the liberal wing of the Democratic Party and a friend of the forgotten at home and abroad.

Some speakers referred to her, in the words of President Harry S. Truman, as "the First Lady of the World."

A new 20-cent commemorative stamp was put on sale by Postmaster General William F. Bolger. It bears a likeness of Mrs. Roosevelt based on a picture taken at Val-Kill in 1960 by Dr. David Gurewitsch, her friend and physician.

The ceremonies were the culmination of a year-long observance that began at a service in the Cathedral of St. John the Divine in New York City, where she was born Oct. 11, 1884.

A candlelight service here Wednesday night recalled Adlai E. Stevenson's eulogy at her death. "She would rather light a candle then curse the darkness and her glow has warmed the world." Mrs. Roosevelt died in New York City in 1962 at the age of 78.

At 9 o'clock this morning, members of her family and friends laid flowers at her grave, next to her husband's in the Rose Garden of the Franklin D. Roosevelt National Historic Site, 80 miles north of mid-town.

Two hours later, the ceremony shifted to Val-Kill, two miles east of the complex named after her husband, which includes a Presidential library and a museum with an Eleanor Roosevelt wing as well as his home.

For Mrs. Roosevelt, who had been orphaned at the age of 9, Val-Kill was her only real home, although she lived at one time or another in the White House, at the Roosevelt Mansion and in an apartment in New York City. Its name is derived from the Fall Kill, a stream that meanders through the property.

"Val-Kill is where I used to find myself," she once wrote. "At Val-Kill, I emerged as an individual."

That process started in 1926, when she first began to use it as a hideaway from what she considered to be the oppressive atmosphere of her husband's home, dominated by her imperious mother-in-law, Sara Delano Roosevelt.

In 1927, she and two friends, Marion Dickerman and Nancy Cook, started a company to manufacture reproductions of early American furniture. They hired local crafts workers to do the work and to train young people in woodworking skills.

Until the company ceased operations in 1936, Mrs. Roosevelt maintained Val-Kill as a combination business venture and private sanctuary while her husband was Governor of New York, between 1929 and 1933, and through his first term as President, starting in 1933. At the President's death in 1945, Mrs. Roosevelt made Val-Kill her permanent home.

In her second-floor apartment in the old factory building, Mrs. Roosevelt received her guests, including Marshal Tito, Jawaharlal Nehru, Haile Selassie, Nikita S. Khrushchev and John F. Kennedy, when he was a candidate for the Democratic presidential nomination in 1960.

Eleanor Roosevelt's cottage at Val-Kill.
Courtesy of Franklin D. Roosevelt Library.

It was also at Val-Kill that she entertained her friends, people she encountered on trains and in shops and the delinquent boys of the old Wiltwyck School for Boys, a former child care agency in the Hudson Valley.

Today, Val-Kill is a complex of five one- and two-story stucco buildings on 179 acres, surrounded by suburban-style homes. With a $700,000 Congressional appropriation, the National Park Service, which maintains the site, has restored the buildings, built a bridge across the kill and bought back some of the furniture that had been sold after Mrs. Roosevelt's death.

THE F.D.R. LIBRARY
(November, 19, 1989)

HYDE PARK, N.Y.—The Franklin D. Roosevelt Library here, the nation's first official Presidential library, will celebrate its 50th anniversary on Sunday with special exhibits, a birthday cake and showings of newsreels of the Roosevelt era.

Under the direction of the National Archives and Records Administration, the Roosevelt Library is one of seven Presidential libraries in the nation. An eighth, the Ronald Reagan Library, is under construction near Santa Barbara, Calif.

In addition, a private non-governmental Presidential library is planned for Richard M. Nixon in Yorba Linda, Calif., where he was born. Mr. Nixon's Presidential papers are in the custody of the National Archives in Washington, where access to some of his taped conversations is a subject of controversy.

The other Presidential libraries are the Gerald Ford Library in Grand Rapids, Mich.; the Jimmy Carter Library in Atlanta; the John F. Kennedy Library in Dorchester, Mass., just outside of Boston; the Dwight D. Eisenhower Library in Abilene, Kan.; the Harry S. Truman Library in Independence, Mo.; and the Herbert C. Hoover Library in West Branch, Iowa.

"The access of the public to the Presidential papers is unique in the world," Don W. Wilson, the Archivist of the United States, said at an anniversary dinner in the library on Wednesday night.

Mr. Wilson said officials of the Soviet Union recently asked the United States for advice on making Soviet historical documents more open to scholars and the public.

The cornerstone of the Roosevelt Library and Museum was laid by President Roosevelt on Nov. 19, 1939. The museum section was opened to the public on June 30, 1941, but the research section of the library was not opened until 1946, a year after President Roosevelt's death.

Today the library is a collection of 45,000 books, 85,000 pamphlets and magazines, 130,000 photographs and 16 million pages of manuscripts. The museum has 23,000 artifacts—pictures, documents, newspaper front pages, and the ship models and stamps that the President collected as a hobby.

Before the Roosevelt Administration, most Presidents considered their official papers to be private property and took them with them when they left the White House. Some papers were destroyed, others sold to private collectors and many were lost.

But President Roosevelt decided that his papers would become the property of the nation, to be housed in a library to be built on the grounds of his home in Hyde Park, in Dutchess County, said Dr. William R. Emerson, director of the Roosevelt Library. "Initially, F.D.R. did not intend for the library to bear his name," Dr. Emerson said. "He looked on it as a place of research, an archival necessity, in no sense a memorial to himself."

But over the years, the Roosevelt Library, which is in a combined museum-library building, has become a popular tourist attraction, with about 350,000 people visiting it a year.

Dr. Emerson conceded, however, that even though it became the first governmental Presidential library, it was not the first Presidential library. That honor goes to the Rutherford B. Hayes Library in Fremont, Ohio. In 1911, the Hayes family gave Spiegel Grove, President Hayes's home, to create a private Presidential library, which is operated by the Ohio Historical Society and the Hayes Foundation.

———————

THE "DATE OF INFAMY" SPEECH
(April 2, 1984)

HYDE PARK, N.Y.—A 43-year-old-mystery—what happened to the reading copy of the famous speech that President Franklin D. Roosevelt delivered to a joint session of Congress on Dec. 8, 1941—has finally been solved.

In the speech, Roosevelt called the previous day, when Japanese planes attacked Pearl Harbor, "a date which will live in infamy" and asked

A sitting room in F.D.R.'s home.
Courtesy of Franklin D. Roosevelt Library.

Congress to recognize that a state of war existed between Japan and the United States.

But when he left the podium in the chamber of the House of Representatives, he left behind on the lectern his reading copy of the speech. When he returned to the White House, the President asked his son James, who was an aide, "Where is the speech?" His son replied, "I don't know."

Since then, archivists have been trying to find it.

"In 1981, the 40th anniversary of the speech, we made great efforts to locate it, but couldn't," said Dr. William R. Emerson, director of the Franklin D. Roosevelt Library here.

The speech was finally found a few months ago by Dr. Susan Cooper, a curator at the National Archives in Washington, during a routine examination in the archives of the papers of the United States Senate for 1941.

Dr. Cooper said in a telephone interview that she had been searching the Senate files for material about the declaration of war against Japan in preparation for a new exhibit celebrating the 50th anniversary of the National Archives.

When she found the manuscript of the speech, she checked with James O'Neill, assistant archivist for Presidential libraries, and Dr. Emerson. They verified that it was the long-lost speech.

"I hadn't known that it was missing," Dr. Cooper said. "It turned out to be very exciting."

"It was pure serendipity." Dr. Emerson said.

The three-page, typewritten manuscript is signed by President Roosevelt, with the added note by an unknown hand, "Dec. 8, 1941, read in joint session."

Roosevelt made the speech, which was broadcast live on radio and recorded, in the House of Representatives, the usual site for a joint session of Congress. The reading copy contains a few minor changes in the President's hand.

The archivist had no explanation of how the speech had made its way into the Senate files, but said it had presumably been picked up by a Senate aide and filed with other documents, such as the resolution declaring war and a copy of the roll-call vote.

The speech will go on display with other historical documents on June 19, in the rotunda of the National Archives Building in Washington, where the Constitution and the Declaration of Independence are on permanent display.

When the anniversary exhibit ends, Dr. Emerson said, he hopes the speech will be sent to the Franklin D. Roosevelt Library here. It contains the reading copies and drafts of all but one of President Roosevelt's 983 speeches—all but the Pearl Harbor one—on file in eight three-drawer, steel filing cabinets.

The library already has on display, however, the first draft of the "Day of Infamy" speech. It consists of three typewritten pages with numerous word changes in the President's hand.

As originally written, the opening paragraph read:

"Yesterday, December 7, 1941, a date which will live in world history, the United States of America was simultaneously and deliberately attacked by naval and air forces of the Empire of Japan."

The President made several changes in the wording of the draft, which transformed the routine beginning into a memorable one. He crossed out the words, "world history" and "simultaneously" and substituted others so that the speech as delivered said:

"Yesterday, December 7, 1941—a date which will live in infamy—the United States of America was suddenly and deliberately attacked by the naval and air forces of the Empire of Japan."

"It's a wonderful example of the architecture of rhetoric," Dr. Emerson said.

CHAPTER 5

Historic Homes

Our ancestors knew how to pick beautiful sites for their homes on the banks of the Hudson River, with spectacular scenery to the west across the river to the Catskill Mountains. Their descendants, though, had problems maintaining them, as you will see from the following articles.

WHITE ELEPHANTS
(August 1, 1977)

TARRYTOWN, N.Y—On a 16-mile stretch of the Hudson River here in the northwestern corner of Dutchess County, 37 manor houses overlook one of the most beautiful vistas in the world—the blue waters of the river against a backdrop of the green-covered Catskill Mountains.

But 14 of those manor houses, where Hudson River aristocrats and the new-rich from New York City lived in a baronial style throughout the 19th century, are now white elephants—threatened by skyrocketing taxes, rising cost of maintenance and occasional vandalism.

The problem of maintaining those white elephants for their historical and scenic value engaged the attention of preservationists from around the country and the local area here the other day on a combined boat and bus tour of endangered river estates.

"The principal problem facing the area is the inability of present landowners to maintain their buildings and open space in the face of ever-rising expenses," a recent planning report said.

This year alone, three of the mansions, all of them dating back to the early 1800s, have been destroyed by fire, razed or left to the wind and rain. Nine more are for sale, four of them adjoining each other near the Kingston-Rhinecliff Bridge.

Standing on the lawn of Edgewater—one of the mansions that has not only survived but that has also been lovingly restored because it has a rich owner—James Biddle, president of the National Trust for Historic Preservation, said, "This 16-mile stretch of the Hudson River is crammed with natural and historic significance that must be preserved."

Mr. Biddle was speaking to about a hundred people, many of whom were on a week-long tour of historic sites in the Hudson Valley. They sailed up the Hudson to Kingston on the *Independence*, a new cruise ship of the American Cruise Lines, and then traveled by bus to the sites.

At Edgewater, they were at one of the few estates actually on the river itself, on a small peninsula in the river between the main line of Conrail and the water. It was built in 1820 by John Livingston as a wedding present for his daughter, Margaret, who married Lowndes Brown, an Army captain from South Carolina.

It was expanded somewhat by Robert Donaldson, a North Carolinian, who bought the property in 1850.

Edgewater's present owner is also a man from North Carolina, Richard H. Jenrette, chairman of Donaldson, Lufkin & Jenrette, one of the nation's

The Vanderbilt Mansion in Hyde Park.
Courtesy of Franklin D. Roosevelt Library.

largest investment counseling firms. He bought it in 1970 from Gore Vidal, the novelist.

Arriving by seaplane from Wall Street just after noon, Mr. Jenrette was the host at a luncheon for the local residents and visitors, all of them concerned with preservation of historic sites.

He laughed when one of the visitors said the way to preserve the Hudson River estates was to find three dozen other rich men like him.

"I don't understand why people haven't discovered this area," he said. "It's not as expensive as buying a big place out in Southhampton or East Hampton and much more convenient."

The endangered area on the east bank of the river runs from Staatsburg in the south to Clermont in the north in the towns of Rhinebeck and Red Hook. At the south end are the Norrie Point State Park and the Ogden Mills Museum; at the north end is the Clermont State Park, the ancestral home of the Livingston family.

In between are 12 estates now occupied by institutions and 22 homes owned by individuals, many of whom are struggling to maintain them. Some owners, unable to keep the estates up, have sold out to developers, but even the developers are having problems, mostly with zoning restrictions.

AN ARCHITECTURAL GEM
(May 5, 1980)

RHINECLIFF, N.Y.—At the age of 88, Margaret L. Suckley is taking steps to preserve Wilderstein, her Queen-Anne-style home here, one of the last of the manorial estates on the Hudson River still in the hands of the family that built it.

Standing on the lawn overlooking the river today, Miss Suckley (pronounced Soo-klee) showed visitors the 35-room structure, every gable looking as if it were on the cover of a Gothic novel, with a five-story circular tower dominating the landscape. Its wooden siding bore only traces of the brown paint that once covered it, the paint on the columns was peeling and the wicker chairs on the wide veranda were faded.

"I am the last of the Suckleys," she said, with no overtone of mystery behind her statement.

But that fact, the high cost of maintenance and the concern that the property may be subdivided after her death were the reasons she cited for deciding to make arrangements now for the future of Wilderstein, which has been described by architects and others as "an architectural gem."

"I just can't afford to keep it up," said Miss Suckley, who walks with a cane but still takes occasional visitors on a tour of the grounds and the house. "It's run down. Everyone thinks it is unique architecturally and it is, but it is much too expensive to maintain."

As a result, Miss Suckley is donating the estate—the land, the house, its furniture and the accumulated papers and documents of 127 years of continuous occupancy—to Wilderstein Preservation Inc., a newly formed nonprofit organization that will maintain and eventually restore it. Miss Suckley will continue to live at the estate.

Her decision to transfer the property was announced at Wilderstein today by J. Winthrop Aldrich, a director of the new group, at the annual meeting of Hudson River Heritage Inc., a regional organization devoted to the preservation of landmarks in the Hudson Valley. He said that the property, which is not open to the public, would be used from time to time for meetings of local organizations.

"This house, its furnishings and the grounds are a remarkable surviving example of high Victorian cultural achievement," Mr. Aldrich said. "It is our intention to work with Miss Suckley and the community at large to preserve these artifacts and their setting in the public interest."

Wilderstein, which is on the National Register of Historic Places, is one of the estates on the east bank of the Hudson River in a 16-mile stretch from Staatsburg to Clermont that is part of a historic district. Its name, meaning stone of the wild man, probably comes from a carving of an Indian head on a huge rock that still stands near the water's edge of the property.

Miss Suckley, whom everyone calls Daisy, is a descendant of the Livingstons of Clermont and the Beekmans of Rhinebeck who obtained their land from the Indians, the Dutch and the British in the 17th century. One of her ancestors was Dr. Thomas Tillotson, surgeon general of the Revolutionary Army.

A friend and neighbor of Franklin D. Roosevelt, Miss Suckley was with the President when he died in Warm Springs, Ga., on April 12, 1945. She also trained Fala, President Roosevelt's celebrated Scotty, at Wilderstein.

Miss Suckley lives alone in the house, with the help of a woman who comes in once a week and a man who works on the grounds from time to time.

The house at Wilderstein was built in 1853 by her grandfather, Thomas H. Suckley. In the late 1880's, his son, Robert, Miss Suckley's father, retained

Wilderstein, the Suckley family home in Rhinebeck.
Courtesy of Wilderstein Collection.

Arnout Cannon Jr., the architect, to remodel the house. It was enlarged to its present 35-room size, with the addition of a third floor and 10 master bedrooms and a distinctive circular tower.

At that time, an onion-shaped stable was built and the 40-acre grounds were landscaped by Calvert Vaux, who was a co-designer of Manhattan's Central Park. J.B. Tiffany was commissioned to provide the interior furnishings and design.

A trained archivist who worked for 22 years at the Franklin D. Roosevelt Library in Hyde Park, Miss Suckley has been busy lately organizing the family's extensive collection of books, documents and paintings.

"I am happy about the transfer," said Miss Suckley. "What would happen if we didn't arrange this? We would have to sell the property, and they would put up houses or maybe even a development."

SAMUEL F. B. MORSE
(May 25, 1980)

POUGHKEEPSIE, N.Y.—The summer home of Samuel F. B. Morse, the artist and inventor of the telegraph, has been opened to the public as a museum by an educational corporation.

The house, surrounded by 106 acres of tall locusts, larches and maples, is an oasis of serenity and Hudson River valley views at the beginning of a strip of shopping centers and commercial development that runs for miles along Route 9 just south of Poughkeepsie, in Dutchess County.

Although it contains a replica of the telegraph, which Morse invented in 1844, and one of his paintings, the house at present reflects more the enthusiasm of the subsequent owners for collecting. After Morse died, in 1872, the Young family acquired the house and over the years filled its 24 rooms with paintings, antique furniture, and numerous bookcases, sometimes with double rows of books.

Its last owner, Annette I. Young, died in 1975, leaving the house and 18 acres surrounding it to a trust called Young-Morse Historic Site Inc., together with more than $2 million to maintain the house "for the enjoyment, visitation and enlightenment of the public."

She also left 88 acres between the house and the Hudson River to the State Department of Environmental Conservation as a wildlife sanctuary. But the state, in a friendly arrangement with the site's trustees, refused the land, which then passed into ownership of the trustees who maintain it as open land.

"The value of this land can hardly be overestimated since it will serve, along with the home site, as a buffer against commercial and other development that has become common along this stretch of Route 9," according to the president of Young-Morse, Kenneth Hasbrouck, a distant cousin of Miss Young.

Mr. Hasbrouck, a retired history teacher, lives across the Hudson River near New Paltz. He is president of the Huguenot Society, which maintains 14 stone houses in New Paltz dating from Colonial days on Huguenot Street, called "the oldest street in America with its original houses."

Morse bought the house in Poughkeepsie in 1847 and called it Locust Grove because of the trees surrounding it. Five years later, with the help of the architect Alexander Jackson Davis, he added an octagonal-shaped wing and a four-story Tuscan tower facing the river.

Just outside the front door today, a plaque put up in 1968 by the New York Chapter of the Morse Telegraph Club reads: "Samuel F. B. Morse, Father of the Telegraph, built this house Locust Grove. It was his summer home 1852-1871."

After Morse's death, his family sold the estate to William Hopkins Young and his wife, Martha. The Youngs, according to Mr. Hasbrouck, were an old New York family that made its money in real estate.

Their son, Innis Young, who died in 1953, collected many of the pictures, paintings and portraits that now fill almost all the available wall space. Their daughter, Annette, who died at the age of 90, was the last of the Youngs.

The house will be open to the public Wednesdays through Sundays.

———◆———

THE LITTLE MAGICIAN
(June 12, 1987)

Q. Who was the first President born a citizen of the United States?
A. Martin Van Buren.

Van Buren, the eighth President (1837-1841), was born in Kinderhook, N.Y., on Dec. 5, 1782, six years after the Declaration of Independence. He was the first President not to have been born during colonial days, which would have made him a British subject.

To learn more about Van Buren, the place to go starting Sunday will be Kinderhook, in northern Columbia County, where his home, Lindenwald, is being rededicated after almost 10 years of restoration. Named after the linden trees that once flourished there, Lindenwald, a National Historic Site, is maintained by the National Park Service.

Van Buren was a lawyer and an astute politician, earning the nicknames of "The Little Magician" and "The Red Fox of Kinderhook." He was the leader of a powerful faction in New York politics known as "the Albany regency."

He held many offices, among them State Senator, Attorney General and Governor of New York, and United States Senator. A strong supporter of Andrew Jackson for the Presidency in 1828, he was rewarded with an appointment as Secretary of State the following year. In 1832, he was elected Vice President for Jackson's second term.

As Jackson's political heir, he was elected President in 1836, becoming the first head of state to come from New York. Almost immediately his administration was confronted with the economic panic of 1837, the nation's first major depression, which led to his defeat in the next election by Willam Henry Harrison

He returned to a simple Georgian building, erected in 1797 on about 225 acres in Kinderhook, and lived there until his death in 1862. He converted the land into a working farm.

Inside the house, he removed a stairway from the entrance hall and changed it into a formal dining room, importing for its large walls 51 panels of wallpaper depicting a French hunting scene. It was used for many of his political dinners. In other parts of the house, he installed Brussels rugs, fine furniture, portraits of some of his political associates—including Jackson and Henry Clay—and cartoons, including some that attacked him.

In that period, he described his occupation as farmer, although he remained active in politics. He ran for the Presidency a third time as the candidate of the Free Soil Party in 1848, when Zachary Taylor was elected.

In 1849-50, his son hired New York City architect Richard Upjohn and made major changes in the building, adding rooms and such modern conveniences as a kitchen range, a bathroom with running water and a furnace. In addition, the red brick exterior was painted a cream color. From a simple Georgian building, Lindenwald was transformed into an eclectic mansion with elements of the Romanesque, Renaissance and Gothic Revival styles.

Martin Van Buren's home in Kinderhook.
Courtesy of the National Park Service.

The site, which had dwindled to 20 acres, was purchased by the United States in 1976, and since then the Park Service has worked to try to restore it as closely as possible to the way it looked in Van Buren's day. The cost was estimated by Park Service officials to be near $2 million.

Today, the three-story building has been repainted the cream color, the French hunting-scene wallpaper has been restored and many of the rooms have been furnished either with original Van Buren pieces or by authentic furniture of the time. A few upstairs bedrooms, although repainted and wallpapered, have no furniture at all.

"We're not sure of what was in them and have no furniture that dates from that time," the superintendent of the site, Bruce W. Stewart, said.

"We hope we will be able to get contributions of some authentic pieces of the time after we reopen."

To get there, take the Taconic State Parkway north, Route 23 west and Route 9H north to the entrance. From New York City, the drive is about two and a half hours.

A GREAT ESTATE
(June 23, 1986)

ANNANDALE-ON-HUDSON, N.Y.—Montgomery Place, a Hudson River estate dating from 1805, has been purchased for $3.75 million by Sleepy Hollow Restorations, which maintains four historic sites in Westchester County.

"Sleepy Hollow is moving from its regional base close to Tarrytown to take on added new responsibilities," said Laurance S. Rockefeller, former chairman of its board of trustees.

The acquisition of Montgomery Place, in the northwest corner of Dutchess County about 75 miles north of Tarrytown, is the first step in a new expansion program, according to Richard F. Halverson, president of Sleepy Hollow Restorations.

"With increasing development of the Hudson Valley, preservation is even more of a pressing issue," he said.

Sleepy Hollow, supported by Rockefeller contributions, maintains Sunnyside, the home of Washington Irving in Tarrytown; Van Cortlandt

Montgomery Place in Annandale-on-Hudson.
Courtesy of Historic Hudson Valley.

Manor in Croton-on-Hudson; Phillipsburg Mansion in North Tarrytown; and the Union Church, with its Chagall and Matisse stained-glass windows, in Pocantico Hills.

Montgomery Place, a 23-room Federal-style mansion on 443 wooded acres, had been occupied continuously for almost two centuries by members of the Livingston and Delafield families.

After the death last year of John White Delafield, his son, J. Dennis Delafield, sold the property to Sleepy Hollow. The organization expects to spend about $2 million for repairs and restoration, with the opening to the public tentatively set for May 1988.

Sleepy Hollow also bought the Annandale Inn, a small restaurant adjoining Montgomery Place, for $325,000 and is now operating the Inn.

Meanwhile, architects, researchers, photographers, carpenters and other workers are busy enumerating the contents of Montgomery Place and planning the restoration of the main building, surrounding barns, carriage houses and cottages.

With sweeping views of the Hudson River and the Catskill Mountains beyond, Montgomery Place sits on a knoll in the center of a 16-mile stretch on the east bank of the Hudson River known as "The Great Estate" area.

Its grounds, with towering locust trees, waterfalls, trails and rustic bridges, retain the quality that led Andrew Jackson Downing, the famous landscape architect of the mid-1900s, to comment that it was "nowhere surpassed in America in location, natural beauty or landscape gardening charms."

To the east, the property includes large orchards with about 5,000 trees producing apples, peaches and pears. For years the fruit has been sold to neighbors.

Inside, behind the Corinthian columns at the front, the mansion is a storehouse of the memorabilia of six generations of Livingstons, one of the most famous families in the United States.

On one dining room wall are portraits of Margaret Beekman and Judge Robert R. Livingston, painted by Gilbert Stuart. They were the parents of Janet Livingston Montgomery, whose husband, Gen. Richard Montgomery, was killed leading an American attack on Quebec in 1775. Mrs. Montgomery began building the house in 1802, and it was completed in 1805.

When she died in 1828, she left Montgomery Place to her younger brother, Edward, who was the 46th Mayor of New York City as well as a Senator from Louisiana, Secretary of State under President Andrew Jackson and Minister to France. His portrait and several of Jackson are among the scores of paintings on the walls.

"It will be years till we find out what we have here," said Kenneth Toole, director of business operations for Sleepy Hollow. "Our intention is not to restore Montgomery Place to a fixed place in time, but to show it as a continuum of a family living in it over the centuries.

———•———

BOSCOBEL
(March 3, 1991)

GARRISON, N.Y.—On May 21, 1961, when Boscobel, the reconstructed Federal-style home of States and Elizabeth Dyckman, was formally reopened here in Putnam County, Gov. Nelson A. Rockefeller called it "one of the most beautiful homes ever built in America."

Built between 1806 and 1808, Boscobel was saved from demolition in 1955 on its original site in Montrose in Westchester County. The General Services Administration, which was building a Veterans Hospital there, had sold it to a house-wrecking contractor for $35, but preservationists raised funds to purchase the building and moved it piece by piece 15 miles north to 45 acres they had bought here. It was rebuilt and refurnished with money largely provided by Lila Acheson Wallace, who founded *Reader's Digest* with her husband, DeWitt Wallace.

Completely restored, Boscobel now stands on a bluff overlooking the Hudson River, with West Point in the distance, as a major museum of the decorative arts of the Federal period of American architecture and furniture. It opened on Friday for a new tourist season.

On 45-minute guided tours, visitors hear the story of the Dyckmans, who built the house. He was a Loyalist during the American Revolution, working for the British in New York City and London. They were married in Trinity Church in New York in 1794.

On one of his many trips to England, Dyckman sent his wife two unusual gold and enamel snuffboxes. Their lids bear carved wooden portraits of Charles II of England on fragments of the royal oak that had sheltered him in the forest of Boscobel when he was fleeing the army of Oliver Cromwell in 1651.

Although the word Boscobel is from the Italian expression for beautiful woods, for Dyckman it was a symbol of his lifelong attachment to England. He chose it as the name for his new home in America, but he died in 1806 before he could live in it.

Mrs. Dyckman lived in the spacious two-story building with her son Peter until her death in 1823. The furniture in the building today is authentic to the period, Boscobel officials said, with almost all of it made in New York by artisans like Duncan Phyfe. But it does not include any original Dyckman articles.

In the formal parlor, which has a big window overlooking the river, are several scroll-back chairs with bright yellow upholstery, as well as a sofa in the same material and mahogany tables. The dining room, also with an expansive river view, has a mahogany table with six bamboo chairs with green cushions along with several sideboards.

Upstairs, Mrs. Dyckman and Peter each had a large bedroom overlooking the river, each with a telescope for watching the boats go by. In the back is a bathing room with a zinc-lined tub, a towel rack and water containers.

Some original Dyckman possessions are in a small museum in the basement, the original site of the kitchen, root cellar, milk house, servants' dining room and slave quarters. On display there, in addition to one of the Charles II snuffboxes, are china, hollow silverware tureens, family Bibles, bills of sale and clothing.

The Boscobel grounds have a large variety of flowering plants that bloom sequentially: in April, there are thousands of daffodils; May has its tulips, and June, its roses. The herb garden and orchards are also open to the public.

Boscobel in Garrison.
Courtesy of New York State Department of Economic Development.

CHAPTER 6

The Hudson River School

Everybody has heard of the Hudson River School of artists. But where did they come from? What has happened to their homes? Over the years, I did scores of stories about Thomas Cole, founder of that genre of painting, and his more prosperous student, Frederic Edwin Church.

FOUR PAINTERS
(June 10, 1988)

In 1825, Thomas Cole went to the Catskill Mountains to paint their rugged cliffs and streams. It was the birth of the Hudson River School of painting, which flourished until the turn of the 20th century and which has now come back into vogue.

Nineteen years later, Cole's most famous student, Frederic Edwin Church, came to study with him in Catskill. Church was 16 years old; he would later build his own home across the Hudson River, south of the city of Hudson. After him came Asher B. Durand, George Inness, John Kensett, Samuel F. B. Morse, Jasper Cropsey, Albert Bierstadt and scores of other artists.

It was the magnificent scenery of the river and the mountains to the west that lured the artists north from New York City, first as summer painters and then as permanent residents.

The artists left a permanent legacy, one that can be seen not only in their art but also in their homes, some of which have been preserved as museums open to the public. And now, at Bard College in Annandale-on-Hudson and at Vassar College in Poughkeepsie, an exhibition called "Charmed Places: Hudson River Artists and Their Houses, Studios and Vistas" shows in paintings, drawings and photographs the places in which many of those artists lived and worked.

At Bard, the exhibition includes paintings by some of the artists of their homes, studios and gardens as well as architectural drawings and old photographs. At Vassar, 20 new color photographs of some of the artists' homes as they exist today, taken by Len Jenshel, a New York City photographer, are on display.

The joint show, which will end on Aug. 12, was put together by Dr. Sandra S. Phillips, a former curator of the Vassar College Art Gallery and now curator of the San Francisco Museum of Modern Art. It is the first exhibition to document and explore the environment of the Hudson River artists, according to Linda Weintraub, the director of the Edith C. Blum Art Institute at Bard. It also traces the relationship between the artists and such Hudson Valley architects as Andrew Jackson Downing, Alexander Jackson Davis and Calvert Vaux.

Only a few paintings by the artists are included in the Bard exhibition, among them a view by Church from his home; a Cole vista of Mount Merino across the river from his home; an Inness painting of the Hudson at Milton, and a Cropsey view of the Hudson.

The famous paintings of the Hudson River School are on display at museums all over New York State, including the Metropolitan Museum of Art, the New York Public Library and the New-York Historical Society in Manhattan; the Brooklyn Museum; the Munson-Williams-Proctor Institute in Utica; and many others.

But the joint exhibition at Vassar and Bard and a visit to some of the artists's homes, not far north of New York City, make a pleasant outing. The Bard museum is open Wednesday through Sunday. The number for information is (914) 758-6822, extension 178. To get there, take the Taconic State Parkway north, Route 199 through the village of Red Hook, and Route 9G north a short distance.

The Vassar gallery is open Wednesday through Sunday, 11:30 A.M. to 8 P.M. Admission is free. Information: (914) 741-6844.

To get there, take the Taconic State Parkway north and Route 55 west, turning left of Raymond Avenue to a blinking light at the college entrance.

In addition, four of the "charmed places"—the homes of Church, Morse, Cropsey and Cole—are now small museums, open to the public. Some of the other homes of Hudson River painters have become private residences; several were destroyed by fire, and others have been extensively remodeled.

CHURCH'S OLANA

The most spectacular home of them all is a 37-room Persian-looking castle that sits on a hill overlooking the Rip Van Winkle Bridge, a few miles south of the city of Hudson. It was built between 1870 and 1874 for Church (1826-1900) and his wife and was called Olana, a word coined by Mrs. Church to mean "our place on high."

The best way to approach Olana is to get off the Gov. Thomas E. Dewey Thruway at Exit 21 in Catskill and take Route 23 east across the Hudson River. As you cross the Rip Van Winkle Bridge, cast your eyes up; directly in front of you is the splendid structure, its pyramidic towers jutting into the sky above the trees, looking like the setting for a tale from the Arabian Nights.

Vaux was the architect, although Church himself designed many of the interiors. The building has a studio wing, but Church did little painting there; he worked in a studio on the grounds, and at his Park Avenue town house in New York. He lived at Olana with his wife and four children assisted by 15 servants, until his death.

A few of Church's paintings are on view in the house, which is furnished in a melange of styles—American-made furniture, Persian rugs, Mexican pottery, Waterford crystal, Canton chinaware, and paintings by a variety of American and European artists.

Now a state historic site, Olana is open Wednesday through Sunday. Reservations are suggested. Information and reservations: (518) 828-0135.

LOCUST GROVE

Samuel F. B. Morse, a painter who is better known as an inventor (1791-1872), moved into the Hudson Valley in 1847, three years after he invented the telegraph. With the help of Andrew Jackson Downing, he remodeled his home into a Tuscan villa, with a four-story tower facing the river.

Today, it is a museum called Locust Grove, an oasis of serenity at the beginning of a strip of shopping centers two miles south of Poughkeepsie on Route 9.

Although the house contains a replica of the telegraph and an English landscape attributed to Morse, it reflects more the collecting mania of the Young family, which owned it after Morse's death. Its 24 rooms are crowded with antique furniture, old paintings and some more memorabilia.

Just outside the front door is a plaque put up in 1968 by the New York chapter of the Morse Telegraph Club. It reads: "Samuel F. B. Morse Father of the Telegraph, built this house Locust Grove. It was his summer home 1852-1871." The initials F. B. by the way, stand for Finley Breese.

Guided tours are held Wednesday through Sunday. Information: (914) 454-4500.

CROPSEY HOUSE

Jasper F. Cropsey (1823-1900) bought 45 acres in Warwick in 1866 and three years later designed and built a studio-house called Aladdin, but he was forced to sell it in 1880. A few years later, he bought a board-and-batten structure in Hastings-on-Hudson and built a studio there close in design to the one at Aladdin.

Sitting on a hill in a four-and-a-half acre plot surrounded by other residences, the yellow two-story Cropsey house is Gothic in style, with gingerbread ornaments. It contains 100 oil paintings, watercolors and drawings by Cropsey. "'Quaint' is the word for the house," said Florence Levins, the curator.

Cropsey lived and worked there from 1885 until his death in 1900. An architect as well as a painter, he designed two churches on Staten Island and several stations of the now demolished Sixth Avenue Elevated line in New York City.

Today, the house, at 49 Washington Avenue in Hastings, just off Route 9, is maintained by the Newington Cropsey Foundation. It is open by appointment only. Telephone: (914) 478-1372.

Olana, the home of Frederic Edwin Church, in Hudson.
Courtesy of New York State Office of Parks, Recreation and Historic Preservation, Olana State Historic Site.

COLE STUDIO

Thomas Cole (1801-1848), a self-taught artist who was born in England, arrived in the United States in 1818. In 1836, he married Maria Barlow and settled in her family home, Cedar Grove, outside Catskill. In 1846, only two years before his death, he designed and built an Italianate studio on the property. That has been destroyed, but an old stable that he also used as a studio still stands.

The Cole house, at 218 Spring Street in Catskill, is a three-story brick structure that stands today between a synagogue and another residence. It is pleasant looking, with nothing to distinguish it from the suburban homes that surround it.

A chain across the driveway shows it is closed for repairs, but it can be seen by appointment. It will reopen to the public on July 6, repainted in its original colors. Information: (518) 943-6533. To get there, cross the Rip Van Winkle Bridge going west and turn immediately onto route 385 south; the house is a few hundred feet on the left.

—————•—————

SUCCESS
(August 12, 1980)

"We have almost been killed by success," reports James Ryan, director of Olana, the Persian-style castle in Hudson, N.Y., once the home of Frederic Edwin Church, the Hudson River School painter, whose "Icebergs" sold last winter for $2.5 million, the highest price ever paid for an American painting.

At times last year, there were long lines of visitors awaiting admission for the 45-minute tours of the startling structure, which mixes Middle Eastern, Latin American, Mexican and North American design. Even though 27,000 people did tour the building, many others were turned away, Mr. Ryan said.

This year, a new admissions policy has been adopted for the castle, which is open Wednesdays through Sundays, 9 A.M. to 5 P.M., from Memorial Day through October. Under the new policy reservations can be made by telephoning (518) 828-0135 for two of the tours, those starting at 10 A.M. and at 3 P.M. In addition, tickets are sold at the gate for tours at other specified times, so that there no longer are lines awaiting admission. On weekdays, tours start every 30 minutes; on weekends, every 20 minutes.

But the tours, which are limited to 12 persons each, have proved so popular that the day's quota of admissions is frequently filled by 1 P.M., especially on weekends, according to Mr. Ryan. "We had to limit access for all to permit access for some and also to preserve the building," he said.

The building and the 400 acres that surround it are on Route 9G, just south of the eastern end of the Rip Van Winkle Bridge, about three miles south of the city of Hudson. The site, which is operated by the State Office of Parks and Recreation, is about 100 miles north of New York City.

The grounds, overlooking the Hudson River and the Catskill Mountains, are open daily from 8 A.M. to dark without charge, for hiking, picnics and walking on nature trails.

But what most people come to see is the five-story house sitting incongruously atop a 500-foot hill. The 37-room mansion was built with flagstones and red-and-tan brick between 1870 and 1874. Church—a man whose eccentricities extended to the spelling of his own name, which he changed in midlife from Frederick to Frederic—designed many of the interiors himself. The architect was Calvert Vaux, a Briton, who came to Manhattan in 1852, and together with Frederick Law Olmstead designed and developed the plans for Central and Prospect Parks.

Church planned his house as a total environment—castle, studio, paintings, furnishings, objets d'art, landscaping—all the expression of his tastes and an escape for himself and his family from the rest of the world and its cares. The castle is built chiefly of a local reddish stone, but it boasts fantastic color and embellishments: arched Persian-style windows outlined with red, yellow and black brick in mosaic patterns; tiles from Iran, Mexico and parts of the United States and fancy stenciled cornices. Its square towers are crowned with soaring multicolor slate roofs. The site is approached by a mile-long driveway winding through heavy woodland, and the castle itself commands a series of artful vistas: rolling meadows, a 12-acre artificial lake, the Hudson River and valley and the Catskill Mountains.

By 1874, the year Olana was completed, Church had traveled to the Middle East, Europe, South America, Mexico and Newfoundland, and had already painted "Icebergs" and "Niagara," which won him a medal at the Paris International Exhibition of 1867.

A few of the paintings by Church and his teacher, Thomas Cole, are on view at Olana, where Church lived with his wife, Isabel, and his four children, assisted by 15 servants, until his death in 1900. The name Olana, choosen by Mrs. Church, is Arabic for "our place on high."

The house is furnished in a melange of styles, with American-made furniture, Persian rugs, Colombian artifacts, Mexican pottery, Waterford crystal, Canton china, paintings by a variety of American and European artists, and a 117-year-old Christmas cactus plant that still blooms.

On entering the central Court Hall, the visitor receives the full impact of Church's passion for the exotic. The room stretches across the entire house, with a brass-railed grand staircase ascending at the rear, a concept Church took from a Persian palace. The formal East Parlor contains furnishings that reflect Church's eclectic taste: European tables and chairs, mother-of-pearl inlaid taborets from Egypt and Morocco, a typical Victorian overstuffed chair, and a fireplace framed with East Indian carvings, to name a few.

Although the mansion's studio, which faces north, has an easel, palettes and other artist's paraphernalia, Church did little painting at Olana. He worked at his Park Avenue town house in New York City and at a studio on the grounds. The Churches also had camps in Maine and North Carolina.

One of the questions visitors frequently ask is, "Where did Church get his money?" According to Mr. Ryan, some of it came from his father, who was in manufacturing and insurance. But Church was also paid large sums for his paintings.

When he died, he left more than half a million dollars—and the estate passed to his son Louis. Louis's widow, Sally, lived there until her death in 1964. The property was about to be auctioned when Olana Preservation Inc., a private organization, was organized as caretaker until the state could take it over. Olana was opened to the public in 1967.

* * *

FAILURE
(May 30, 1994)

CATSKILL, N.Y.—On a clear day in the 1840's, Thomas Cole, the founder of the Hudson River school of painting, could sit on his porch here and look to the west to the Catskill Mountain scenery that he put into his paintings.

Today, almost 150 years after his death, Congress is considering bills to make his home a national historic site and the focus of an artists' historical park encompassing the mountains and streams depicted in his work.

Most of the land painted by Cole and other artists now falls within the Catskill Park and Forest Preserve, largely owned by the state. That would not

The Thomas Cole house in Catskill.
Courtesy of National Park Service.

change under the proposed legislation, although the Federal Government would be authorized to accept donations of additional land.

Local groups said their main concern was preserving the Cole house and studio, which they said are threatened by neglect.

Senator Daniel Patrick Moynihan has called for immediate action to save the buildings. "The house needs work," he said, "and should not endure another winter like the last one in its present state."

A similar bill has been introduced in the House of Representatives by Gerald Solomon, a Glens Falls Republican, whose district includes the Cole House.

The two-story brick Federal structure is painted light yellow and sits on 3.5 acres here, across the road from a gasoline station on a street with suburban-type houses. Trees have grown high enough to block any view of the Catskills from the porch.

The house, which was purchased by the Thomas Cole Foundation in 1982, is closed to the public. It will be open for visits in July and August on Wednesdays through Sundays, said Donelson Hoopes, guardian of the site.

But there is little to see in the house. Sparsely furnished, it contains only a few artifacts from Cole's day, including a palette and some brushes he used, but none of his paintings. The exhibits include color transparencies of his major works, which are in museums around the country.

The foundation says it cannot maintain the property properly and has offered to donate it to the Government if it becomes a national historic site.

"It belongs to the nation," said Ira Spanierman, an art dealer in New York City who is president of the foundation. "It's the spiritual birthplace of American landscape painting. It should be a national shrine."

The foundation bought the house from the Catskill Center for Conservation and Development, a private nonprofit organization that had acquired the property in 1979 from Edith Cole Silberstein, Cole's great-granddaughter.

Cole lived in the house and worked in a studio at the rear of the property from 1836 until he died in 1848 at the age of 47.

Born in England in 1801, he came to the United States as a boy and became a self-taught artist. Interested in landscapes, he made several trips into the Catskill Mountains area, producing the "romantic realist" paintings that brought him fame.

He frequently walked from his home through the village of Catskill, along a trail that is now State Route 23A, to the Kaaterskill Falls, which became one of the most painted landscapes of the 19th century. Typically, he would stop and sketch, making notes for paintings to be created later in his studio.

Within a 15-mile radius of his home are more than 10 sites he painted and as many more painted by artists of the Hudson River school, including his most famous pupil, Frederic Edwin Church.

In contrast to the neglected condition of the Cole house, Church's opulent home Olana, which resembles a well-preserved Persian castle, sits on a hill on the east side of the Hudson River, little more than a mile away. Filled with paintings, furniture and objects collected over the years, it is a state historic site and a popular tourist attraction.

Testifying before a Senate subcommittee on May 17, Marie Rust, North Atlantic regional director for the National Park Service, quoted estimates that it would take $3.5 million to restore and develop the Cole site and another $350,000 a year to maintain it.

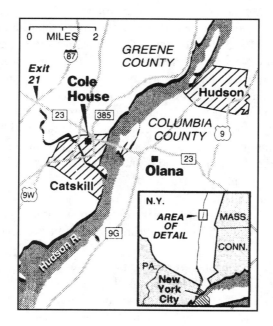

Chapter Seven

A Capital City

I like Albany. I like its public buildings, its museums, and its restaurants. And I am constantly amazed by how many New Yorkers have never visited Albany and who seem to reject the idea when it is broached. They are missing plenty.

EXPLORING ALBANY
(June 7, 1976)

As a new session of the Legislature opens, Albany again takes center stage, the focus of attention for returning lawmakers and people intent on doing business with New York State. But there is more than state business in the capital, as visitors willing to explore just a few steps beyond the legislative halls can discover this weekend.

Like most capitals, Albany has two faces. It is the working home of 40,000 state employees, and it is also a city where 110,000 people live year-round, oblivious to the city's governmental functions. The city and its roguish past is described by William Kennedy, the novelist, in his new book, "O Albany! City of Political Wizards, Fearless Ethnics, Spectacular Aristocrats, Splendid Nobodies and Underrated Scoundrels."

For the casual visitor, however, the roguish side of Albany is invisible. What is most surprising to an outsider is the city's architectural diversity and beauty. Its skyline is dominated by the huge marble and glass Empire State Plaza complex of state offices, but the State Capitol itself could be mistaken for a French chateau, and the Executive Mansion is a prime example of Victorian busyness. Perhaps the most handsome building in town is the Gothic headquarters of the State University, which overlooks the Hudson River, a copy of the Flemish Cloth Guild Hall in Ypres, Belgium.

HISTORY

It was the beaver that attracted the first settlers to Albany. In 1614, the Dutch established a trading post, Fort Nassau, on the site to trade trinkets to the Mohican Indians for beaver pelts. When Fort Nassau was destroyed by ice in 1617, the Dutch established Fort Orange there. The first permanent settlers came in 1624.

In 1652, Peter Stuyvesant ordered the settlement's name changed to Beverwyck, Dutch for "town of the beaver." When the British took possession in 1664, the name was changed to Albany. Following the American Revolution, in 1797, Albany, because of its central location, became the state capital.

THE STATE CAPITOL

Built between 1867 and 1898, the State Capitol sits on top of a hill on State Street, set off with pyramidal red-tile corner dormers, with traces of Second Empire, Romanesque and Renaissance elements. It is one of the few state capitols in the country without a dome.

The New York State Capitol in Albany.
Courtesy of New York State Department of Economic Development.

The interior is working space—offices for the Governor and chambers for the Senate and Assembly, with a visitors' gallery for the public. Tours are conducted daily between 9 A.M. and 4 P.M., with no admission charge. The number for tour information is (518) 474-2418, but reservations are not necessary.

THE STATE MUSEUM

From the A train in New York City's IND subway to the elk of the Adirondacks, the State Museum is a fascinating collection of memorabilia about the people and nature of the Empire State. The permanent displays include dioramas of New York City and the Adirondacks, with another one in preparation for upstate New York.

The museum, which is on the south end of the Mall, is open free 10 A.M. to 5 P.M., daily except Thanksgiving, Christmas and New Year's.

THE EXECUTIVE MANSION

A Victorian structure of 40 rooms whose first occupant was Gov. Samuel J. Tilden in 1875, it is now the home of Governor Cuomo and his family, one block south of the Mall. The public rooms are open for guided tours. They include the reception hall, the drawing room, the dining room, and the County Room on the second floor, with a painting or other art work depicting each of the state's 62 counties.

Tours are given Thursdays only, at 1, 2 and 3 P.M., with reservations required at least a week in advance, from (518) 474-2418.

THE MALL

Officially it's the Gov. Nelson A. Rockefeller Empire State Plaza in honor of the man who pushed it through, but everybody calls it the Mall. Built at a cost of $2 billion, it has been derided as "Nelson's Edifice Complex," but it has become a major tourist attraction as well as the working place of 13,000 state employees.

The Mall's dozen marble and glass structures cover 98 acres just south of the Capitol. Among them are office buildings for the Legislature and the courts; a Cultural Education Center housing the state library (with 4.5 million books, the third largest in the country) and the State Museum; the Erastus Corning Tower (named for the former Mayor of Albany), 42 stories high, the tallest building in the state north of New York City (with an observation deck open free to the public from 9 A.M. to 4 P.M. daily), and the astonishing upturned elliptical building for the performing arts called the Egg.

The buildings are connected by an underground concourse with shops and eating places. Its walls are covered by paintings by such artists as Helen

The Executive Mansion in Albany.
Courtesy of New York State Department of Economic Development.

Frankenthaler and Mark Rothko. Free tours of the Mall start at 11 A.M., 1 P.M. and 3 P.M. daily from Room 106 in the concourse.

THE ALBANY INSTITUTE

Just one block north of the Capitol, at 125 Washington Avenue, is the Albany Institute of History and Art, a small, delightful museum. The current exhibition is a collection of landscape and topographical prints of the early 19th century (through Jan. 15). Opening on Jan. 15 is an exhibition about state inventors and inventions. Another exhibition this month and next is a retrospective of the metal works of Samuel Yellin, the architectural blacksmith. The museum is open free Tuesday through Sundays.

NEW MUSEUM
(June 7, 1976)

ALBANY—Ten stuffed animals—a moose, two beavers, three gray wolves and four black bears—have been moved from the old State Museum here to the new State Museum, which opens for its first preview tomorrow.

The stuffed animals, with their hides refurbished and their fur carefully groomed, are the only exhibits from the old museum, housed on the fifth floor of the State Education Department Building, that will be used in the new museum, situated on the modernistic Empire State Plaza.

At 4:30 P.M. on June 30, the doors will close on the old museum, with its old fashioned cases of gems, stones, table maps, mounted birds and animals, whales and a life-size model of the Cohoes mastodon. All the exhibits except the 10 stuffed animals will be put into storage, donated to other museums and educational institutions or—in rare instances—sold.

The following day, the new museum will open, with its first permanent exhibit devoted to the Adirondacks wilderness as part of the theme "Man and Nature in New York State," and an open-air exhibit on the forces that helped shape New York State. The stuffed animals are part of several different dioramas of Adirondacks Mountains scenes.

Other permanent exhibits, now being planned, will cover New York City-Long Island and upstate New York. But for those nostalgic for city life, the museum has already installed an old-fashioned city traffic light, a manhole cover and an old fire hydrant in one of its hallways.

At the south end of the plaza, the museum occupies one floor covering 4.5 acres of ground in a 10-story building which bears the bureaucratically conceived name Cultural Education Center. The building will also house the State Archives and the State Library, which are to move in—also from the Education Department Building—in 1977.

The opening of the museum marks another step toward completion of the controversial billion-dollar brainchild of former Gov. Nelson A. Rockefeller, which is about two years behind schedule. The cost of constructing the entire plaza, which was started in 1964, was put at $985 million by the General Services Administration. But critics, including State Comptroller Arthur Levitt, have said that, with interest charges, the cost will exceed $1.5 billion.

From the State Capitol, the plaza opens up to the new cultural center at the south end, with a huge granite staircase leading up from a terrace to an open-air exhibition level. Above that, the center's marble walls are broken by tall and narrow glass windows.

"We call that gun-portal architecture," said Fred Van Daacke, a senior historical planner for the State Museum, as he conducted a tour of the building. "It's almost as if we were prepared for the British coming again."

Scores of workers were busy in the building, installing carpeting, polishing the brass and completing some of the exhibits in preparation for a press preview and for official visitors before the formal opening day.

"We're 99 percent complete now," Mr. Van Daacke said, as he watched a worker adjusting logs on one of the dioramas, a reproduction of a logging run in the tree-cutting years in the Adirondacks.

In addition to the Adirondacks display inside the building, the museum will also open a Bicentennial exhibit, entitled "Forces," on the open-air terrace gallery. According to museum personnel, the three forces that shaped New York society were materialism, diversity and change.

Among the items in the "Forces" display will be Horatio Alger books, "hard times" tokens, posters advertising English classes for foreigners, Dutch furniture, a brass lantern, and a modern washing machine, radio and refrigerator.

The museum and the terrace will open officially over the four-day July 4 weekend, with concerts and ceremonies each day. During the summer the museum will be open from 10 A.M. to 9 P.M., with no admission charge.

"The museum's aim is to try to get visitors to experience the exhibits as if they were the real thing," Mr. Van Daacke said. As part of that attempt, he said, the dioramas were made large, the explanatory texts were kept short and photographs were blown up to become backdrops, instead of using paintings.

According to another museum official, G. Carroll Lindsay, director of public programs, the new museum is different because it is "theme oriented."

"No object in the exhibit halls is treated separately as a historic or scientific phenomenon," he said.

All the exhibits in the new museum were planned and constructed by members of its staff. The architect for the building and for the entire Empire State Plaza was Harrison and Abramovitz of New York City.

THE EMPIRE STATE PLAZA
(May 28, 1978)

ALBANY—Sixteen years after construction started, the modernistic Empire State Plaza, covering 98 acres of downtown Albany, is now complete.

On Friday, the last building to be completed, the inverted oval Meeting Center that everyone calls "the egg," was formally dedicated. Soon John C. Byron, the man who supervised construction of the billion-dollar project, will retire and his office will go out of existence.

Incongruously set in the middle of Victorian Albany between the baroque State Capitol and the turreted red-brick Governor's Mansion, the plaza consists of 10 office buildings for state employees, the State Library and Museum, and the Meeting Center, constructed in a "Buck Rogers" style of glass and steel towers faced with enormous quantities of marble.

Looking down from the window of his 41st floor office, Mr. Byron can see only one brown spot in the vast open spaces between the buildings. It is one of the few unfinished things that he will leave behind, an area that will become a park for children.

Over the years, the controversy surrounding the plaza, mainly because of its design, cost and financing, has gradually died down, and today, the plaza has become one of the major tourist attractions in the state, admired by many visitors.

"It's absolutely magnificent," said Harold Hein of Thornwood, N.Y., who recently made his first visit to the plaza. "It's so beautifully done and dramatic in appearance. It is certainly an improvement over the slums that were here before. I had heard that it was called 'Rocky's Folly,' but I certainly don't agree with that."

When the construction, pushed by then Gov. Nelson A. Rockefeller, was started, the project was called many other names, including "Rocky's erector

The Governor Nelson A. Rockefeller Plaza, or "the Mall," in Albany.
Courtesy of New York State Department of Economic Development.

set" and "Rocky's edifice complex," but recently even Democratic critics have muted their comments because of the apparent tourist approval.

However, a recent move to rename the project the "Gov. Nelson A. Rockefeller Plaza" has apparently died in the Democratic controlled State Assembly, ostensibly because it would cost too much to change all the signs and papers in the area.

Even though the name is officially the "Empire State Plaza," everyone in Albany calls it simply "The Mall," a contraction of its first name, which was "The South Mall."

"Despite all the other names, it's still the South Mall legally," Mr. Byron said. "That's the name on all the contracts and legal documents and it's the only name with any legal significance."

The cost of the project, for construction alone, was put by Mr. Byron at $985 million—about twice the original estimates. But, according to its critics, notably Arthur Levitt, the State Comptroller, the real cost to the taxpayers, including financing charges, will be nearer $2 billion.

"But, you know, the construction cost is not that high, considering today's inflation and the cost of other major projects," Mr. Byron said. "Why, the Olympic Stadium in Montreal alone cost $800 million."

Some criticisms of the plaza are still being made by visitors, however— lack of adequate parking space, inefficient use of office space and huge distances between buildings.

One project under consideration by the state is the use of small tractor-driven carriages, such as those used at the World's Fair, to transport people on roadways that would flank the large reflecting pools in the center of the plaza, Mr. Byron said.

Mr. Byron, a civil engineer who is 62 years old, has been with the Office of General Services, which supervises the construction and operation of all state buildings, since he got out of the Army in 1946. He has been involved with the Mall since it was started, becoming director of construction in 1971.

As he looked back, Mr. Byron said the biggest challenge had been the pouring of concrete for the peculiarly shaped, inverted "egg."

"There's been nothing like it," he said. "We had to construct rings around the concrete before we poured, and as we poured it, we had to make the shell self-supporting. We put hundreds of ring gauges in the concrete, sending information to a computer to monitor the stresses. We found that the stresses were less than we had predicted."

Another problem with the egg was that the concrete was poured in the summer, when the outside temperature was high.

"We knew that the outside temperature of the shell could not exceed 160 degrees and we also knew that concrete gives off heat when it sets," he said. "What we did was to use ice instead of water in mixing the concrete. That made for a slower increase in heat as the concrete set, and that's how we solved the problem."

Mr. Byron is "an old-fashioned, rare, dedicated individual," said his boss, John Egan, deputy commissioner of the Office of General Services. "He never seeks publicity or personal aggrandizement."

But his colleagues recognize him as "the man who built the mall."

THE STATE LIBRARY
(February 23, 1978)

ALBANY—Leonard Di Chiaro and Charles Rothe are checking 25,000 books out of the state library every day this week but they have no intention of reading any of them.

They took them from the old state library, housed in the State Department of Education building directly across the street from the State Capitol, about a half-mile across town to the new state library on the south end of the Empire State Plaza.

Packed in cardboard boxes, the books were carried in 27-foot trailer trucks driven by Mr. Di Chiaro and Mr. Rothe as part of a movement of 4.5 million books, journals, maps, manuscripts, newspapers and magazines in the library collection. The move, which started on Feb. 8, is expected to be completed by the end of March.

The two truckers are part of a 72-man moving team from the Neptune World Wide Movers of New Rochelle, which is working 16 hours a day, five days a week, under a $490,000 contract to complete the move in time for a spring opening of the new library.

In its modernistic new home, the library shares a building called the Cultural Education Center with the State Museum and the State Archives. The museum has already opened, drawing thousands of visitors a day.

The library directors are planning to have the institution, which is celebrating its 160th birthday this year, in full operation in time for the Governor's conference on the future of libraries in the state, which will open in Albany on June 5.

When the new facility is opened, it will have a computerized index catalogue, open stacks for public browsing and research, large amounts of shelf space with room for expansion, and splendid views of the Hudson River and the Helderberg Hills from its floor-to-ceiling windows.

The new library consists of two parts—the sixth, seventh and eighth floors of the Cultural Education Center, each about the size of three football fields, and a well-lighted cavernous basement containing three floors of bookshelves, the equivalent of about two football fields, filled with bookshelves six feet high.

"One of the things we are excited about in the new building is the better level of service we will be able to provide through technology to meet the changing information needs," said Peter J. Paulson, director of the new library, in an interview.

In addition, the library's annual budget of $3 million has been raised by 6 percent and it has received permission to fill vacancies on its staff to bring it up to the 180 positions authorized, Mr. Paulson said.

Its major functions are to provide reference materials for the State Legislature and other government offices, to service materials for the blind and the visually handicapped, to be a central repository of books on call from libraries throughout the state through an interlibrary loan system, and to be a reference center for the public.

Mr. Paulson said that the library would be better able to provide those services in the new building than in the old, which he said was overcrowded, poorly lighted and inefficient.

But there are those who regret leaving the old library, which has been housed in the Education Department building since 1912. Its main reading room on the second floor is a huge domed structure, several floors high, with stained glass windows, serviced by creaky elevators grinding upward from seven tiers of dusty, stacked books in the basement. It has some open shelves of general reference works and large collections of genealogy and local history books.

"I'm going to miss this place," said Joan Hoose, a librarian, on a tour of the old building. "But there will be better lighting in the new stacks in the new building and we'll like that."

Not everything is going to the new library, according to William De Alleaume, a principal librarian who is supervising the move. Left behind will be bulk newspapers being converted to microfilm, some state documents, some archival material, an old textbook collection and the old index-card catalogue.

The catalogue, which contains more than three million index cards in 2,000 file drawers, is being converted to magnetic tapes, with users having access through computer terminals. Just two terminals will be ready for use on opening day.

In the meantime, most patrons of the new library will be able to use a temporary index system in which books have been catalogued on small microfiche transparencies which contain hundreds of entries that can be read on a device resembling a small television screen. The entire collection has been catalogued in two drawers by that method instead of the 2,000 drawers needed for the index system.

CHAPTER EIGHT

The Most Beautiful Road

My nominee for the most beautiful major road in New York State is the Taconic State Parkway, from Westchester County north to the northern end of Columbia County, where it ends in the Berkshire Spur that connects the Massachusetts Turnpike to the New York State Thruway.

THE TACONIC STATE PARKWAY
(August 14, 1987)

Many years ago, Lewis Mumford described the Taconic State Parkway as a consummate work of art, fit to stand on a par with our loftiest creations. It is still a beautiful parkway, with its scenic qualities increasing the farther north you drive on it.

The Taconic is 105 miles long, from the northern suburbs of New York City to the hilly, rural Hudson Valley. Like all major roads leading out of metropolitan New York, it is crowded on Friday and Sunday evenings, but at other times, it is a pleasure to use, evoking those bygone days when people went for a drive just for the fun of it.

As a gateway to the countryside, the Taconic is twice an attraction. Not only does it lead to nearby tourist areas, but it can also be enjoyed for its beauty, something one can hardly say about the crowded Northern State Parkway on Long Island or the narrow, winding and sometime exasperating Bronx River Parkway.

A summer outing on the Taconic State Parkway can begin where the road starts, at the Kensico Dam Plaza at Valhalla in central Westchester County. Already, the Taconic is different. There, in front of the huge masonry wall that holds back 32.6 billion gallons of New York City water, a large grassy expanse invites a brief stop, perhaps for a picnic. It was there that construction of the parkway started in 1929, but it was not completed until 1963.

Once on the road, a slight detour after only 4.2 miles of driving is well worth taking—on Route 117 and then 448 west 2.6 miles to Pocantico Hills, the Rockefeller family home. The major attraction there is the lovely small Union Church and its stained-glass windows.

High above the Union Church's altar, a Matisse rose window reflects the sun in a leafy motif of green, yellow, blue and white. At the opposite end of the church a Chagall window of vivid blues, reds, yellows and greens shines down. On the side walls, eight more Chagall windows, seven representing Old Testament prophets and one in memory of Michael Rockefeller who died in New Guinea, catch the sun's rays, too. Information: (914) 631-8200

Returning to the Taconic, a 12-mile drive through the fashionable central Westchester suburbs of Pleasantville and Chappaqua leads to a bridge that crosses the Croton Reservoir to the entrance of the Franklin D. Roosevelt State Park.

ROOSEVELT PARK

Named after the 32nd President of the United States (1933-1945), the park offers swimming in a pool, boating on a lake and picnicking on the grass as well as fields for playing softball and soccer (and ski trails in the winter). Information: (914) 245-4434.

About 12 miles farther north, the Taconic begins a climbing, curvy path through the hills of the Clarence Fahnestock State Park in Putnam County, where a reduced speed is recommended. To get to the park, exit at Route 301 and go less than a mile west to the entrance.

FAHNESTOCK PARK

The 12,000-acre Fahnestock State Park, named after Clarence Fahnestock, a local doctor who died in France in World War I, is open year round. In the summer, it offers hiking trails, tent and trailer camping, bridle paths, boat rentals, fishing holes and a beach for swimming; in the winter, ice fishing, skating, cross-country skiing, snowshoeing and snowmobiling as well as a few camping sites. Information: (914) 225-7207.

Thirteen miles beyond the park, the vistas on the Taconic open up with a spectacular view of the hills of Dutchess County, and the parkway becomes an even more pleasant and enjoyable ride.

After passing the intersection of Interstate 84, the next site of note is Shenandoah, the only gas station on the parkway. The State Department of Transportation, which maintains the parkway, says it has closed five others because of lack of business and inability to find responsible operators. Shenandoah is also the only rest stop on the parkway.

From there, it's seven miles to the James Baird State Park, which does have restrooms and a host of recreational facilities.

BAIRD PARK

Named after a local contractor who donated the 590 acres to the state, James Baird State Park provides a 50-meter Olympic-sized swimming pool, picnic grounds, soccer fields, basketball, volleyball and tennis courts and an 18-hole golf course. Information: (914) 452-1489.

Back to the Taconic, it's 6.3 miles north to Route 44 and then four miles on that road east to the village of Millbrook, in the center of the horsey hunt area of Dutchess County, where you are just as likely to park next to a Mercedes as a Jeep.

A scenic view of the Taconic State Parkway.
Courtesy of New York State Department of Transportation.

MILLBROOK

Millbrook is a good place for a lunch stop, with French, Italian and country inn restaurants as well as a diner on or near Franklin Avenue, which is Route 44 through the center of the village. It is also an antiques center, with scores of dealers clustered in a few shops.

Returning to the Taconic, it's a 20-mile drive to the first overlook now open on the parkway, just over the county line in Columbia County. Up to last year, there were many others open farther south, but the state closed them down because of excessive illegal dumping of household garbage by travelers returning to the metropolitan area. It was too expensive to clean up, the state said.

From there, it's only 2.3 miles to the entrance to Lake Taghkanic State Park, the last park on the parkway. Its name is pronounced the same as the parkway. The word is derived from the name of a spring used by Indians hunting in the area. One translation for the spring's name is "water enough" and another, "come and go."

TAGHKANIC PARK

Lake Taghkanic State Park's 1,569 acres are largely devoted to low-cost family programs—with cabins and cottages available (advance registration necessary), two bathing beaches on Lake Taghkanic, picnic areas, boat rentals, softball fields and walking trails. Information: (518) 851-3631.

Leaving Lake Taghkanic, it's exactly 21 miles through the hill country of Columbia County to Route 203, the exit leading to the village of Chatham, still relatively unspoiled by creeping boutiquism.

CHATHAM

A likely first stop is the Bakery, at the corner of Routes 203 and 66, where the locals meet for breakfast, lunch and dinner. A walk on Main Street will bring you to an old-fashioned 5-and-10-cent store, a railroad crossing at grade level, and many old-fashioned supply stores. Well worth a detour is the Shaker Museum in Old Chatham, with 8,500 items in three buildings covering more than 200 years of Shaker history in the United States. Information: (518) 794-9100. To get there from Chatham, take Routes 66 and 13 north, following the signs seven miles to the entrance.

For all practical purposes, Chatham is the end of the Taconic, but the parkway does go on for about four miles more to its intersection with the Berkshire Spur of Interstate 90. If you do continue, take the Spur west nine miles, paying a 25-cent toll.

There you have two options: returning to the Taconic, retracing your path on the southbound lanes, or going south more leisurely on Routes 9 and 9H, through the apple orchards and farm stands of Columbia County.

Sooner or later, though, it will be necessary to return to the Taconic for the trip home. One good choice is to continue south on Route 9 to Rhinebeck, in northern Dutchess County, which has several fine restaurants. From there, take Routes 308 and 199 east to the Taconic, making it a parkway round trip.

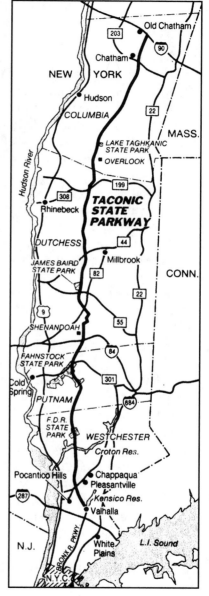

SOME MORE SCENIC ROADS
(June 13, 1986)

With the Hudson Valley entering the full bloom of summer, it's a good time to tour the area's most scenic roads—officially certified by the State Department of Environmental Conservation.

The roads—80 miles of them in the Hudson Valley—were identified as among the state's most beautiful because of the vistas they afford and the "substantial opportunity" they offer travelers to appreciate the cultural, historic and topographical features of the region, according to the Conservation Department.

A good place to start a Hudson Valley tour is by crossing the Tappan Zee Bridge, which carries one of the official scenic roads. Continue west on Interstate 287 to the Palisades Interstate Parkway, an unofficial scenic road.

After about 10 miles north on the parkway, exit left on Route 17A and then drive north on Seven Lakes Drive through the Harriman State Park to Bear Mountain.

Instead of crossing the Bear Mountain Bridge at the Bear Mountain traffic circle, go north on Route 9W to Highland Falls and continue north through West Point on Route 218. West Point is well worth a stop to see the military museum and the panoramic views of the Hudson River.

Route 218 is the Storm King Highway, which climbs along the west bank of the Hudson River around the mountain for which it is named. If mountain roads bother you, an alternative is to continue north on Route 9W, another official scenic road, to Cornwall.

Either way, you will find yourself going north on Route 9W through the city of Newburgh, where a turn to the east on Route 17K for a short distance will take you to Washington's headquarters on a bluff overlooking the Hudson River. The headquarters is open 9 A.M. to 5 P.M. on weekends.

If by this time you have had enough driving, cross the Newburgh-Beacon Bridge, which is a scenic road, too, and proceed south through the city of Beacon on Route 9D. Farther south, Route 9D becomes one of the valley's scenic roads.

From Route 9D it's a short jog west to either Cold Spring or Garrison. Each village has a riverside park for Hudson River- watching and restaurants.

A LONGER TOUR
For those who want a longer Hudson River road tour, go north from Newburgh on Route 9W through the apple tree country around Marlboro and

Highland to Ulster Park. There, River Road goes off to the right (east) for a short loop close to the river. It returns to Route 9W just south of Kingston. Proceed farther north on Route 9W through Saugerties and Catskill. Just north of Catskill, turn right for a short distance on Route 23 and then left on Route 385, which skirts the river, through Athens and Coxsackie to New Baltimore.

For the return trip, the best way is to retrace Route 385 south to the Rip Van Winkle Bridge, another scenic road, across the Hudson River. From the bridge, you will be able to glimpse Olana, the Persian castle-like home of the artist Frederic Edwin Church, which is a state historic site on a hill on the east bank, well worth a detour.

Take Route 9G south a short distance to the Olana entrance, or continue south on it through Columbia and Dutchess Counties to Annandale-on-Hudson. There, turn right (toward the river) to River Road.

Its name is really a misnomer because, although close to the Hudson, it offers no river views but traverses the back ends of many large river estates. It runs south through the campus of Bard College, where a pleasant stop is the college's art gallery.

For a meal break, turn left on Route 308 a short distance to Rhinebeck where there are several restaurants to choose from.

Return to River Road, past the Rhinecliff railroad station, and follow the road, which changes its name several times before it reaches Route 9. South of Staatsburg, Route 9 becomes an official scenic road. If you want to stop to watch boats on the river or for a picnic, try either the Norrie Point State Park or the Vanderbilt Mansion, both of which have entrances on the right on Route 9.

If by this time you have had enough of Hudson River scenery, turn east (left) on East Park Road at the traffic light in Hyde Park to the Taconic State Parkway. Although it has no official designation, the Taconic is one of the most scenic roads in the Hudson Valley, a bonus for weary homebound motorists.

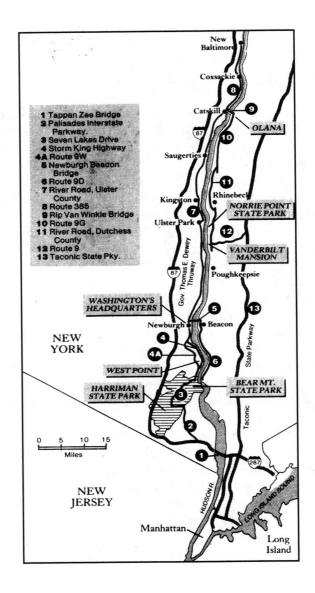

CHAPTER 9

The Foliage Season

Every year, it was a delight to write the annual fall foliage story. The problem was how to find something new to say about the changing leaves, which more or less were the same each year. I finally devised a pattern of describing a different kind of trip in the valley each season, touching on its many other kinds of attractions. Following is an example of those foliage stories.

A FOLIAGE TRIP
(October 14, 1983)

The foliage season is approaching metropolitan New York—a little late and a little more muted than usual because of the long dry summer and an autumn that has been a little warmer than usual.

The normally vivid fall colors of the leaves may be somewhat more subtle this year, but there will still be a spectacular display starting this weekend in the Hudson Valley and northwestern Connecticut, and a little later in nearby New Jersey, Connecticut and Westchester.

As the days grow shorter and the nights longer, the annual tide of color is slowly sweeping down from the north toward the metropolitan area. Last weekend, the color was reported to be at its peak in the Adirondack region—at places like Lake Placid, Old Forge, Indian Lake and the Prospect Mountain Veteran's Memorial Drive at Lake George.

In New England, always a major area for foliage watching, reports indicated that the foliage display was at least a week late. In the Catskill Mountains, the colors were reported to be nearing their peak at least a week later than usual.

Nevertheless, farther south the low-lying sumacs and the climbing wild Virginia creepers, the first of the leaves to turn, are dark red and purple, indication that the crimson of the sugar maples and the golden yellow of the hickories are not far behind.

"This weekend should see the peak of the foliage in the Hudson Valley," said Jerry Gotsch, a state forester based there.

The peak is coming a week after the Columbus Day weekend for two reasons. One is that the holiday this year came a bit earlier than usual, on Monday, Oct. 10, to make a three-day holiday weekend, instead of on the traditional Oct. 12, the day Columbus discovered America. The other is the weather.

"The warm and dry weather has delayed the turning of the foliage," said Dr. George Stevens of the Connecticut Agricultural Experiment Station in New Haven.

Last month, the nights were not cold enough to turn McIntosh apples the bright red that consumers like. And this month, the nights have not been consistently cold enough to trigger the chemical reactions that bring bright colors to the leaves.

In a normal pattern, the leaves start to turn when night temperatures drop to 40 degrees or lower. The changes in light and temperature slow the complicated processes in the leaves, which gradually lose their ability to produce chlorophyll, the chemical that makes leaves green.

As the chlorophyll disappears, the colors it masks in the green leaves become more apparent. Carotene, which produces yellow colors, emerges in the leaves of poplars, tulip trees, birches and sycamores. In other trees, anthocyanins are produced, turning maple leaves red, ashes purple and oaks brown.

Recent research has shown that the cool nights of autumn inhibit the flow of sugar out of the leaves. In daytime, brilliant sunshine promotes sugar synthesis and its transformation into anthocyanin. But botanical scientists still do not know what initiates the color changes in the autumn—cool weather, dessication, long nights, some inborn timer or a combination of these.

The entire chemical process that changes leaf colors takes 30 to 60 days, depending on the species of tree. During the final stages, cork layers form at the base of the leaf stalks, cutting the leaves from their supporting branches, and they fall to the ground, signalling winter.

Here are some of the common trees and the colors they acquire:

Early turning trees—sumac, red to purple; shadblow, reddish to bronze; willows, yellow-green; ashes, yellow-green; locusts, yellow-green; black gum, scarlet.

Early to middle turning trees—sugar maple, bronze, orange and red; sassafras, orange to scarlet; cherry, reddish; sour gum, brilliant red; birch, yellow; hickory, yellow.

Late turning trees—oaks, dark red to brown; white ash, yellow; beech, yellow to bronze.

Following are 10 recommended one-day foliage tours in nearby New York, New Jersey and Connecticut. They are short because finding overnight lodging in any of the inns, motels, or hotels in the areas has been almost impossible during the height of the foliage season; most were filled with advance reservations long ago.

A few words of caution: First, restaurants in the areas will be crowded, so make reservations, be prepared to wait or take along picnics. Second, because so many people will be out foliage-watching, the roads could be made dangerous by slow drivers and by cars stopping suddenly so that their occupants can get a better view.

1. FOLIAGE AND PAINTING

After you have viewed the foliage in the Hudson Valley, you may want to see how some of the painters of the Hudson River School viewed it. An exhibition of 19th century American landscapes called "All Seasons and Every Light"

The Mohonk Mountain House, west of New Paltz.
Photograph by Matthew Seaman.
Courtesy of the Mohonk Mountain House.

opens today at the Vassar College Art Gallery in Poughkeepsie and runs through Dec. 16. It includes 50 paintings, a dozen works on paper and four sketchbooks by such artists as Frederic Church, Jasper F. Cropsey, Asher B. Durand, Sanford R. Gifford, Charles Moore, William Trost Richards and Aaron D. Shattuck. The gallery is open with no admission charge. The scenic way to get there is via the Taconic State Parkway, which is one of the premiere foliage routes in the Northeast, north to Route 55, Route 55 west to Raymond Avenue on the outskirts of Poughkeepsie and Raymond Avenue left to the college entrance.

2. FOLIAGE FROM A TRAIN

If you'd like to see the foliage from a train window as well as a car window, the place to go is Arkville in Delaware County. At the refurbished Union Station there, the Red Heifer sightseeing train of the Delaware and Ulster Rail Ride leaves several times a day for a 50-minute round-trip to Fleischmanns along the banks of the Bushkill Creek.

3. LEAVES AND APPLES

The foliage weekend is also the time when the state's Golden Delicious apples are ready for picking. Apple experts call this year's crop one of the best ever for quality and taste. Other apples available for pick-it-yourselfers and at roadside stands include Red Delicious and Northern Spy as well as the more traditional McIntosh. There are two major apple-growing areas near metropolitan New York, one in Ulster County on the west bank of the Hudson and the other in Columbia county on the east bank. The scenic way to the Ulster County apple area is up the Palisades Interstate Parkway to the Bear Mountain Bridge and then north on Route 9W through Marlboro, Milton and Highland. Turn left on Route 299 into New Paltz and then go south on Route 32. For the trip home, take Route 32 south to Interstate 84 east to the Taconic Parkway south. The scenic approach to the Columbia County apple area is up the Taconic State Parkway to Route 82 (do not take the first crossing of Route 82 in southern Dutchess County). Take Route 82 west to Route 9H and turn north for a trip through dozens of apple orchards and fruit stands. A pleasant place for a picnic is Lindenwald, the home of Martin Van Buren, the eighth President, on Route 9H in Kinderhook.

4. COLORS FROM THREE STATES

The northwest corner of New Jersey is pleasantly rural with several areas of foliage interest. For a three-state tour, cross the George Washington Bridge and continue on Interstate 80 to Route 209 at the Delaware Water Gap in

Pennsylvania. Follow Route 209 north, with its views of New Jersey to the east, to Port Jervis in New York State. Take Route 23 southeast back into New Jersey and continue to Newfoundland. Switch there to Route 210 north to Greenwood Lake and then take Route 511 south along the banks of the Wanaque Reservoir back to Route 23 for the return trip.

5. MASSACHUSETTS

For a full-day trip covering parts of New York, Connecticut and Massachusetts, a scenic approach is up the Hutchinson River Parkway, Interstate 684 and Route 22 all the way to Route 23 in Hillsdale. Turn right there on Route 23 through the Taconic Hills into South Egremont, Mass., with many antique shops, and continue to Great Barrington. Take Route 7 south to Sheffield, Mass., and Canaan, Conn., continuing south along the banks of the Housatonic River. Among the pleasant places to stop are Cornwall, with its covered bridge; the Kent Falls State Park, about three miles north of Kent; and the covered bridge at Bull's Bridge. For the return, continue south on Route 7 to Interstate 84 at Danbury, turning west there to Interstate 684 south.

6. DUTCHESS COUNTY

The northwest corner of Dutchess County has several parks with Hudson River views. Among them are the Franklin D. Roosevelt home and museum at Hyde Park, the Vanderbilt Mansion in Hyde Park and the Ogden Mills and Ruth Livingston Mills State Park in Staatsburg. The Roosevelt home, which was damaged by fire last year, is not completely restored, but the ground floor is open daily from 9 A.M. to 4:30 P.M. Also open to the public during the same hours is the F.D.R. Museum, with its Presidential mementos, and a wing devoted to Roosevelt's wife, Eleanor. To get there, take the Taconic State Parkway north to the Salt Point Turnpike, turning west and following local Routes 115 and 41 to Hyde Park, turning south a short distance on Route 9 to the entrance. The entrance fee includes admission to the Vanderbilt Mansion, a few miles north on Route 9, a baronial structure with pleasant grounds for walking. Farther north on Route 9 is the Mills Mansion, part of a state park. There are usually few visitors to the Mills Mansion, which is in need of extensive repairs, but the park and the area around it are pleasant places from which to view foliage.

7. BEAR MOUNTAIN SCENE

Bear Mountain and West Point are among the closest and most pleasant places from which to view the foliage in the metropolitan area. To get to either, cross the George Washington Bridge and take the Palisades Interstate Parkway, which passes through some of the most beautiful scenery in the area, north to the Bear Mountain Bridge, where there are several options. One is to park near the Bear Mountain Inn, (914) 786-2751, which is open for lunch and dinner every day, and to walk around Hessian Lake. Several areas are available for picnics. Another is to head along Seven Lakes Drive, taking the Perkins Memorial Drive to the top of Bear Mountain, 1,300 feet high, with its sweeping views of Hudson scenery (no parking fee).

To prolong the trip, take Routes 9W and 218 north a short distance to the grounds of the United States Military Academy at West Point, which welcomes the public every day, with no admission charge. Stop at the entrance visitors center and get a map for self-guided driving or walking tours. Among the major points of interest: Trophy Point, overlooking the river, with several links of the chain that was used in the Revolutionary War to bar British ships from coming up the river, and the West Point Museum, with its flags, uniforms and other military items. For the trip home, take Route 9W south to Interstate 87 across the Tappan Zee Bridge.

8. FROM THE CATSKILLS

Over the years, the most consistently beautiful foliage views have been in the northern Catskill Mountains. To get there, take the Gov. Thomas E. Dewey Thruway north to Exit 21 at Catskill. Following Route 23 west, climb slowly along the northern rim of the mountains, with several stops offering panoramic views, to Windham. Normally a summer resort, Windham has several fine restaurants. Continue on Route 23 to Prattsville, turning left there on Route 23A to Hunter and Tannersville, which are resort villages with dozens of motels, hotels, restaurants and boutiques. From Tannersville stay on Route 23A, but drive carefully the next several miles to Palenville because the road is steep, with twists, hairpin turns and warnings, and continue to Route 9W. For a quick trip home, turn north on Route 9W a short distance back to the Thruway. For a slightly longer trip with the opportunity to see thousands of chrysanthemums in bloom, turn south at Palenville on Route 32 to Saugerties wiich is holding its annual chrysan-themum festival at Seaman Park, on Route 9W just north of the village. Chrysanthemums of every conceivable color are in bloom—a striking con-trast to the foliage colors. For the return trip, the Thruway is one mile west of Saugerties.

9. CONNECTICUT

The northwest corner of Connecticut, with its many sugar maples and traditional New England villages, is one of the most popular areas for foliage tours. Take Interstate 684 north to Interstate 84, turn east there and go north on Route 7 and east on Route 4 toward Sharon. Just before you reach the village, you may want to stop for a walk and a spell of bird watching at the Sharon Audubon Center, which has 11 miles of walking trails. At Sharon turn right on Route 41 to Lakeville and Salisbury, both of which have good restaurants. A little east of Salisbury, turn right on Route 126 into Falls Village on the Housatonic River and then continue south on Route 63 into Litchfield. Turn right on Route 202 to Bantam, New Preston and New Milford, where the road joins with Route 7 for the return trip.

10. KENSICO RESERVOIR

A water view somehow enhances the beauty of the foliage. One way to experience this is by touring the perimeter of the Kensico Reservoir in central Westchester County, just north of White Plains. Take the Major Deegan Expressway north to the Cross County Parkway, turn one mile east on it and then go north on the Bronx River Parkway to the Kensico Dam Plaza. The foot of the masonry dam is a good place to picnic. Turn right on a local road a short distance until Route 22, following it north on the east bank of the reservoir, turning left on Route 120 at the north end. Turn left again at Nannyhagen Road and left once more on West Lake Drive to the reservoir's aerators where there is room to park. Bear left at the aerators to a road that crosses the top of the masonry dam back to Route 22 for the trip south.

CHAPTER 10

Flowers

New York is a growing state—of not only farm crops but flowers of many kinds. Once it was the violet capital of the world, and today it is arguably the anemone capital of the world. It also produces fifty-five species of orchids. Like many other states of the Northeast, it is also the home of a booming greenhouse industry, supplying home owners with flowers, plants, and trees of various kinds. I tried to reflect all that in many stories about plants and flowers.

WILD ORCHIDS?
(October 6, 1991)

SCHENECTADY, N.Y.—Orchids growing wild in New York State?

Yes, within the city limits of Schenectady, as well as in the Adirondack and Catskill Mountains—hardly the environments conjured up by the popular image of orchids as tropical plants that require careful nurturing

In fact, according to Dr. Charles E. Sheviak, curator of botany at the State Museum in Albany and a specialist in North American orchids, orchids can thrive where people have built ponds, roads and drainage ditches, created sandy beaches, cut down trees and opened up pastures.

Dr. Sheviak's prime example of how limited development can help a rare orchid, even in the relatively cold climate of New York, is the regeneration of a population of nodding ladies'-tresses (Spiranthes cernua) here in Schenectady.

"This shows how some of our rare plants can flourish despite massive disturbances by man," he said, as he bent down over a small, white orchid growing with dozens of others on the sandy bank of a recently constructed pond just beyond a school and some city streets.

Other examples he cited include thriving stands of fringed orchids, rein orchids and nodding ladies'-tresses on excavated road shoulders in the Adirondacks, and rose pogonias and grass pink orchids in roadside ditches on Long Island. The key, Dr. Sheviak said, is that the development must be in open areas to the sun.

While cautioning that not all development activity is good for the environment and plants, he said that efforts to protect the environment can sometimes be counterproductive, especially for orchids.

"I have seen examples of preservation in order to save a species that have resulted in the disappearance of the species," he said. "By eliminating the disturbances that would have preserved the species, they have been destroyed."

As an example, he mentioned an area of southern Arizona, where fringed orchids, rein orchids and nodding ladies'-tresses had grown in a field grazed by cattle. In an attempt to save the flowers, he said, the cattle were barred.

"The result was that the orchid population declined," he said. "In part, the reason they had survived was that the cattle had cut the grass down, permitting light and sun necessary for the growth of the orchids, and their hoof prints in the soil opened up additional sites for the seeds to become established."

The nodding ladies'-tresses here represent one of 55 species of orchids native to New York State and one of 215 in North America (of 30,000 species known throughout the world). A small plant about the size of a pencil, a member of this species grows to a height of between 6 and 12 inches, with small white flowers spiraled on its stem.

Its flowers droop slightly, the origin of the word nodding in its name. When seed pods form, they resemble braided hair. A prolific seed producer, one plant can manufacture as many as 400,000 seeds, Dr. Sheviak said.

A rare plant like most orchids, the nodding ladies'-tresses is listed by the state as a protected plant, which means a person who picks one can be fined $25. But it is not on the state's list of threatened or endangered species.

On a field trip to demonstrate the resurgence of the nodding ladies'-tresses, Dr. Sheviak walked down a dirt path to the site of the new pond, with a large sandy bank at its north end and tracks of the main line of Amtrak between New York and Chicago at the south end. Five years ago, it was a swampland.

"This is about as disturbed an area as you can find," Dr. Sheviak said, referring to the large amount of earth moved to create the pond and its banks.

Today, the soil around the pond is a mosaic of plant life, crowded with asters, wild strawberries, cudweed, boneset, bog club-moss and sapling willow, birch and cottonwood trees as well as the nodding ladies'-tresses.

Because of the sunny, open space created, the nodding ladies'-tresses found a congenial home, he said, speculating that the first seeds had been brought in by the wind.

"They are an opportunistic species and respond very well to new sites being opened up," Dr. Sheviak said.

HYBRID ANEMONES
(February 14, 1973)

RHINEBECK, N.Y.—Despite February's cold and snow, the "anemone capital of the world" is in full bloom here in the northwestern corner of Dutchess County.

Every day before sun-up, a handful of workers report to each of the three greenhouse complexes near this village to cut the brilliantly colored flowers, pack them and ship them by bus, truck and plane throughout the eastern part of the United States.

The hybrid anemones, a favorite flower of Americans before holidays such as St. Valentine's Day, are produced commercially only in the Rhinebeck area, according to their growers. A New York horticulturist reported, however, that hybrids had been grown in France and Australia many years ago, but not commercially.

In the natural form, anemones are short plants in the same family as the buttercup, with small flowers. The hybrids are taller and larger, with more-brilliant blooms in various shades of red, blue, white, pink, lavender and combinations of colors. They grow only in greenhouses, under carefully controlled conditions.

"Anemones are a cold crop," Richard Battenfeld, one of the growers explained. "They don't like it hot."

Anemone seeds and bulbs are available to home gardeners, but the hybrid growers say they do not produce the same kind of flowers.

"You just can't grow them at home," Mr. Battenfeld said the other day.

"If you wanted to break into the business, it would take $100,000 and 10 years of time," according to James E. Ashton, a Cooperative Extension Service agent in Dutchess County.

About 15 miles north of Poughkeepsie, Rhinebeck is the hub of the area, at the intersection of Route 9 and 308, but none of three anemone-growers are actually in the village. F. W. Battenfeld and Sons is six miles to the east in the town of Milan; the Riverside Nurseries, two miles to the west in Rhinecliff; and Ralph Pitcher and Sons, about halfway between Rhinebeck and Red Hook to the north.

The area owes its prominence as the anemone capital to the growth of the vast Hudson River estates in the late 1800s. At their height, the estate owners imported gardeners from abroad and built large greenhouses.

When estate life declined after the turn of the century, local gardeners moved some of the greenhouses and converted many into beds of violets. At one time, there were as many as 150 violet growers in the area, which became known as "the violet capital of the world." But violets dropped in popularity and the greenhouse owners turned to other flowers.

Roswell Cole, then assistant postmaster of Rhinebeck, began experimenting with anemones, with seeds imported from the Netherlands. When he retired in 1948, he devoted full time to anemones, planting them by hand, trying to develop new, colorful blooms in sufficient quantities for the commercial market.

Today, at 80 years of age, Mr. Cole, now retired for the second time, is a consultant to the family-owned Riverside Nurseries, operated by his two sons,

Anemones growing in Battenfeld's greenhouse in Rhinebeck.
Courtesy of Battenfeld's Greenhouses.

Donald and Roger. It is the largest of the three producers, with an acre of beds under glass in 10 greenhouses, sending 600 dozen flowers to market a day. They expect to increase that to 1,000 dozen a day before Mother's Day.

Riverside Nurseries and its two competitors cooperate in the exchange of seeds and information. Their operation is essentially alike, cutting flowers from September through May and planting seeds and nurturing plants from April until the cutting season starts. A striking similarity in all three enterprises is that they are family owned and operated, with only a small number of employees.

One day last week, for example, Mr. Battenfeld, his mother, his wife and his son, Fred, and two helpers were at the sorting table in a darkened room, preparing flowers for market. They had been up before daybreak, cutting the flowers from the 75,000 plants in their greenhouses

"We've got to pick them while it's dark," Mr. Battenfeld explained, "because the buds open in the light."

A few miles to the north, Kenneth Pitcher and his assistant, Jack Schwan, were at work, packing 25 dozen flowers in an insulated box for air shipment to Miami. The Pitcher greenhouses are operated by Kenneth and Donald Pitcher, sons of its founder.

The Pitchers are the only ones of the three producers who sell at retail. A small sign outside the door of their work shed says, "$2 to $4 a dozen." In New York, at a retail florist, anemones depending on quality and season sell for up to $10 a dozen.

Mr. Schwan, who takes a personal delight in pollination experiments, trying to find new color combinations, has a goal beyond producing plants for each year's crop. Like his competitors he is on a quest for the one elusive anemone that none of them has been able to produce yet, one with a yellow flower.

THE LAST VIOLET GROWER
(April 13, 1979)

RHINEBECK, N.Y.—The last major commercial grower of violets in the East will close down six of his seven remaining greenhouses here tomorrow, the day after Easter, and the violet corsage and nosegay, symbols of romance in bygone days, will fade like the flower into nostalgia.

At one time, back in the 1920s and 1930s, this small village on the Hudson River in the northwest corner of Dutchess County was known as "the Violet Capital of the World," with 150 growers producing millions of flowers in 400 greenhouses.

Today, there is only one large-scale grower left, and he is going out of business, largely because the growth of the bluejean generation and the decline of the long formal evening gown have made corsages almost obsolete, with a consequent decline in the sale of violets.

"There's no great demand for violets anymore," said Don Roy, assistant manager of S. S. Pennock Company, one of the big wholesalers in the New York City flower market. "We have a small quantity on hand because there is no great demand for them."

"They just don't go for corsages anymore," said Eugene Trombini, whose family has been growing violets here in Rhinebeck since his father started the business in 1924. Trombini Brothers is the last wholesale grower of violets east of the Mississippi River.

Standing in one of his greenhouses the other day, Mr. Trombini was preparing the last shipments to go out for sale to a few customers who still believe that a violet corsage is part of Easter Sunday finery.

"It's time to give up the business," Mr. Trombini said, citing the rising cost of fuel oil to heat greenhouses, the difficulty of finding part-time labor to pick the flowers, and the declining sales.

Tomorrow, Mr. Trombini, who is 61 years old, will go to work full time as Highway Superintendent for the Village of Rhinebeck, facing asphalt, gravel and trucks every day instead of the lavender and purple blooms of the violet plants. His brother Walter, who was the other part of Trombini Brothers, will retire.

The Rhinebeck area developed as one of the nation's leading producers of winter-grown flowers in greenhouses because of the rise in the late 1800s of the Hudson River estates, where wealthy landowners built huge greenhouses and imported gardeners to care for them.

When the great estates began to decline in the early 1900s, local residents bought the greenhouses and converted them into beds of flowers such as violets, which grow only in cold weather, with the height of the season between February and April. When the violets declined, some of the greenhouse operators began to grow hybrid anemones, which remained one of the major floral products of Rhinebeck.

Mr. Trombini's father, Frank, bought his first greenhouse in 1924 and gradually expanded until he operated 17 of them, all devoted to violets. At the height of the business the Trombinis had six million plants blooming and employed 25 workers to pick flowers and tie them into bunches of 50 each.

———•———

THE BEAUTIFUL WEED
(June 13, 1982)

ALBANY—One of the most beautiful flowers of the summer, purple loosestrife, is spreading so fast that it is endangering the flora and fauna of wetlands in upstate New York and other parts of the Northeast, according to a Cornell University botanist.

The plant grows to a height of five or six feet, bearing spikes of crimson or purple flowers in the summer and fall, usually in flood plains and marsh-lands and on the banks of rivers. For soil scientists, the presence of loosestrife is a telltale sign of a wet soil.

"Few people dispute the beauty of this plant," said Dr. Richard A. Maleci, a wildlife biologist at the State College of Agriculture and Life Sciences at Cornell, but he called its spread "alarming."

"Unlike other wildflowers that grace the countryside briefly and then die, purple loosestrife, an import from Europe, is extremely hardy, prolific and aggressive," he said. It crowds out native wild plants such as cattails, smartweeds, rushes and sedges that provide cover for birds and other wildlife.

"Invasion of this exotic perennial plant already has resulted in the elimi-nation of many native plant species from a number of wetland areas in the Northeast," Dr. Maleci said.

"Purple loosestrife forms clumps of semi-woody stalks that are resistant to decay," he said, "producing a gradual elevation of the ground level because of debris trapped in a tangle of roots and stems. That blocks sunlight to other plants attempting to grow beneath, reducing or excluding some moisture-lov-ing plant species."

As an example of the aggressive territorial characteristics of the plant, Dr. Maleci cited its spread over the 6,000-acre Montezuma National Wildlife Refuge at the northern end of Cayuga Lake in the Finger Lakes. In 1951, sparse stands were noted, increasing to about an acre in 1956, he said, but now the purple loosestrife covers 1,000 acres.

Although newly established stands of loosestrife may provide cover for spring-breeding ducks and shore birds, Dr. Meleci said, "the usefulness and availability of this cover is often of short duration because the developing clumps become rank and impenetrable to these birds after two or three years."

As a result, he said, the wetlands become less suitable for water fowl, and other marsh inhabitants, such as song-birds. Furbearing animals, reptiles and amphibians, may also be affected negatively.

The first loosestrife seeds entered this country about a century ago, presumably as "hitchhikers" on a ship from Europe, Dr. Maleci said. The plant is now found in much of the Northeast, including New Jersey, Massachusetts, Rhode Island, Vermont and Pennsylvania as well as New York. It has also reached north into Quebec and Ontario and is spreading rapidly to the Middle West as far as Minnesota and Wisconsin, he said.

"In the East, New York State is among the hardest hit, especially in Federal and state wildlife refuges," Dr. Maleci said. "If left unchecked, the detrimental effects of loosestrife encroachment will continue to place an additional stress on wildlife resources that are plagued already by the loss of valuable wetland habitats."

So far, according to a Cornell report, control measures such as pulling up individual plants, mowing, burning or applying chemical weed killers have not proved effective. One experiment that shows signs of promise is growing Japanese millet, a highly competitive plant, but the report said experimenters doubted whether complete eradication of loosestrife was possible in the near future without adversely affecting native vegetation.

THE BEST JOB
(August 14, 1988)

RED HOOK, N.Y.—Richard S. Mitchell has what some people call the best job of all the 210,000 employees of the New York State government.

As the official state botanist, Dr. Mitchell roams the state looking for wildflowers and other plants to include in a new encyclopedia of New York's trees, shrubs and plants.

"Yes, but I spend an awful lot of time behind a word processor, too," he said.

One of his assistants, J. Kenneth Dean, said, "It's a pretty good job, but sometimes at the end of the day, when you come back plastered with mud, covered with poison ivy, you know it's hard work."

121

Dr. Mitchell, who is 50 years old, has been the state botanist for the last 13 years, working out of an office in the State Museum in Albany. Before he came to New York he was professor of botany at the Virginia Polytechnic Institute in Blacksburg.

In New York, his publications testify to his work in the field and at the computer. He compiled "A Checklist of New York State Plants," which lists all of the 3,400 plants in the state, with a box next to their names so plant-lovers can check off species they have seen in the same way that bird-lovers keep track of birds they have spotted.

He also is the author of "Rare Plants of New York State" and has completed six volumes of an encyclopedia, "New York Flora," with 40 more to come.

"Actually, I am a little frustrated," he said. "For years we have been trying to get people to work on our encyclopedia, but we are short of staff. At the rate we are going, it may take 100 years to finish it."

Dr. Mitchell's goal is to record the significance to man of each species in the state—trees, weeds, poisonous plants, medicinal herbs, edible plants, flowers and endangered species. He said about 85 percent of the state's plants remained to be studied in detail.

Like any other state employee, Dr. Mitchell faces problems resulting from cutbacks in funding because of the state's budget deficit. He has only $800 to finance his field expeditions this year, instead of the usual $3,000.

But instead of facing hostile politicians in Albany as Governor Cuomo does, Dr. Mitchell braves heat, mosquitoes, mud, poison ivy, sudden thunder-storms and sometimes even irate landowners in the field.

"I once saw him fall through a bog mat over his head." Mr. Dean said.

On a foray here the other day when the temperature exceeded 90 degrees, Dr. Mitchell continued his quest for a rare plant that the Federal Government thinks is extinct—the micranthemum. For 12 years, he and Mr. Dean have been looking for the micranthemum, so far without success.

A member of the figwort family, the micranthemum is so rare that it does not have a common name. A tiny plant, it bears the imposing scientific name of micranthemum micranthemoides.

It was last seen in the United States in New York in 1938, but Dr. Mitchell thinks it may have survived in the tidal marshlands of Cruger's Island in the Hudson River in northwestern Dutchess County.

Cruger's Island, once a battleground between rival Indian tribes, today is a remote wilderness peninsula of 56 acres jutting into the Hudson. It received its name from John Cruger, a prosperous New York City merchant and descendant of two New York mayors of the same name. New York State bought the property in 1981.

Years ago, the micranthemum was reported in the marshes of Delaware Bay near Philadelphia and in Maryland, but recent government-sponsored searches have not found any.

"It's a tiny creeping plant with oval leaves that creeps on mud," he said. "It has tiny flowers, somewhat like a snapdragon, less that a quarter of an inch in size."

Dr. Mitchell, accompanied by Mr. Dean, drove his 4-wheel drive station wagon down a narrow lane to a set of railroad tracks. He parked, got out and walked across the tracks into a one-foot wide path through a jungle of weeds and bushes in marshlands near the Hudson River.

He stopped to point out Joe Pyeweed, cone flowers, honeysuckle, sweet cicely and cornflowers. On all sides, the red berries of bittersweet stood out among the green leaves. Purple loosestrife grew taller than his head.

"They're like good friends," Mr. Dean said. "We see then all the time."

"Watch out!" Dr. Mitchell cried. "That's a monster poison ivy."

"It's the biggest one I have ever seen," Mr. Dean said, as he ducked under the leaves.

"There's a nice yam out there. Look at that heart-shaped leaf," Dr. Mitchell said. "It looks like a philodendron, doesn't it?"

Near the end of the path, Dr. Mitchell pointed to an area covered with periwinkles, or false myrtle, indicating that there had once been a house where the flowers grew.

"There's just one chance in 10 million that there's a micranthemum out there," he said.

He jumped over some mud to explore a nearby marsh. "No luck," he said.

What was visible were large stretches of pickerel weed with beautiful purple flowers and cattails as far as the eye could see. Beyond them, water chestnuts covered hundreds of acres of low tidal waters.

Dr. Mitchell, his shirt wet with sweat, returned to the starting point near the railroad tracks.

"I have a feeling that the micranthemum is out there somewhere on the Hudson," he said.

Mr. Dean pointed to a nearby tidal marsh filled with wild rice plants.

"I'll bet it's hidden in there someplace," he said. "We're discouraged but we have to keep looking for it because it is important."

A BOOM IN BLOOMS
(February 18, 1992)

EAST GREENBUSH, N.Y.—At Becker's Farm here, flowers, house plants and seedlings fill five greenhouses, with red and pink geraniums flourishing in the 80-degree moist heat. Outside, a new parking lot has been completed and a new greenhouse is under construction.

Becker's Farm is part of the fastest growing segment of agriculture in New York and the Northeast—supplying trees, shrubs, plants and flowers for homeowners.

"In the Northeast, it's the only segment of agriculture that is growing, and it is growing by leaps and bounds," said Dr. Carl F. Gortzig, professor of horticulture at the College of Agriculture and Life Sciences at Cornell University in Ithaca.

In New York, greenhouses and nurseries are the second biggest cash producers for the state's farmers, behind the state's dairy industry. But they are the largest segment of agriculture in New Jersey, Connecticut, Massachusetts and Rhode Island.

With $343 million in farm income from nursery and greenhouse products, New York ranked fourth in the nation in 1990, behind California, Florida and Texas, according to Federal statistics. New Jersey was 10th, with sales of $227 million, and Connecticut far down on the list, with sales of $134 million.

The nurseries grow trees and shrubs outdoors for planting outdoors. Greenhouses, which occupy much less space, produce potted plants for hanging in homes as well as seedlings of flowers and vegetables for home gardeners.

The United States Department of Agriculture reported a combined national farm income of $8.1 billion in 1990 from growing trees, shrubs and plants, up 11 percent from the $7.3 billion the year before. The figures for 1991 are not yet available.

The major reason for the growth of the industry is that the sales of nursery and greenhouse products are tied directly to housing starts, which boomed in the 1970s and 1980s, according to Dr. George J. Wustler, specialist in floriculture at Rutgers University in New Brunswick, N.J.

In addition, the environmental movement has brought about a renewed interest in planting trees by both individuals and corporations, and supermarkets are selling large numbers of potted plants and cut flowers.

"There is a strong link in the sale of plants through landscaping architects to new offices and corporate headquarters," Dr. Gortzig said. "Today, any business, instead of paving up to its front door, is landscaping to give it an environmental image."

The current recession has affected the nursery business more than greenhouses, said Dan O. Barnhart, executive director of the New York State Nursery and Landscape Association. Because of the drop in housing starts and a consequent decrease in planting of trees and shrubs, he estimated that nursery sales might be down as much as 17 percent last year and so far this year.

But greenhouse sales have proved to be more immune to the economic downturn, experts said, because people continue to buy plants and flowers on holidays and other occasions and to work in their home gardens.

"Oddly enough, it seems that when times are difficult, people find flowers an attractive but modestly priced product," Dr. Wustler said.

Despite the economic cycles, more young people are entering the nursery and greenhouse business, said Robert Mungari, director of the Plant Industry Division of the State Department of Agriculture and Markets.

He reported 2,729 wholesale growers and 5,016 retail sales outlets in New York State, up slightly from last year.

Becker's Farm here is an example of the changes the young generation can bring. The business is on 82 acres on Routes 9 and 20, a major four-lane highway, surrounded by shopping centers, restaurants, motels, shops and a few residences here in a rapidly growing area of Rensselaer County, four miles southeast of Albany. It is operated by David Becker and his wife, Karen and his father, Frank Becker Jr., and his wife, Cynthia.

It was started as an apple orchard by David Becker's great-grandfather, but converted into a greenhouse operation by his father.

At the age of 37, David Becker returned to the farm in 1990 with his wife after working for 17 years as a manager of various Agway farm supply stores upstate. "Being self-employed attracted me the most," he said.

The Beckers immediately began to expand and make plans to stay open all year. They converted the old cold-room where apples were once stored into a germination room where plants are grown from seeds under fluorescent lights.

Last year, they sold 7,500 geranium plants; this year they have planted 12,500.

Now, in mid-February, they are growing 50 varieties of house plants in pots, as many varieties of bedding plants for gardens, herbs and vegetable seedlings like tomato, pepper and cucumber. They also plan to sell fruit and vegetables, seeds, fertilizer and other garden supplies. At this time of year, all the Beckers are busy inside the greenhouse putting soil in pots, planting seeds, transplanting seedlings, hanging potted plants and labeling the plants in preparation for opening day.

Looking up as she sorted boxes of labels for the plants in one of the greenhouses, Cynthia Becker said, "it's always springtime here."

A PALETTE OF PLANTS
(September 1, 1994)

RED HOOK, N.Y—Norman Greig stood in a field on his 500-acre farm here in the middle of an unfinished work of art—a growing maze of sorghum grass with pathways cut for people to walk through and, perhaps, get lost.

Although the grass is only three feet high at the moment, it will be eight feet tall when the growing season ends in October. It will then be a finished work of art tall enough to hide anyone who enters the maze.

Mr. Greig, who maintains a dairy herd and grows apples, berries, vegetables and flowers for the pick-it-yourself trade, is a practitioner of a new art form, crop art. He is one of 14 farmers in Dutchess County who have created large pictorial images and sculptures on their farms for the first time this year, using crops and the soil.

Among their works, some visible from the road and all from airplanes, are portraits of cows, an American flag, a quilt, pumpkins, a green apple with a worm, and even the New York State tourist logo, "I♥NY."

"Our purpose is to bring attention to the lively changing agriculture of Dutchess County," Mr. Greig said.

"We are in an area where agriculture is being redefined, and we are producing more and more for retail markets."

While the number of dairy farms in the county has fallen to 50 from 120 over the last 10 years, he said that roadside farmer's markets selling fruits and vegetables had increased from a dozen to 75 in the same period.

Mr. Greig, who is also president of the Dutchess County Farm Bureau, an organization of farmers, is trying to keep farming and farmers viable in the county. One of the bureau's innovative methods is to bring tourists—and customers—to the farm by creating the crop art.

"I think it is a first," Mr. Greig said. "I don't think it's ever been done before like this in the United States."

He said he had talked about crop art at many farm meetings and had found both skepticism and interest but no reports that it had been tried elsewhere to attract tourists or as a marketing tool for agriculture.

The idea of art on Dutchess County farms came when Mr. Greig read an article about Stan Herd, who is considered one of the pioneers of crop art. Mr. Herd, who lives in Lawrence, Kan., started in 1981 with a portrait of Santanta, a 19th-century Kiowa Indian chief, on a 160-acre plot near Dodge City, Kan.

"There have been earthwork artists before and there have been a lot of people over the years who have written messages on the ground," Mr. Herd said in a telephone interview. "But I was the first at bat making pictorial representations on the ground."

Mr. Herd is now working in New York City, creating a landscape image along the Hudson River between 68th and 70th Streets. "Gateway to the Countryside" is composed of various plants, rocks and earth, and is visible from Amtrak trains and by motorists driving north. "It's a month away from reaching its peak," he said.

In Kansas, Mr. Herd's best-known work was a 20-acre piece called "Sunflower Still Life," a Van Gogh-like depiction of a table with a vase containing sunflowers that turned yellow as the growing season advanced. It was created in 1985 and disappeared into the landscape in 1988.

Among his other pieces are a portrait of Will Rogers and an 18-acre vodka bottle for an advertisement.

In Dutchess County, the crop artists use the dark brown soil as their canvases and their pigments are grass, clover, flowers, green corn and pumpkins. Instead of brushes, they use tractors, plows and hay-cutting machinery.

The cost to the farmer, who receives no outside financing, has been minimal, Mr. Greig said. "We have the equipment, we have the materials, and we do it in our spare time."

For most farmers, the conception, too, originates on the farm, he said, although some have consulted professional artists. At the Breezy Hill Orchard and Cider Mill in Clinton Corners, for example, Elizabeth Ryan-Zimmerman, the farm operator, worked with three artists. Carole Field came in to collaborate on "Farm Quilt," a two acre-design. Stephen Falatko designed an archway using corn, gourds, seeds and fruit. Claude Bailey created a 12-foot sculpture from used tractor parts.

On Route 82 in Stanfordville, Mike Doyle, manager of the Rocky Reef Farm, has created a green Black Angus bull, 200 feet from head to tail, by planting clover within the outlines of the bull and another shade of green grass around it.

In Clinton, on Fiddlers Bridge Road, Emil and Viola Schoch have carved out "I♥NY" in grass that covers four acres on their Christmas tree farm. The letters are each 20 feet wide and 100 feet long.

Peter Barton has created an American flag of 3,200 red, white and blue impatiens on his farm in Beekman and also a much larger, 18-acre picture of a green apple, made of pumpkin plants, with a worm in it.

Mr. Greig is so enthusiastic about crop art that he has a second art work growing and a third that he is just starting.

The growing one, called "Harvest Medley," is a one-and-a-half-acre pumpkin patch now covered by the green leaves of the pumpkin vines, interspersed with stalks of corn and scarecrows. When the leaves die in October, the giant pumpkins, some of them weighing around 400 pounds, will become visible.

He has also laid out a black and white portrait of a Holstein cow on an acre. He plans to use about 500 chrysanthemums—dark purple ones for the black part, white ones for the white, and reds for a bell around "Daisy's" neck.

"Farmers are not thought of as artists, but they really are," Mr. Greig said. "Agriculture is a rich visual experience. Much of it is done for very practical reasons, of course, but what we do is beautiful visually, and we are proud of it."

A list of the farmers, their art works and their locations is available from the Dutchess County Tourist Promotion Agency, 3 Neptune Road, Poughkeepsie, N.Y. 12601.

Chapter 11

Trains

The most memorable person I met in all my years of covering stories in the Hudson Valley was Lettie Gay Carson, a fellow resident of the Town of Ancram. An indomitable woman, she fought for years to retain train service in the Harlem and Hudson Valleys, winning the admiration of many residents and even of her opponents. She lost many battles, but she never gave up. She must be turning in her grave as Metro-North now talks about expanding service on both the Harlem and Hudson Divisions, something they scoffed at when they curtailed service many years ago.

THE LAST PASSENGER TRAIN
(March 26, 1972)

CHATHAM, N.Y.—The last passenger train from Chatham to New York City rolled southward into oblivion this week, leaving in its track hard feelings, bitter words and a controversy about the future of transportation in the Upper Harlem Valley of New York State.

On Monday night, its sister train left Grand Central Terminal and ended its run some 60 miles south of Chatham, at Dover Plains, N.Y., the new terminus of the Harlem Division of the Penn Central.

As a result there is no passenger train service any more at nine previously scheduled stops—State School, Wassaic, Amenia and Millerton, in Dutchess County, and Copake Falls, Hillsdale, Craryville, Philmont and Chatham, in Columbia County.

Posted on the door of each station is a pink slip, reading:

"Effective March 20, 1972, Train 935 departing Grand Central Terminal, New York at 4.25 P.M. will terminate at Dover Plains, N.Y. Effective this date service between Dover Plains and Chatham is discontinued."

The decision does not affect passenger service in the Lower Harlem Valley, one of the chief commuter areas around New York City. Trains will continue to serve stations like White Plains, Brewster, Pawling, Dover Plains and intermediate points. The line will also continue to carry freight to Chatham.

The only hope for restoration of passenger service farther north lies in a bill before the State Legislature that would authorize the state to operate trains to Chatham, between New York and Montreal and from Albany toward Boston. The bill is now before the Assembly's Ways and Means Committee, but its passage is dubious.

However, the backers of rail service are not giving up the fight. They have sent telegrams urging Governor Rockefeller to intervene and are asking local residents to support them.

"I'm going to continue to work for the legislation and restoration of rail service," said Mrs. Gerald Carson of Millerton, vice president of the Harlem Valley Transportation Association, who has been one of the driving forces behind the campaign to keep the trains.

Mrs. Carson's organization is also opposed to the extension of bus service in the area and will present its view on Tuesday in Millerton at a public hearing before a state Department of Transportation examiner. Before the rail service was discontinued, Resort Bus Lines, Inc. applied for permission to operate buses from Chatham to New York on a route roughly paralleling the railroad tracks. The bus company now provides service from Pittsfield, Mass., to New York City through Millerton and then south on a different route.

"We don't hate buses—we think they ought to run east and west and serve as feeders for rail service," Mrs. Carson explained.

She and other rail supporters recall that only 20 years ago the Upper Harlem Division of the New York Central Railroad boasted five trains a day, some of them with club and dining cars. The fast trains made the 127-mile trip to Chatham in two hours and 45 minutes.

In recent years, however, the line has deteriorated. The number of trains dropped to one a day in each direction and the scheduled running time rose to three hours and 45 minutes, with frequent delays.

The number of passengers dropped, too, but no precise count was made. A railroad spokesman said that the train never carried "more than a bus load of passengers," but Mrs. Carson contended that the train carried more and that more people would have traveled if the railroad gave good service.

The decision to curtail passenger service came suddenly last Monday, ending more than a year of controversy, which pitted the railroad, supported by the Interstate Commerce Commission, against vocal local residents, supported by the Attorney General of New York.

The local group, the Harlem Valley Transportation Association, maintains that the Chatham line was really part of a commuter network feeding into New York City, that "many" passengers were affected and that the railroad was deliberately trying to kill the branch.

On the other hand the railroad contended that only a handful of passengers rode the trains, that it lost money on the run and that the Upper Harlem Valley was far beyond the commuter area.

The Penn Central had scheduled discontinuance of the line as far back as May, 1970, when Amtrak declined to take over the Chatham trains. They continued to operate, however, when the Attorney General's office contended that they were within the commuter area and therefore, not subject to abolition.

A year later, in May, 1971, the Interstate Commerce Commission held hearings on the subject and on June 28, ruled that the Chatham run was intercity and not commuter. On the same day, Governor Rockefeller vetoed a bill that would have extended the power of the Metropolitan Transportation Authority to Chatham.

The Attorney General's office appealed the I.C.C. ruling and it was this appeal that was tried last week, paving the way for the end of the passenger service.

A Metro-North train on the Hudson Line,
with the Bear Mountain Bridge in the background.
Photograph by Frank English. Courtesy of Metro-North railroad.

A typical reaction in the area came in an editorial in *The Lakeville* (Conn.) *Journal*, which is published four miles from the Millerton station:

"The Penn Central could not have demonstrated its contempt more pointedly than by the stealthy way it chose to end passenger service on the Upper Harlem Valley Line. By halting the northbound train at Dover Plains Monday, thereby stranding passengers to other points, it showed the same public-be-damned attitude that has characterized its approach ever since the ill-starred merger of the Pennsylvania and the New York Central."

THE LAST FREIGHT TRAIN
(April 13, 1980)

MILLERTON, N.Y.—The last train from Millerton, an engine and four freight cars, rolled slowly down the tracks here the other day, ending 128 years of rail service to this agricultural community in the northeast corner of Dutchess County.

Its departure signaled one more step in the gradual curtailment of branch-line rail service in New York State. The lines have been maintained since 1976 by subsidies from the state and Federal governments to Conrail, which was established in that year to take over the properties of eight bankrupt railroads in the Northeast.

In 1976, there were 35 operating branch lines with 218 miles of track in the state. They served 192 customers by taking their shipments to and from the main lines of the major railroads. Under pressure from the shippers, the state leased the branch tracks from the bankrupt railroads and, with the help of a $2.3 million annual Federal subsidy, paid Conrail to keep the local freight trains rolling.

Even with the subsidy, business on the branch lines declined, mainly because of the uncertainty of service. By 1979, there were only 13 of the lines left in operation. At that time, the State Department of Transportation offered the lines to local communities and other interested parties. The offer brought mixed results.

Private operators took over branch lines in only two areas of the state. Rail-Service Associates, based in Syracuse, is operating 75 miles of track on one line, the Ontario-Midland in Wayne County, and 15 miles on another, the Ontario-Central in Ontario County. The New York and Lake Erie Railroad is operating on 15 miles of track in Cattaraugus County.

With Federal subsidies scheduled to end Sept. 30, the state intends to get out of the branch railroad business completely, according to Robert J. Colucci, a rail expert with the State Transportation Department.

"What we are trying to do now," he said, "is to get local communities to buy the tracks and maintain them, with Conrail operating freight trains, at $1 a year." Negotiations are in progress in seven upstate areas, he said.

As the state's fiscal year closed on March 31, New York ended its subsidies to two financially troubled branch lines, which have ceased operations. They were the Malone branch in Franklin County, which ran from Malone to the Canadian border, and the Millerton branch, which ran 14 miles north from Wassaic. The demise of the railroad in the upper Harlem Valley was especially ironic for Millerton, which was named for Sidney Miller, a construction engineer who helped build the rail line between 1850 and 1852. It was at that time that the New York and Harlem Railroad was extended to Chatham, in the northern part of Columbia County. It connected there with the Boston and Albany Railroad.

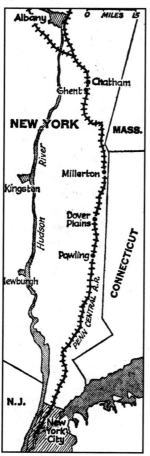

At one time, the Upper Harlem Division was a busy passenger and freight line. But in 1972, passenger service to Chatham ended. Now the passenger service extends only as far north as Dover Plains and the freight service to Wassaic.

Some rail experts suggest that there were too few shippers to keep the Millerton branch in operation. But for Lettie Gay Carson, president of the Harlem Valley Transportation Association, which has fought for years to save the line, the reason was that transportation officials in Albany and Washington had supported road and highway construction, not railroads.

"It's terrible," she said. "In these days of energy shortage, it is absurd to be cutting rail service rather than expanding it."

In Millerton, the few shippers who used the line are making plans to receive supplies, such as feed and propane gas, by truck. There is also talk of converting the empty railroad station into a boutique or an ice cream parlor.

CHAPTER 12

River Towns

Between New York City and Albany, small cities grace the banks of the Hudson River—and there is a newspaper story in every one of them, almost every day.

Obviously, a paper with a city orientation could not cover them all, but I tried to visit most of them occasionally, trying to find something there that would interest a general reading public. And the following articles tell some of those stories.

KINGSTON
(July 11, 1983)

The city of Kingston, 100 miles north of New York City, is trying to regain its importance as one of the state's major river ports. Its waterfront, at the confluence of Rondout Creek and the Hudson River, is bustling with new activity—several marinas, a cruise boat, a maritime museum, shipbuilding, a trolley museum, an art gallery and even an old tugboat.

But do not expect another South Street Seaport. Kingston is a small city—population 27,000—and the riverfront development is on a small scale.

Kingston is more than a tourist town. It is the seat of Ulster County and a blue-collar working city, with a huge International Business Machines manufacturing facility as the major employer. Kingston's waterfront also has oil tanks, junk yards and a wholesale fish establishment. "This is not Disneyland—this is for real," one local official said.

HISTORY

More than 300 years old, Kingston played a part in the colonization of America and in the American Revolution. Only seven years after Henry Hudson discovered the river that bears his name, the first Dutch settlers set up a trading post on the Rondout Creek, seeking beaver and other furs from the Indians.

But relations with the Indians were not all cordial. The Esopus Indians burned the settlement in 1653 and massacred the inhabitants. But soon after, Peter Stuyvesant, the doughty pegleg Governor of New Netherland, ordered a stockade built at the north end of the village—and today this stockade area is one of Kingston's prime tourist and shopping centers.

Originally called Esopus, the settlement's name was changed to Wiltwyck by order of Governor Stuyvesant, and in 1664, when the British took possession of the Dutch colony, its name was changed once again, to Kingston.

During the American Revolution, when the Hudson Valley was a major battle area, the city was briefly the capital of New York State as the British advanced up the Hudson and the new state government fled to Kingston. On April 20, 1777, the state's first constitution was adopted there, and on July 30 of that year, George Clinton took the oath of office as New York's first Governor. But shortly after the first State Senate met in Kingston, the British captured and burned the town.

The foundation for Kingston's growth was laid by the completion of the Delaware and Hudson Canal at Rondout Creek in 1828. Barges from

Homesdale, Pa., traversed the mountains behind Kingston with anthracite coal destined for the furnaces of New York City. The Rondout waterfront became the home base of the Cornell Steamship Company, which carried coal, bricks and cement to New York from 1837 to 1964. Its key location, about halfway between Albany and New York City, made Kingston the busiest port on the Hudson for years.

In the mid-1800's, the *Mary Powell*, queen of the Hudson River steamers, and many of the Hudson River dayliners put in at Kingston, which became the gateway to the tourist areas of the central Catskill Mountains. It still is a gateway, even though changing times, the automobile and the truck ended the colorful steamship era in the early 1900's.

MARITIME MUSEUM

In an attempt to recapture the nostalgia of the golden age of the Hudson steamers, Kingston's new Hudson River Maritime Center has just opened its first section, the gallery, in a restored three-story building at 41 Broadway, close to the waterfront. Appropriately, its current exhibition is of the steamers, with models of the *Mary Powell* and others, like the *Saugerties*, the *Ansonia*, the *City of Kingston* and the *Ulster*, as well as pictures, models of tugboats and equipment including a foghorn that blows when you pull the handle. The gallery is open Thursday through Sunday.

Under construction a few hundred yards away at Rondout Landing is the center's new museum. Its building is shared by a group of shipbuilders and riggers who are restoring sailing boats tied up at their bulkhead. So far, these professionals have been glad to interrupt their work to explain briefly what they do and how they do it.

Although the museum is not scheduled to open until September, one major exhibition is already in place—a steam tugboat, the *Mathilda*, a Hudson workhorse dating back to 1899. Formerly at the South Street Seaport Museum, she now sits on land, just outside the museum.

TROLLEY MUSEUM

How is a trolley museum connected to the river transportation of the Hudson? In the days when the tourist-filled steamers docked at the end of Kingston Point, they were met by trains that carried the people into Kingston and to the Catskill Mountains. The tracks are still there, recently bought by the city for the use of the new Trolley Museum of New York, which has just opened near 1 Rondout Landing.

At present, the Trolley Museum is providing a short train ride along Rondout Creek from the Maritime Museum, but it hopes to extend the ride to Kingston Point by next year, thus duplicating the old-time connection. But instead of a trolley car, as in years past, a car powered by a gasoline engine with room for 40 passengers is being used.

By next year, the museum plans to have in its collection seven trolleys, including four from New York City, an old car from New York's elevated line, two Hudson Tube cars and an IND subway car. As soon as an overhead 600-volt electric line is installed, some of the trolleys will begin operation, the association says.

At present, the mile-long ride passes marinas, blackberry patches and a sign that reads "No Parking Trolley Traffic." And there is a guide who jumps down at each intersection with a red flag to stop other vehicles.

CRUISES

For people who don't own a boat, one opportunity to get out on the river is offered by the 68-foot *Marion T. Budd*, which starts from 1 Rondout Creek. Weekdays throughout the summer, there are buffet cruises.

All cruises require reservations, at (914) 255-6515.

SENATE HOUSE

The Senate first met in Abraham Van Gaasbeek's store and home at the edge of the stockade area on Sept. 9, 1777. He inherited the building through marriage with a descendant of Wessel Ten Broeck, who built it about 100 years earlier.

Today, the renovated house and an adjacent stone museum, both built of rough-cut blue stone, are operated as a state historic site. The house consists of a kitchen with a beehive oven, a bedroom and a parlor, where the Senate sat for six weeks while the Assembly met in the nearby Bogardus Inn.

On Oct. 16, the senators fled to Poughkeepsie as the British under Maj. Gen. John Vaughan captured and burned the city, which he called Esopus. The Van Gaasbeek house was the only one of about 300 buildings to survive. The general explained his action this way: "Esopus being a nursery for almost every villain in the country, I judged it necessary to proceed to that town. On our entering the town, they fired from their houses which induced me to reduce the place to ashes, not leaving a house."

The story of the Vaughan campaign and the wanderings of the state government are told in the museum, a few steps from the Van Gaasbeek house. It contains three exhibitions now: one on the prestate government of New York; another of the paintings of John Vanderlyn, who lived from 1775 to 1852; and the third of the paintings of Ammi Phillips, another early New York painter.

Tomorrow is "Sojourner Truth Day" in Ulster County, honoring the black woman abolitionist leader who was born there as a slave in 1797.

———•———

HUDSON
(October 21, 1994)

HUDSON, N.Y.—This small city on the banks of the Hudson River is casting a nostalgic eye back to its bawdy history, when it was widely known as "the little town with the big red-light district."

Other cities organize tours of their historic districts or gardens, but on Saturday, Hudson is focusing on self-guided tours of a street once lined with houses of ill repute.

The buildings along Columbia Street, now mostly private homes, will not be open to the public. From the outside they look like ordinary houses, with no signs of their former use.

The occasion for the tours is a publication party for a book by Bruce Edward Hall called "Diamond Street," as Columbia Street was once known. It is a history of the prostitution and the underworld of gambling and gangsters that flourished alongside the respectable merchants and residents of the city until a state police crackdown in 1950.

Hudson was organized in 1783 by Quakers from Nantucket and Martha's Vineyard who needed an inland port for their whaling ships. Over the city's early years, they tolerated grog shops and bawdy houses for the transient trade of sailors and wagon drivers.

At its height, in the 1920s and 1930s, when Diamond Street was renamed Columbia Street, the main street of prostitution had 15 brothels, with a total of 50 to 75 prostitutes. The going rate in those days was $2 for 20 minutes with a prostitute.

At that time and even later, Hudson had a wide reputation as a center of vice. Mayor John Scalera remembers that when he was a soldier at Fort Leonard Wood in Missouri, other soldiers there knew of Hudson. The Columbia County District Attorney, Paul Czajka, said that when his father was in the Army in Europe, everybody knew of Hudson's reputation as a red-light city.

Herbert Weintraub, a retired merchant, said, "When my sister went off to the University of Michigan, my father told her to say she was from Albany, not Hudson, because of the city's reputation."

Mr. Weintraub, who was born and raised in Hudson and who operated a paint store on Warren Street, the main business street of Hudson, said he had fond memories of old Hudson and the red-light district.

"It was a marvelous cottage industry," Mr. Weintraub said. "The girls were customers as well as prostitutes. Hudson was prosperous in those days." Mr. Weintraub's nostalgia was shared by many longtime residents, who said the prostitutes helped the city's economy through purchases at drugstores, dress shops, jewelry stores and beauty parlors.

Stephen Durham, who grew up in Hudson and later bought his house on Columbia Street from Mae Gordon, a former madam, in 1972, said: "Things were better in those days. There was a lot of money circulating."

As a boy, Seymour Silverman delivered milk from his parents' pasteurizing plant on Columbia Street to many brothels.

"I always remember them with great fondness," said Mr. Silverman, who now lives in Westchester County. "They were very kind. They were a group unto themselves. They kept their houses neat and orderly and caused no trouble at all."

"Prostitution flourished in Hudson, along with gambling and bootlegging, because generations of local police officers and public officials either averted their eyes or were corrupt," said Mr. Hall, whose book was published by Black Dome Press.

"Hudson was a schizophrenic city then," he said. "It was a virtual shopping center of vice while at the same time respectable citizens held their church suppers, lived and worked and ignored the vice around them."

The era of organized prostitution ended in 1950 when state troopers, without informing the local police, raided the brothels and arrested many madams, who never came back.

Today, there are no houses of prostitution here, local officials say, but there are frequent arrests of street-walkers.

"Our major crime problem in Hudson now is criminal mischief and minor larceny," Mayor Scalera said.

But Mr. Czajka, the District Attorney, who has his office here, thinks Hudson has a more serious crime problem.

"My theory is that the city of Hudson has an institutional corruption history," he said. "In the old days it was gambling and prostitution, today it is gambling and drugs. The biggest crime problem in the city arises from drugs."

Hudson today has a population of 7,800, down from 11,000 at its height. It remains a divided city, said Mr. Hall, with wealthy weekenders from New

A madam and employees in one of Hudson's bawdy houses.
From Diamond Street, The Story of the Little Town with the Big Red Light District,
by Bruce Edward Hall. Courtesy of Black Dome Press.

York City, 120 miles to the south, and a permanent local population of working men and women and merchants.

"The local residents think the book and the history are a riot," he said. "The weekenders are huffy about it. They don't want anybody to touch their image of Hudson as a 'Currier and Ives' village, which it is not. They want Hudson to be known for its antique shops and boutiques."

"I don't think the book runs down Hudson; rather, it enriches its history. It's the story of desperate women who had to survive, who had no other way of making a living. Those were the days before welfare and unemployment insurance. Some of those women got offers of money for sex and they decided that shoes for their children were more important than virtue."

NEWBURGH
(February 17, 1981)

NEWBURGH, N.Y.—George Washington slept here—in his headquarters overlooking the Hudson River—almost every night for 16 1/2 months in 1782 and 1783 while awaiting the official end of the Revolutionary War.

This weekend the headquarters, now an official state historic site, is celebrating the 259th anniversary of his birth with a program of music, lectures, dancing, a quilting bee and story telling as well as drill, musket and artillery demonstrations.

The program, which started yesterday, will continue today and tomorrow, without charge to the public, from 1 to 5 P.M., ending with a series of nonalcoholic toasts honoring Washington and the adoption of the Bill of Rights 200 years ago.

For most visitors, though, the major attraction is the 6.5 acre Washington headquarters complex itself, on a bluff on the west bank of the Hudson, about 60 miles north of New York City. The complex consists of a fieldstone headquarters building, a red-brick two-story museum built by New York State in 1910 and a limestone 40-foot-high Tower of Victory, erected in 1887.

On April 1, 1782, Gen. George Washington, Commander in Chief of the Revolutionary Army, established his headquarters here, about 12 miles north of West Point, in a house owned by Tryntje Hasbrouck, the widow of Col. Jonathan Hasbrouck. Mrs. Hasbrouck received the news of her temporary eviction "in sullen silence," according to the historians of the house.

Washington's Headquarters in Newburgh.
Courtesy of New York State Office of Parks, Recreation & Historic Preservation, Palisades Region, Washington's Headquarters State Historic Site.

Mrs. Washington joined her husband there and stayed most of the time until he left on Aug. 19, 1783. With the Washingtons were several personal servants, from two to six aides-de-camp and about 55 soldiers who acted as bodyguards. Several miles away, at New Windsor, the Revolutionary Army of about 9,000 soldiers camped while a treaty of peace with the British was being negotiated in Paris.

Washington lived and worked inside the headquarters building, which was divided into two sections: a bedroom, dressing room and parlor in which he and Mrs. Washington lived, to the right as visitors enter, and his military offices, to the left.

In the center hallway, near a large stone fireplace without sides, is a small dining room, with a table set with napkins, pewter cutlery and china of the time and several chairs. Washington had his major meal there at midday, usually with some of his senior officers; he had a light meal at night with Mrs. Washington.

Their bedroom was small, about 12 feet by 12 feet, sparsely furnished with a canopied double bed, folding chairs, a mirror on the wall, a chest of drawers and a trunk for clothes. It also contains a small table where Washington usually had breakfast with Mrs. Washington.

None of the present furnishings were there during the Washington occupancy, said Thomas A. Hughes, director of the headquarters site. "There's nothing I can say for sure that Washington himself used in this building," he said. But, he added, all of the items on display dated back to the Revolutionary period or are reproductions.

Washington himself described the parlor as "Mrs. Washington's room." In it, she entertained the wives of officers at tea. Today, the room is furnished with pieces of the period and a green wool rug. In the center a table is set with a teapot and some playing cards. Nearby on a small table is a tea caddy with an unusual lock and key, presumably to keep uninvited people from using it. Around the walls are nine chairs for Mrs. Washington's guests.

On the opposite side of the house, Washington maintained his military headquarters in two rooms, one his office and the other a "war room" for his aides. Washington's room contains a chair "that he might have used," said Mr. Hughes, a desk with a reproduction of his expense account book on display, a table cluttered with papers and maps, and several small trunks containing rolled-up documents.

Adjacent is the room where his aides worked at two tables, with several candles to provide light. On the tables are inkwells, quill pens, sand for blotting the ink, rolled up maps and papers, The whitewashed walls are devoid of any decoration, not even the maps that one might expect in a war room.

A short distance away, the two-story museum displays maps, dioramas and exhibitions showing the major events of the Revolutionary War in the Hudson Valley and how the soldiers of the time lived.

The best way to Washington's Headquarters is up the Taconic State Parkway, west on Interstate 84 across the Hudson River to Route 9W, then south on 9W for 1.6 miles, turning left on Broadway (Route 17K) for a half-mile to Liberty Street. Turn right for three blocks on Liberty Street to the entrance of the parking lot.

———•———

THE "COLLAR CITY"
(January 22, 1989)

TROY, N.Y.—Back in 1820, Orlando Montague, a blacksmith, complained to his wife, Hannah, that he did not have a clean white shirt in the evening when he came home from work. Mrs. Montague solved the problem by cutting collars off her husband's shirts, providing a clean one for him to wear whenever he wanted.

Her invention of the detachable collar gave rise to a new industry in Troy, detachable collars and shirts. A hundred years later Cluett, Peabody & Company had become the largest industry in town, manufacturing detachable collars, Arrow shirts and other items of apparel.

Troy is still known as "the collar city." But its last tie to the detachable collar is being broken. Cluett, Peabody has announced that it is closing its administrative and sales offices in Troy, consolidating operations in Atlanta.

Cluett, Peabody, which employs about 10,000 people in 12 factories, is a subsidiary of West Point-Pepperell Inc., the nation's largest publicly held textile manufacturer. West Point-Pepperell is the object of a hostile takeover bid by Farley Industries, a Chicago-based company that manufactures Fruit of the Loom underwear and other products.

Cluett, Peabody's move, scheduled to start in March, will leave 385 people jobless, although some have been offered a transfer to Atlanta. But there will be no problem finding jobs for those who stay, according to Steven G. Dworsky, the City Manager.

"Our economy is as strong as it ever has been in terms of jobs," he said, citing a low unemployment rate and the growth of light technological and service industries in town.

145

William Downs, the agent of the Amalgamated Clothing and Textile Workers Union, which represents some of the employees, agreed. "But," he added, "it's ironic that the announcement of the closing comes just at a time when Troy is celebrating its bicentennial."

On Jan. 5, 1789, some of the 50 settlers of the tiny community of Vanderheyden met at Ashley's Tavern and decided to give their village the short and more easily remembered name of Troy.

The village, near the junction of the Mohawk and Hudson Rivers about 150 miles north of New York City, grew rapidly. It became the steel capital of the United States, providing guns for the War of 1812 and for the iron-clad *Monitor* of Civil War fame.

With factories prospering along the banks of the Hudson River, Troy stretched seven miles long and only a mile and half wide, with elegant Victorian mansions testifying to its prosperity and many one and two story frame houses for its predominantly blue-collar families.

After the Civil War, Troy began to decline as Pittsburgh rose as a steel center. Like many other industrial cities, Troy went through hard times with plants, warehouses and stores standing vacant.

But today, Troy, with a population of 55,000, is bustling. Some of the vacant warehouses have been converted into apartments, the long vacant Hendrik Hudson Hotel downtown is filled with offices and commercial ventures, and the riverfront has been turned into an urban park.

"It's gotten to the point where it's hard to find a parking space downtown," Mr. Dworsky said.

The focus of Troy's yearlong bicentennial celebration is Uncle Sam, Troy's most famous character.

Samuel Wilson arrived in Troy in 1789 and went into the meat-packing business. During the War of 1812, he supplied the Army with barrels of meat, stamped with the initials U.S. According to the legend accepted in Troy, the soldiers began to refer to their meat supplier as Uncle Sam. Trojans can point to evidence that proves to their satisfaction that Samuel Wilson was the original.

One is the inscription on his tomb in Oakwood Cemetery that reads: "In Loving Memory of 'Uncle Sam' the name originating with Samuel Wilson 1766-1851 during the War of 1812 and since adopted by the United States."

And just last year, President Reagan signed a bill designating Sept. 13, 1989, Wilson's 223rd birthday, as an official Uncle Sam Day throughout the United States.

Although Troy has been a manufacturing town for most of its existence, its main industry has been and still is education. It is the home of the oldest engineering college in the United States, Rensselaer Polytechnic Institute,

146

founded in 1824; Russell Sage College; the Hudson Valley Community College, and the Emma Willard School, founded in 1821.

Not only is R.P.I. the largest employer in the city, it is a spark plug for technological growth in the area. It operates a technological park for new industry on the outskirts of Troy and an "incubator" program on campus to help new high-technology businesses get started.

So far, according to Mark P. Rice, the director of the incubator program, it has helped 45 new companies. Seventeen are still on campus; 16 have prospered and moved to the technological park or nearby; 6 have merged with other companies; 3 lost their principals to academia, and 3 went out of business.

As an example of the kind of new business that the college is helping, Mr. Rice cited Unique Bathing Supplies, which entered the program on Jan. 1. It is the brainchild of Douglas Williams, who devised a bath tub for the elderly and the disabled. It has a side door that opens to let the bather enter before it is filled with water and then closes to become watertight.

Other fledgling companies are producing solar collectors, robot control systems, automated test equipment, materials for dental and medical implants and other highly technical products.

In return for low rent, the new entrepreneurs receive space and access to libraries, computers, laboratories and faculty consultants. For the college, it means helping students and graduates enter the business world and strengthening the local economy by nurturing innovative technology, Mr. Rice said.

THE TV-LISTING CAPITAL
(November 12, 1992)

GLEN FALLS, N.Y—This small city on the banks of the upper Hudson River is the world capital of television program listings.

Glen Falls (population: 15,000) gained this distinction because of a young man who wanted to live in a rural atmosphere near Lake George, where his family had a summer home.

Today the town that calls itself "the gateway to the Adirondack Mountains" is home to two companies that furnish the television programs printed in 3,000 daily and weekly newspapers in the United States, Canada and Mexico with a combined circulation of 120 million.

It all started with James E. West, whom even competitors call "the father of television program listings."

He grew up in Scarsdale and went to Ithaca College in Ithaca, N. Y., majoring in business. After working for a year at the *Reader's Digest* in Westchester County, he came to Glens Falls, about 200 miles north of New York City and 9 miles south of Lake George. "I moved up to be near the lake," he says now.

To earn a living at the age of 25 in 1965, he started a shopping paper, distributed free. In it, he included television schedules, mostly of stations from the nearby Albany-Schenectady area.

Looking for a printer, he met Raymond Kennedy, then publisher of the *Hudson Register-Star*, about 90 miles to the south. Mr. Kennedy noticed that the programs were the same ones received in Hudson. He offered $50 a week for the rights to print the television log in his newspaper.

"I took the money, I needed it," Mr. West said.

More importantly, he got the idea that other newspapers in the area would pay for and print the same log.

Out of that grew a television listing guide for the area and then expansion into other areas, to Philadelphia and New Jersey.

Today the company he founded has grown into a large enterprise called TV Data Technologies Inc. It has 196 employees who furnish television programs for 2,700 weekly and daily newspapers, including large ones like the *Washington Post* and the *Chicago Sun-Times* and small ones like the *Independent*, a twice-weekly in Hillsdale, N. Y.

"The charge ranges from $30 for a small weekly to $600 for a large metropolitan daily," said Kathleen F. Warn, vice president for sales and operations.

The privately owned company grosses from $15 million to $20 million a year and is profitable, she said, but she declined to give any specific figures. Its owner is Cable South Management, a privately held partnership based in Birmingham, Ala., which also owns cable companies and radio stations.

Mr. West, 53, is a consultant for the company. He still lives in the Glens Falls area with his wife, Greta, a schoolteacher.

"The company grew around a person, Jim West, and an idea," said Charles Stackpole, president of TV Data Technologies.

The idea was so good that one of Mr. West's associates, Ted Zoli, who helped him convert to computer operations, began a competitive company.

That company, now called Tribune Media Services, is owned by the Tribune Company of Chicago. It has a staff of 114 supplying television listings to about 300 clients, mostly large dailies including *USA Today*, *The New York Times*, the *Chicago Tribune* and the *Daily News* in New York, with a combined circulation of about 50 million.

"Its charge to its newspapers ranges from $250 to $1,500 a week, largely based on the newpaper's circulation," John B. Kelleher, its general manager, said. He declined to give any figures on profits or loss.

The companies are in the Town of Queensbury, just across the city line from Glens Falls, drawing labor from a wide upstate area.

Their only competitors are two small companies in Texas and *TV Guide*, which has 108 editions and a circulation of 14.6 million, according to its research department.

The two Glens Falls companies operate roughly the same way. They gather information from television stations, networks, cable companies and other sources by fax, computer, telephone or old-fashioned mail. They then put it together in the familiar form of individualized television grids or logs.

"The major problem facing the industry," Mr. West said, "is how it is going to help the consumer cope with the growing number of television channels, especially with the widely predicted 500 channels and the 'information superhighway'."

Mr. Kelleher, 32, a computer specialist, is pessimistic about the future of the printed word as a television guide. "I do not see paper and ink guides 20 years from now," he said, predicting that the schedules would be available on the screen soon.

Arthur J. Bassin, a consultant for Cable South, said, "The great challenge is consumer acceptance. Will they accept electronic listings or print?"

----•----

NEW YORK'S ARSENAL
(July 24, 1988)

WATERVLIET, N.Y.—In an age of atomic bombs and intercontinental ballistic missiles, old-fashioned cannon still pour out of the Watervliet Arsenal, which this month is celebrating its 175th anniversary of producing arms for the United States Army.

"We are the only big-gun arsenal in the United States," said John Swantek 3d, its public affairs officer.

The arsenal is on the west bank of the Hudson River about eight miles north of Albany, covering 140 acres in the city of Watervliet. An active mili-

The commandant's quarters at the Watervliet Arsenal.
Courtesy of Department of the Army.

tary base, it has 11 Army officers who direct the work of 2,462 civilians who manufacture the cannon.

"We are considered a 'warm base', meaning that our machinery and technology are kept up for rapid expansion if necessary," Mr. Swantek said.

The arsenal is also a "go go" base, that is, Government-owned and Government operated, and a closed base, with only its museum open to the public, he said.

Its history dates back to 1813, when it was established to supply artillery for the Army during the War of 1812. None of its original buildings stand now, but over the years about 100 buildings were erected to house expanding production in war and peace.

Today, it is one of three arsenals operated by the United States. One in Rock Island, Ill., manufactures small arms and equipment and the other, in Pine Bluff, Ark., concentrates on chemical weapons.

Working five days a week, 24 hours a day, the Watervliet Arsenal produces a medley of huge cannon—105-millimeter and 120-millimeter guns for the Army's tanks and 155-millimeter howitzers for its artillery.

But the largest gun the arsenal handles is a 16-inch cannon from the battleship New Jersey, sitting on a lathe in a huge building, ready to be relined for use once more. It is 65 feet long, weighs 120 tons and can fire a 2,300-pound projectile 26 miles, as it did during the Vietnam War.

At one time, in the early 1950's, the arsenal manufactured an even larger cannon to handle atomic projectiles, but no longer does. One of them sits idle just inside the entrance gate, a monument to changing technology.

A plaque reads:

280 m m M66 Cannon
"Atomic Annie"

Manufactured at Watervliet Arsenal, it is the largest bore U.S. cannon produced since World War II. It had the ability to fire a nuclear-armed projectile 48 miles. The M66 carriage, gun and twin transporter weighed 168,000 pounds. The unit is no longer in service.

"The arsenal was very proud of that cannon," Mr. Swantek said. "But we don't make them anymore. Today, a soldier can carry an atomic weapon on his shoulder."

The actual number of cannon produced at the arsenal and their value are classified information, but some statistical information is available. The arsenal has orders for 1,584 cannon that are 120 millimeters, for 355 that are 155 millimeters, and for 98 mortars that are 60 millimeters, according to Mr. Swantek.

Its major production is for Army use, but the arsenal also sells arms abroad. Last year, its figures show that it sold $20 million in cannon to Egypt, Japan, Morocco, Norway and Bahrain, with Egypt, the largest customer, spending $4.5 million.

"Our bread and butter item is the 120-millimeter cannon, which is used on the Abrams tank, the main battlefield tank of the Army," Mr. Swantek said.

The 120-millimeter cannon—the number refers to the size of the internal bore through which a projectile is shot, about 4.7 inches—is manufactured in a gun shop that is the size of four football fields.

The metal comes to the arsenal in stubby pre-formed cylinders of high-alloy steel with a hole through the center. Heated to 1,900 degrees Fahrenheit, they go into a 150-foot-long rotary forge, manufactured in Austria, in which four 1,600 horse-power hammers, guided by computers, pound them into the proper shape and length. The internal bore is protected from collapsing by an inserted slug.

After air-cooling, a process that takes from 18 to 20 hours, the cylinder, now about 17 feet long, about three times its original length, is taken to a finishing machine shop. There, the interior bore is prepared for firing, and the cannon is measured, tested for flaws, polished and prepared for delivery.

After a long automated process guided by computers, the cannon receive their finishing touches by hand. Workmen with small drills resembling those used by a dentist remove burrs while others using buffing discs on hand drills polish them.

"We check the old-fashioned way, by hand," said Peter Bessette, a senior industrial specialist at the arsenal. In one corner of the finishing building, Del Pierce, a quality control inspector, used a caliper to measure the diameter of a completed 155-millimeter cannon, which should be between 12.498 and 12.500 inches.

"It looks pretty good," he said. "I'd say it passed."

As one of the last steps, a workman taps onto the breech, or loading, end of the cannon, the initials of the commanding officer as a pledge that the cannon is of excellent quality. Most of them still bear the initials of R. T. W., for the previous commanding officer, Col. Robert T. Walker. But from now on, the initials J.H.M. will be inscribed for Col. Joseph H. Mayton Jr., who has just taken command of the arsenal.

CHAPTER 13

Lighthouses

Everybody recognizes the romance of lighthouses. I found them an irresistible source of news when the Coast Guard abandoned them and local historical societies and other interested groups banded together to save them.

There are seven lighthouses on the Hudson River between New York City and Albany—under the George Washington Bridge in Manhattan and at North Tarrytown, Stony Point, Esopus Meadows, the Rondout Creek, Saugerties and between Hudson and Athens. Only two of them—completely automated—are at work performing their original purpose of guiding river traffic. The others are tourist attractions, one of them even a bed and breakfast place, as you will see in the following articles.

RONDOUT
(September 17, 1984)

KINGSTON, N.Y.—The old lighthouse at the confluence of the Hudson River and the Rondout Creek still blinks at night as a navigational aid, but it will soon have an added function—as a museum to tell the story of lighthouses in the river.

The 2 1/2 story, cream-colored brick lighthouse, in the river near the west bank, has been leased from the United States Coast Guard, its owner, by the Hudson River Maritime Center here for 20 years at a rental of $1.

It will continue to act as a marker for ships plying the Hudson River between New York City and Albany, with its light turned on and off automatically by light sensors. But the building, now being restored by the City of Kingston, will be open to the public for the first time as well.

"There's something magic about lighthouses," said Marita Lopez-Mena, the director of the Maritime Center. "People are eager to get out and see it. We're already swamped with calls from organizations that want to hold meetings out there."

But the Rondout Lighthouse will not be ready to receive the public until next spring because of the difficulty of access. It can be reached only by boat.

On a trip to the lighthouse Thursday by launch, Jay Hogan, the city's superintendent of public works, climbed up over a stone jetty and then up a short flight of temporary wooden stairs to reach the base of the structure.

"We have applied for a permit to build a new landing dock, and when we get it, we will have a new entrance," he said. Permits are required from the Army Corps of Engineers and the State Environmental Conservation Department.

Mr. Hogan said the city also planned to build a stone walkway on top of the battered jetty that now runs about 2,000 feet from the shoreline into the river to the lighthouse.

The restoration of the lighthouse is being managed by the City of Kingston, the Maritime Center and the Hudson River Heritage Task Force, an arm of the Environmental Conservation Department. The city contributed $15,000 for the project, the task force, $7,500, and the state, $50,000. The museum is expected to contain pictures, maps and models of ships and lighthouses.

The idea for restoring the lighthouse came from Elise Barry, now an architectural consultant in Rhinebeck, N.Y., just across the Hudson from the lighthouse. When Miss Barry was a graduate student at the Pratt Institute in

Brooklyn in 1977 and 1978, she wrote her thesis on the adaptive reuse of Hudson River lighthouses.

She was asked by the State Office of Historic Preservation to put together the information necessary to obtain historic site status for them, which was granted in 1979. She also acted as a consultant to the task force to find a way to preserve them.

The Rondout Light, which was built in 1913 to replace an older one, is one of two remaining active lighthouses in the Hudson. The other is the Hudson-Athens lighthouse, farther north. Earlier this year, it became the first to be taken over by a private non-profit organization.

Like the Rondout Light, Hudson-Athens is in fairly good shape. It too is not yet open to the public, pending a fund-raising drive and repairs organized by the Hudson-Athens Lighthouse Preservation Committee.

Five other lighthouses, all inactive, remain in the river, with navigational lights either on steel poles or bridges nearby. They are near Tarrytown, close to the Tappan Zee Bridge; Saugerties; Esopus; Stony Point; and perhaps the most famous of them all, the Jeffrey's Hook Lighthouse under the George Washington Bridge. The Jeffrey's Hook Lighthouse, better known as "the little red lighthouse under the big gray bridge," was made famous in a children's book.

Until the 1950s, the beacons were operated by full-time lighthouse keepers, who lived with their families under the lights. But the development of radar for navigation made both the lighthouses and their keepers largely obsolete.

In 1954, some of the lighthouses were abandoned and others, near creeks or danger points, were automated. In 1980, the Coast Guard received permission from Congress to lease the historic structures at little or no rent.

When the first lease was granted to the Hudson-Athens preservation group, the Coast Guard said it hoped other organizations would follow. At that time, Capt. David Naus, chief of the Aid to Navigation Branch of the Coast Guard in the Third District, based on Governors Island, said unless private organizations responded, unused lighthouses might have to be demolished

Under the new lease, the Coast Guard continues to operate the lights. The responsibility for doing so at Rondout falls upon William Spinnenweber, a 56-year-old part-time employee of the Coast Guard, who bears the old-fashioned title of "lamplighter."

Every night, Mr. Spinnenweber, who lives about a mile downriver in Port Ewen, checks the light visually to make sure it is on. About once a week, he goes out by boat to make an inspection and to replace bulbs, if necessary. On foggy nights, he has an added duty. He drives to the shore near the light and flicks the switch on a pole, which activates a foghorn.

"It's a seven-day-a-week job," he said, "If I get stuck, my wife knows how to care for the light. And I have an uncle who is trained to replace me, too."

HUDSON-ATHENS
(November 24, 1986)

HUDSON, N.Y—From the bottom of the Hudson River came the message: "The currents are a bit of a nuisance down here."

The words, calmly spoken, came from Peter Miller, a marine diver, who was walking on the riverbed, inspecting the foundations of the Hudson-Athens Lighthouse, the northernmost lighthouse between New York Harbor and Albany, about 150 miles north of New York City.

Despite the fast-moving currents, Mr. Miller, a Newburgh police detective on weekdays, made an underwater circuit of the structure in just under three hours. He found the riprap—rocks placed as protection against wave erosion— gone on the east side, which faces the main river channel. The rocks were a victim of ice floes and of waves made by passing ships, tankers and barges.

He also found some wooden piles exposed, but in excellent condition, and some wooden supporting beams eaten away.

"It's phenomenal," said Dan Rohe, a consultant on diving who was supervising the project. "It's in very good shape, better than we expected."

Mr. Miller's underwater tour was part of a series of inspections that Hudson River organizations have made of some of the lighthouses that have been abandoned by the Coast Guard.

"We can't afford them," said Lieut. Jeff Anderson, an officer with the Aids to Navigation Branch of the Coast Guard, based on Governors Island in New York Harbor. "It's a lot easier to maintain a light pole in the river than a big old structure."

But for Hudson River organizations, the lighthouses are beautiful, nostalgic reminders of an age when lighthouse keepers and their families lived on the river, maintaining the lights and the foghorns for riverboats and ships plying the deep channel between New York City and Albany.

"They are charming structures and there's something romantic about them that should be preserved," said John Doyle, executive director of the

The Hudson-Athens Lighthouse.
Courtesy of Hudson-Athens Lighthouse Conservancy.

Heritage Task Force for the Hudson River Valley, a private, nonprofit organization that is paying for the underwater inspections.

From New York City to Albany seven lighthouses are still standing; all are on the National Register of Historic Places.

The best known is the Jeffrey's Hook Lighthouse in Manhattan, under the George Washington Bridge, made famous by a children's book, *The Little Red Lighthouse under the Great Gray Bridge*. It was built in 1899 and deeded to New York City in 1953.

Farther north are lighthouses at North Tarrytown, built in 1883; Stony Point, built in 1883; Esopus Meadows, built in 1880 and rebuilt in 1913; Rondout Creek in Kingston, also built in 1880 and rebuilt in 1913; Saugerties, built in 1835 and rebuilt in 1934; and Hudson, built in 1874.

The Coast Guard has relinquished possession of all, either by deed or lease, even though it maintains lights on Kingston-Rondout and Hudson-Athens.

The Kingston-Rondout Lighthouse has been leased to the Hudson River Maritime Museum, which is planning to open a branch in it, and the Hudson-Athens structure to the Hudson-Athens Lighthouse Preservation Society.

At Hudson-Athens Lighthouse, which is on the west side of the main river channel between the city of Hudson in Columbia County and the village of Athens in Greene County, Mr. Rohe made a quick visual inspection of the structure. It seemed to be standing level in the river.

"I'm pleased at that," he said.

The lighthouse sits on a pedestal of nine feet of granite blocks, each about two feet high, resting on wooden piles driven into the river. On top of the pedestal is a two-story red brick house, where the lighthouse keeper and his family used to live. Attached to the house is a 2 1/2 story red brick tower with the navigation light.

Accompanying Mr. Rohe were Mr. Doyle; Frances Dunwell, Hudson River program coordinator for the State Department of Environmental Conservation; and Lynn Brunner, chairman of the Hudson-Athens Lighthouse Preservation Society, which is trying to raise funds to restore the lighthouse.

Mrs. Bruner is a daughter-in-law of the last lighthouse keeper, Emil Bruner, who retired in 1949, when the lighthouse was converted to automatic operation.

"We want to put it back to what it was in 1874 to show what life was like for a lighthouse keeper and his family," Mrs. Bruner said. "A lot of people think it was romantic, but it really was very hard, being isolated there, sometimes running out of food, boiling water for everything."

SAUGERTIES
(June 17, 1990)

SAUGERTIES, N.Y.—A half-mile out into the Hudson River, the old Saugerties Lighthouse, abandoned 36 years ago, is getting a new lease on life as a historical landmark, a tourist attraction and a restored aid to navigation.

One of seven lighthouses on the Hudson River between New York City and Albany, the Saugerties light sits at the confluence of the Esopus (pronounced Ee-SOAP-us) Creek and the river as a legacy of the days when the village was a thriving river port.

"We see it as a reminder of Saugerties's past, back in the 1800s when its factories shipped iron, glass and paper to New York City and even abroad, said Clifford C. Steen, president of the Saugerties Lighthouse Conservancy, which is restoring the lighthouse.

Mr. Steen, a house painter and paper hanger, is a trustee of the village of Saugerties, which has about 4,000 residents. It is 101 miles north of New York City on the west bank of the Hudson River.

In the early 1900s the Saugerties Night Line sent passenger boats downriver to New York City every evening, returning the next day. Ferries ran across the river between Saugerties and Tivoli as well.

Today, those factories, boats and ferries are gone and the Esopus Creek has become a recreational waterway with two marinas for pleasure boats, several homes with their own docks and a Coast Guard station that maintains buoys and lights on the Hudson.

The Coast Guard retains a simple functional light mounted on a small steel tower on the south side of the mouth of the Esopus Creek. Opposite it on the north side is the old lighthouse, a two-story stuccoed red brick building with a glass cupola on top that once flashed the warning light for river pilots.

"We have finished stabilizing the structure, and now we are working on the interiors," Mr. Steen said.

Mr. Steen and his working crews go out to the lighthouse on a small barge, from the dock of John and Virginia Rapp in Saugerties. They climb up an inclined wooden gangway to the structure, which sits on a masonry base, surrounded by riprap rocks to protect it against the river currents.

The only other way to the lighthouse is by a cruise boat, the *Sea Explorer*, which is based at the Rondout Creek in Kingston. Under the command of John Cutten, its owner and captain, she takes visitors on tours on weekends.

Inside the lighthouse, a worker is laying bricks, restoring old walls. Beams have been replaced but are still visible through holes in the ceiling.

The Saugerties Lighthouse.
Photograph by Allen Bryan.

Through a hole in the floor, one can see the top of a large cistern, which collected rain water in the days when the lighthouse was working.

The first lighthouse at Saugerties was built in 1838, but it was replaced by a more modern one in 1869. It remained in operation until 1954, when the Coast Guard abandoned it and other lighthouses on the river, replacing them with automated lights.

Since then state officials, local organizations and lighthouse buffs have worked to save the lighthouses from decay and demolition.

"The stabilization and repair of New York's large and varied collection of historic lighthouses in one of our office's priorities," said Austin N. O'Brien, an official of the State Office of Parks, Recreation and Historic Preservation in Albany.

"These highly visible landmarks reflect an important episode in the state's maritime history, and most are in critical need of preservation due to long-term exposure to harsh weather conditions."

Perhaps the best-known of the Hudson River lighthouses is the one at Jeffrey's Hook in New York City under the George Washington Bridge, called "the little red lighthouse under the great gray bridge," after a book by that name. It was given to the city by the Coast Guard after it was abandoned in the 1950s.

From New York City north, lighthouses remain standing at Tarrytown, Stony Point, Esopus Meadows, the Rondout Creek in Kingston, and Hudson-Athens, as well as at Saugerties. State, municipal and conservancy groups are active in trying to preserve them. All seven are listed on the National Register of Historic Places.

In 1987, after several years of negotiation, the Saugerties Lighthouse Conservancy bought the lighthouse here for $1, with the help of an enabling act by the State Legislature.

So far the conservation group has spent about $200,000 in restoration work, using public and private money, Mr. Steen said. It will take "a couple of hundred thousand more" to complete the restoration, he added.

"If we had the money, we could complete it this year," he said.

When the restoration is almost finished, the Coast Guard plans to restore the light atop the old lighthouse, said Chief Boatswain's Mate Don Fillman, in charge of the Saugerties Coast Guard Station. He said he hoped that could be done by the end of the summer.

For Mr. Cutten, the cruise boat captain, the work of the conservancy and the restoration of the light is saving taxpayers "a lot of money."

"Without the conservancy, the government would either have to tear the lighthouse down or restore it, which costs money," he said. "This way, the government has the use of a navigational aid and saves money that way. As a taxpayer, I appreciate that."

Reconstruction of the Saugerties Lighthouse.
Photograph by Cara Lee. Courtesy of Scenic Hudson.

CHAPTER 14

PCBs

Not everything is lovely on the Hudson River. Back in 1973, I wrote a story about how the river was improving, pollution decreasing, and fish returning, but that was just before the state discovered polychlorinated biphenyls in the river, dumped over many years by General Electric plants at Fort Edward and Hudson Falls.

More than twenty years later, state, Federal and local officials are still wrestling with the problem of cleansing the river of PCBs, with no solution in sight.

A PRIMER
(May 22, 1985)

ALBANY—Last month, New York State extended what had been a ban on commercial fishing for striped bass in the Hudson River to include New York Harbor and both shores of western Long Island because of contamination by PCBs.

The PCB problem—with its impact on commercial fishing and suspected impact on human health—has been a matter of public concern since 1976. At that time, the General Electric Company, which had been dumping the chemicals into the upper Hudson River, agreed to stop and to pay a $3 million fine to the state.

Since then, the State Department of Environmental Conservation, with financing from both the Federal and state governments, has been working on a $26.7 million plan to clean up PCB sediments from the river bottom.

PCBs—polychlorinated biphenyls—are not only a problem in New York. Earlier this week, the Westinghouse Electric Corporation agreed to clean up six sites of PCB dumping near Bloomington, Ind., at a cost to the corporation of between $75 million and $100 million.

Following is a series of questions and answers on the PCB problem in New York State, based on interviews with state fish and water experts:

Q. When will we be able to eat striped bass from the banned waters again?

A. The most optimistic estimate by fish experts at the State Department of Environmental Conservation is in "less than 10 years," if the agency can proceed with a disputed plan to dredge PCB-laden sediments from the Hudson River. But if that proposal is not put into motion, they say, it may be several decades.

Q. What is the state's plan?

A. To deposit the PCB sediments from the river bottom in a clay-encapsulated tomb on land. Because of lack of money, the state has scaled down its original objective and now plans to clean up only one-third of the contaminated silt in 20 "hot spots." That would mean dredging and burying 700,000 cubic yards of sediment, containing 110,000 pounds of PCBs.

Q. Who will pay?

A. Of the $26.7 million, the Federal Environmental Protection Agency is contributing $20 million, or 75 percent, and the state $6.7 million, or 25 percent.

Q. What is holding it up?

165

A. There is no approved land disposal site. The state picked one, on an abandoned farm south of Fort Edward in 1982, but local residents won a suit barring it. At present, the state is studying about a dozen alternative sites.

Q. What is the state's timetable?

A. Under an agreement with the E.P.A., the state has until May 1987 to come up with an approved site and two years more, until May 1989, to start dredging. The state hopes to start dredging in the fall of 1988 and complete the project in two years. After that, it will take several years more for the PCB levels in the river and the fish, to fall to acceptable standards.

Q. What are acceptable levels?

A. The E.P.A. has determined that more than two parts of PCBs per million in fish is a potential danger to human health. The latest tests, made in 1984, show that striped bass in the Hudson averaged 4.8 parts per million. That level of contamination has remained relatively constant since 1980.

Q. How dangerous are PCBs?

A. Both state and Federal authorities are worried that an accumulation of PCBs in the human body can cause cancer. Those concerns are based on findings that PCBs can cause cancer in laboratory animals, although no direct link to human health problems has been demonstrated. As a result, the state has warned women and children not to eat any striped bass from the banned areas and men to eat not more than one meal a month of the fish.

Q. What are PCBs?

A. A group of about 200 different kinds of chemical compounds, composed of chlorine, carbon and hydrogen. As a class they are colorless liquids that are fire-resistant, good conductors of heat, but poor conductors of electricity. Because of that, they were used for many years as insulating materials in the manufacture of transformers and other heavy electrical equipment.

Q. How did they get into the Hudson River?

A. Between 1945 and 1976, they were discharged as waste products from two upstate General Electric manufacturing plants, one at Fort Edward and the other at Hudson Falls. Under an agreement with the State, G.E. halted its used of PCBs and their discharge into the river in 1976, paying a fine of $3 million and agreeing to spend $1 million more in research. In addition, the state believes that smaller amounts of the chemical have been deposited in New York waters by small factories in New York City and New Jersey.

Q. Where are the PCBs now?

A. Of 600,000 pounds of PCBs deposited in the river, scientists estimate that about 377,000 pounds are in sediments between Fort Edward and Troy.

About 200,000 pounds are concentrated in "hot spots" of contamination, defined as those with concentrations of 50 parts per million or more, and 177,000 pounds in "cold spots" of lesser contamination. In addition, about 150,000 pounds have migrated downriver into the lower Hudson. The remaining 73,000 pounds are scattered beyond New York City or along river banks or in some small dredged land deposits.

Q. Why can't nature take care of the PCBs?

A. A group of researchers at General Electric recently reported discovering that bacteria occurring in nature have broken down some of the PCBs into a less toxic form. But Henry G. Williams, the State Commissioner of Environmental Protection, says the evidence is not strong enough to wait and see if nature can do the clean up. More over, his technical experts believe that unless the dredging is done soon, the upstream PCBs will be washed down the river, making the situation even worse than it is now because there would be more contamination in the area where striped bass spawn.

Q. Are there alternatives to the state's plan?

A. Yes, but all of them are in the early stages of research or development. The alternatives include a process of heating the sediments until the PCBs separate, a chemical method of separation and a process that uses steam to convert the PCBs into a gas that can be burned.

The third plan is similar to the process just announced by the Westinghouse Electric Corporation, in which it will burn PCBs together with municipal wastes to produce steam or electricity.

All other plans would still require dredging, although they would eliminate the burial step. In addition, preliminary work is also going on into a biological method in which bacteria would be used to destroy PCBs in place on the bottom of the river.

Q. What is likely to happen?

A. Sometime this summer, the state will announce the location of a dozen possible alternative burial sites. In the fall, a State Siting Board will be appointed to select one of them. Whichever one is selected will certainly be challenged in the courts, leading to further delay.

If the state wins approval in the lower court, appeals will delay the project even further. If the state loses, it faces a difficult choice—trying to find still another site, pushing one of the alternative methods or killing the project.

BURIAL SITE?
(January 3, 1986)

ALBANY—A state plan to dredge PCBs from the bottom of the Hudson River has met another snag—the objections of the upstate town selected as the tentative site for burial of the toxic chemicals.

Residents of the town, Fort Edward in Washington County, won a court suit two years ago that barred state use of a site there the first time it was selected by the Department of Environmental Conservation as the burial site.

State officials, who have begun studying the ground at another site in Fort Edward, said they felt the new location met the legal objections to the first site. The state's $26.7 million project calls for burying the PCBs, or polychlorinated biphenyls, in clay-encapsulated tombs.

Local residents and officials are still against using any site in their town.

"I am against the dredging of PCBs until they have a method of permanently destroying them," said Daniel H. Hayes, the Town Supervisor. "I don't think anyone should be forced to have PCBs buried on their land."

Thomas West, an attorney for a local organization opposed to the dredging, known as Cease, for Citizen Environmentalists Against Sludge Encapsulation, said it was against "spending that much money on a program that has not yet shown that it will have a significant effect on the environment."

The state has tentatively selected a 150-acre site on the north edge of Fort Edward, next to an existing town landfill. "It has good soil, has the proper zoning and seems to be environmentally acceptable," said Russell Mt. Pleasant, the state official in charge of the PCB project. "We are now on the site making geological and other engineering surveys.

He said the state was gathering the new data to prepare a supplemental environmental impact statement before the appointment of a new siting board. The state has not yet acquired the land or reached an agreement with the town to incorporate its landfill into the PCB disposal site.

If there are no further lawsuits that would cause delays, Mr. Mt. Pleasant said that the state hoped to appoint the siting board in 1986, prepare the site in 1987, dredge in 1988 and finish the job in 1990.

Fort Edward, a 27-square mile town on the east bank of the Hudson about 40 miles north of Albany with a population of 6,500, has been the focus of a PCB controversy ever since it was determined in 1976 that the chemical was a possible cause of cancer in humans.

Until that year, the PCBs were discharged into the Hudson as waste products from two General Electric plants in Fort Edward and nearby Hudson

Falls. In 1976, G.E. halted its use of PCBs, paying a fine of $3 million to the state for violating the Clean Water Act and agreeing to spend $1 million more in PCB research.

PCBs once were used in the manufacture of electrical equipment because of their good insulating qualities. Tests have shown that they can cause cancer in animals, and there are concerns that they may be dangerous to human health.

As a result, the state has banned commercial fishing for striped bass in the Hudson because of their levels of PCBs and has warned the public not to eat the fish more than once a month.

The state has estimated that 600,000 pounds of PCBs were deposited in the river between 1945 and 1976 and that more than half of them remained on the river bottom, just south of Fort Edward. It has prepared a plan to dredge some of the PCB-laden sediments from what it calls "hot spots" of contamination.

In 1982, a state hazardous waste siting board approved the use of a 25-acre abandoned farm in Fort Edward as the burial place. But Cease won a court decision barring use of that site because the court held it was in violation of the town zoning laws.

Following that, the Federal Environmental Protection Agency held up its appropriation of $20 million, three-quarters of the cost of the project, until the state, which would pay one-quarter of the cost, or $6.7 million, found a new site and re-examined the river to see if the "hot spots" were still there.

Since then, the state has resurveyed the "hot spots" but has not yet announced its findings.

A BAN ON STRIPED BASS FISHING
(April 22, 1986)

ALBANY—New York State will ban all commercial fishing for striped bass in its waters because of unsafe levels of PCBs in the fish. As a result, striped bass will be virtually unavailable in restaurants or stores in the metropolitan area.

Since last summer, commercial fishing for striped bass has been banned in all state waters except those off eastern Long Island.

But on the basis of new study, the State Department of Environmental Conservation said the levels of PCBs—polychlorinated biphenyls—in the fish in all waters exceeded the safe limits set by the Federal Food and Drug Administration.

"This leaves little alternative but to close the commercial striped bass fishery," Clarence Bassett, assistant commissioner of the department, said today. "We have no choice but to act."

The ban does not deal with recreational fishing for striped bass. But to conform with Federal efforts to prevent overfishing, the state plans either to impose a statewide moratorium on recreational bass fishing or to raise the size limits on fish that can be kept.

The decision to extend the ban on commercial fishing in effect reverses a decision made last year by the Cuomo administration.

At that time, commercial striped bass fishing, which had been banned in the Hudson River since 1976, was halted off western Long Island and in New York Harbor.

But eastern Long Island, with its major fishing industry, was exempted by the administration, which explained that even though PCBs had been found in fish from the region, more samples were needed.

The Governor, who was traveling out of state today, could not be reached for comment.

With the new regulation, which will take effect before the fishing season opens May 8, the two major striped bass fisheries in the Northeast—New York, which once provided about half the striped bass for the region, and Chesapeake Bay—will be closed. This will virtually halt the supply of striped bass to market. Chesapeake Bay was closed last fall because of overfishing.

Small amounts of the fish come from other states, but authorities are considering banning out of state fish to avoid confusion over their origin.

In addition to its impact on consumption, the new prohibition will affect the livelihood of 240 commercial fishermen who had permits to catch striped bass off Long Island in 1985. They caught 466,145 pounds of fish off eastern Long Island last year with a dockside value of $858,769, according to state figures.

Richard Mill, executive secretary of the Long Island Fishermen's Association, said of the decision: "We don't think there's been enough study. But we don't have the experts on our side."

He said the decision would affect all fishermen because bass fishermen would now turn to other types of fish.

170

Haul Seining for striped bass.
Photograph by Cara Lee. Courtesy of Scenic Hudson.

"That means fewer fish for more fishermen," he said. "You see, most guys don't want to leave this way of life. So they try to hang on as long as they can."

The Department of Environmental Conservation defines the marine waters of eastern Long Island as those east of an imaginary line from Mastic in the south to Wading River in the north.

In its new report, the department said it had studied 444 striped bass collected during the 1985 fishing season, most of them provided by fishermen. Almost all the fish were contaminated with more that two parts per million of PCBs, the safe limit set by the Food and Drug Administration.

"The PCB findings were not too much different from those we found last year," said Lawrence Skinner, a fish ecologist for the department. "There is no increase in the PCBs. But last year we had only seven samples from eastern Long Island, and this year we have a much larger sample, something we can really rely upon for data."

Striped bass are especially vulnerable to PCB contamination because they spawn in the Hudson and stay there longer than other fish, such as shad. In addition, they contain more fat, where the PCBs concentrate, than other species of bass, such as the sea bass.

PCBs, which are believed to cause cancer, were dumped in the river as waste products over a period of years from two upstate General Electric plants. The chemicals, which have special insulating qualities, were used in the manufacture of heavy electrical equipment.

Since then, the state has been preparing a plan to clean up the river by dredging some of the PCB-laden sediment from the bottom and burying it on land. But the plan has been halted by the resistance of towns selected for the PCB burial.

Over the last year, the State Department of Health has warned the public not to eat striped bass from the Hudson River, New York Harbor or the waters of western Long Island, and to eat no more than one meal a month of bass from eastern Long Island marine waters.

Despite the new prohibition, the department has not changed its cautionary notice, according to William Fagel, a spokesman. He added, "We are in the process of reviewing our advisories and I would suspect they would be changed to reflect the new report."

The regulations on recreational fishing, which are sure to raise objections from sport fishermen, must be issued to conform to a Federal plan to protect the striped bass population in Chesapeake Bay and other northeastern waters, the department said.

"If a moratorium on recreational fishing were enacted, it would also have the benefit of conserving the dwindling Chesapeake Bay stocks and adding an increased measure of protection for unknowing consumers who might eat illegally marketed PCB-contaminated striped bass," the department said.

Public hearings on the proposed new recreational limits will be held Tuesday at the Suffolk County Community College on Long Island and on Wednesday at the Bear Mountain Inn in Rockland County. No changes can be made for at least 60 days, unless an emergency is declared, according to Mr. Bassett.

The new measures to protect the public from PCBs in the Hudson River and adjacent waters come 10 years after the chemicals were discovered in the river.

———•———

A RITE OF SPRING
(April 2, 1992)

NYACK, N.Y—In an annual rite of spring, shad and striped bass are returning to the Hudson River to spawn.

For the dwindling number of commercial fishermen on the river, the fish, although plentiful, are a mixed catch—a legacy of a 16-year-old controversy about toxic PCBs in the river. The bass, considered unfit for human consumption, must be thrown back while the shad are kept for sale as a gourmet delight.

The difference stems from the eating habits of the fish, which both return to the river of their birth to lay eggs. The striped bass eat small fish in the river and thus accumulate PCBs, while the shad do not feed in their six-week sojourn in the river and remain PCB free.

PCBs, or polychlorinated biphenyls, were deposited in the river over a 30-year period ending in 1976 from two General Electric plants in Fort Edward and Hudson Falls. Until that time PCBs were used in manufacturing electrical equipment because of their excellent insulating qualities.

Although little has been done officially on state plans to cleanse the river of PCBs, the PCB levels of the contaminated fish are declining, according to the State Department of Environmental Conservation.

"But you still can't eat the bass; that's the anomaly," said Christopher Letts of the Hudson River Foundation, a nonprofit group that conducts education programs about the Hudson.

Despite the gradual improvement in the Hudson, the state is still backing a controversial plan to dredge contaminated sediments from the river bottom and bury them on land.

If nothing is done, state environmental officials said, future floods in the upper Hudson River could possibly carry PCBs now buried in the river sediment downstream to the spawning areas of the bass.

The plan is now under review by the Federal Environmental Protection Agency as part of a complete re-examination of the PCB problem. Its recommendations, which could range from doing nothing at all to approval of the state plan, are not expected until the summer of 1993.

Meanwhile, fish seem to be flourishing in the river; said Robert Gabrielson, president of the Hudson River Commercial Fishermen's Association, who has been fishing in the Hudson for 50 years.

In addition to large numbers of striped bass and shad, the river supports a population of "millions of catfish," blue crabs and American eels, he said. If commercial fishing for them were permitted, he said, "the economic value to the Hudson Valley would be enormous."

"There's been no decline in the fish, only a decline in fishermen," he said, attributing it to the state ban on commercial fishing for striped bass. "When I was a young man, there used to be hundreds of fishermen on the river. Now there are only 40 to 50."

In 1991, the last year for which figures are available, the state issued 90 commercial shad fishing licenses, down from 144 in 1988.

One of the license holders, Ron Ingold of Edgewater, N. J., fishes in the shadow of the George Washington Bridge. Mr. Gabrielson, another license holder, and his son, Robert Jr., fish out of Nyack, just north of the Tappan Zee Bridge.

Mr. Ingold and Mr. Gabrielson set nets in the river, trapping the fish as they swim upriver in the flood tides twice a day. Using old-fashioned muscle power, they pull the nets up by hand and remove the fish, which weigh three to four pounds, one by one.

Coming into the Burd Street Marina here in two boats last Monday, the opening day of the shad season, the Gabrielsons unloaded several boxes of fish.

Mr. Gabrielson pulled the boxes of shad into his ice house for shipment later to the Fulton Fish Market in New York. He left the others containing striped bass with two technicians from the Department of Environmental Conservation, Peter Liebig and Robert Morse, for PCB testing.

The Federal Food and Drug Administration guidelines for safety in fish are less than 2 parts per million of PCBs. The limit is based on studies showing that PCBs could cause cancer in laboratory animals, but there is no conclusive evidence showing that it is a human carcinogen.

Hudson River shad fisherman John Mylod.
Courtesy of Scenic Hudson.

In its latest official report, dated December 1991, the State Department of Environmental Conservation said that PCB levels in striped bass had markedly declined in the lower Hudson River. In 1978, the average level was 18.1 parts per million, dropping to 6.1 in 1980 and 2.79 in 1990.

"While this report presents some good news about PCB levels in striped bass in the Hudson, it is not a clear sign that all is well," said Thomas C. Jorling, commissioner of the department. "Concentrations of PCBs remain high enough to present a risk to the public health and the environment.

THE STURGEON GENERAL
(July 25, 1994)

STAATSBURG, N.Y.—They call Dr. Mark B. Bain "the sturgeon general."

Although his official title is Associate Professor of Fish Biology at Cornell University in Ithaca, along the Hudson River here he has earned the new, unofficial rank as the coordinator of several programs researching the life and habits of sturgeon. More particularly, Dr. Bain and his associates are trying to find out why the sturgeon population has plummeted, not only in the Hudson River but all along the East Coast.

Although the commercial fishing season ended on June 15, Dr. Bain and his crew are out almost daily, working under research permits. Sailing a 27-foot fishing boat based at Norrie Point State Park here, a few miles north of Poughkeepsie, the researchers seek the two species of sturgeon that live in the river. They capture the fish with nets that entangle their gills.

The team examines, tags and releases the smaller species, the shortnose sturgeon, which can grow to 3 feet in length and weigh between 10 and 20 pounds. It is a federally protected endangered species, off limits to fishermen.

But most of their attention is focused on the larger species, the Atlantic sturgeon, which can reach 7 feet and weigh up to 700 pounds. Along the East Coast, it is a vanishing species, although it is not yet listed as either threatened or endangered.

Although his research is not scheduled to end until 1996, Dr. Bain has already come to one conclusion, based on the number of fish caught: the population of the shortnose sturgeon is increasing, while that of the Atlantic sturgeon is decreasing rapidly.

Dr. Bain offered three possible reasons for the Atlantic sturgeon's decline: overharvesting of the fish, poor reproduction due to some unknown environmental cause, and competition from the increasing numbers of shortnose sturgeon.

Other experts singled out overfishing, especially in the waters off the Atlantic Coast, as the probable major cause. John Waldman, a research specialist for the Hudson River Foundation, said the high price of sturgeon roe, sometimes running to $50 a pound, was a powerful incentive for overfishing.

The results are unmistakable, the experts agree. Paul Perra, program director of the Atlantic States Marine Fisheries Commission in Washington, an organization of 15 states from Maine to Florida, cited these figures: In 1890, seven million pounds of Atlantic sturgeon were caught off those states; 201,000 pounds were landed in 1990 and 67,000 pounds in 1993.

Dr. Bain, 38, was born in Pittsburgh, where three rivers meet. He got involved in fish research, he said, because "I've always been interested in fishing and the water and the outdoors." He got his doctorate in fish biology from the University of Massachusetts in 1984.

At work, Dr. Bain typically wears an informal collegiate uniform—a white T-shirt with a red "C" for Cornell and gray shorts.

"Mark's job is to take disorganized viewpoints and get them to work together," said Clay Hiles, executive director of the Hudson River Foundation, a non-profit research organization based in New York City. "We say to the scientists, here's the money, but you have to share the information and send it to our coordinating genius." The foundation is supporting a three-year, $1 million research program into the sturgeon.

Aside from size, Dr. Bain said, one difference between the two species is that the shortnose sturgeon lives its entire life in the river, while the Atlantic sturgeon lives in the ocean but comes into the river in May and June to spawn.

Another difference, he said, is that the Atlantic sturgeon—like related species in Europe and Asia—is a major commercial fish, whose roe is processed into caviar and whose flesh is smoked.

In an effort to restore the population of Atlantic sturgeon, the fisheries commission last year required the states either to limit or ban fishing for the species. New York limited the length of the fishing season and banned catching fish under five feet.

As a result, only 22 commercial fishermen applied for licenses last year and only about half of them fished, according to Kathryn A. Hattala, a marine biologist with the State Department of Environmental Conservation, who monitors the river.

Everett Nack, Hudson River fisherman, with Atlantic sturgeon.
Photograph by Steve Stanne. Courtesy of Scenic Hudson.

Last year, they caught 104 fish weighing a total of 6,200 pounds, down from 35,000 pounds in 1992 and 74,000 pounds in 1991, she said.

While Dr. Bain is working on the river, he is also coordinating research for three groups. One is trying to use DNA to determine the sex of immature fish, which is not readily apparent; another is using strontium and calcium formations in the ear bones of fish to determine how much time they spend in salt and fresh water; and the third is experimenting with Caesarean sections to extract roe for caviar without killing the fish.

While the research could hold the promise of a better future for the Atlantic sturgeon, the work of Dr. Bain and his team will also have more immediate effects. In the last week of June they captured a female Atlantic sturgeon, and the United States Fish and Wildlife Service took it to a hatchery in Pennsylvania, where its roe will be extracted and used to produce baby sturgeon for planting in Chesapeake Bay.

CHAPTER 15

Harry the Hawk and Other Animals

The most interesting animal stories I wrote were about Harry the Hawk, an actor at the City Opera in New York City, who was arrested one day by a policeman from the State Department of Environmental Conservation and carted off to an avian jail. Here is that story and what happened subsequently.

ARRESTED
(November 13, 1981)

NEW PALTZ, N.Y.—A hawk named Harry that had a bit part in the New York City Opera production of "Der Freischutz" was seized by conservation officers last week a few hours before curtain time and has become a leading character in a wildlife legal battle.

Among other things, the court fight could determine what is best for Harry—an actor's life on stage or a raptor's life in the wild. In the meantime, the bird is being held virtually incommunicado by the state, according to his keeper.

State conservation officials contend that the stage-trained bird was illegally kept by an internationally known expert on birds of prey and should be retrained by a "federally licensed rehabilitator" and then be set free in the wild.

But the bird expert, Dr. Heinz K. Meng, a professor at the State University at New Paltz, who was keeping Harry between performances, denies the state charge and contends that releasing the hawk would amount to killing him.

The opening act of the real-life drama began on Nov. 5 when 30 state and Federal conservation officers raided 11 sites in New York State to inspect birds held by falconers, all of whom hold licenses to raise or train wild birds. Twelve persons were charged with illegal possession of hawks, and 13 birds were seized.

The raid concluded an undercover operation into illegal falconry practices, according to conservation officials. There were no charges that birds were mistreated, but of illegal holding or transfer of hawks and falcons, which are violations less serious than misdeameanors.

One confrontation occurred at the aviary here of Dr. Meng, a biology professor and pioneer breeder of peregrine falcons. Dr. Meng said he had worked all his life to restore endangered bird populations and deeply resented the raid.

He said he showed five conservation officers 20 birds in breeding chambers, as well as three peregrine falcons, one hybrid Lanner falcon, one gyrfalcon and one Harris hawk, all sitting on outdoor perches.

The Harris hawk was Harry, a 16-year-old bird owned by William Robinson of Saugerties. Harry, who resembles a golden eagle but is a bit smaller, was to appear that night in the opera, flying across the stage in front of Max, the hero, who shoots him with a magic bullet.

Harry had appeared in the opera on three recent occasions and Dr. Meng was paid $300 for each appearance and his handling services.

Harry, the operatic hawk.
Photograph by Heinz Meng.

Over Dr. Meng's objections, the officers took Harry away, charging that Dr. Meng had violated his scientific collector's permit by acquiring him without prior written approval from state officials.

"It's ridiculous," said Dr. Meng, who has pleaded not guilty. No hearing date has been set. Conviction could bring a fine of up to $250 and loss of license.

Dr. Meng had been keeping Harry between the performances in New York and he said both the bird's owner and the agent for its appearances had the necessary permits.

With no time to get a stand-in, the flight of the bird across the stage on Nov. 5 was left to the audience imagination. But on Tuesday night, a red-tailed hawk owned by Nancy Washo of Pleasant Valley appeared.

Capt. Earl T. Washburn, chief of the law-enforcement branch of the regional office of the Department of Environmental Conservation in New Paltz, said Harry was being retrained to be introduced to the wild. He declined to say where.

"I hope they are not planning to let Harry go because that would be the equivalent of killing him," Dr. Meng said. "Harry is a tame bird used to humans and has never hunted for himself. There is no way an imprinted bird of that kind can be retrained to return to the wild."

———•———

RELEASED
(December 6, 1981)

NEW PALTZ, N.Y.—Harry, the operatic hawk, came home in triumph today to the aviary where he was seized a month ago by wildlife conservation officers.

Under a court order, the officers returned him to his owner, William Robinson of Saugerties, in a brief ceremony in the regional offices of the State Department of Environmental Conservation here.

"I am very pleased to see him," Mr. Robinson said. "But he does look a little fat."

Mr. Robinson carried Harry in a large white box to the nearby home and aviary of Dr. Heinz K. Meng, professor of biology at the State University College at New Paltz and an internationally known expert on birds of prey.

Harry is a 16-year old Harris hawk, resembling a golden eagle but slightly smaller, with a bright yellow beak and a brown body. According to Mr. Robinson, Harry will resume his career as a wandering player as soon as the bird becomes trim again.

"The hawk is the star of my wildlife lectures series," said Mr. Robinson, who makes his living lecturing in schools.

Although the first act in the real-life drama of Harry, who was seized at the Meng aviary a few hours before he was scheduled to appear in a bit role in the New York City Opera production of "Der Freischutz," ended in a legal victory for his keeper, the story is not over.

On Dec. 18, Dr. Meng must appear in a local town court, where he will face a charge of violating his scientific collector's permit by not having the state's written permission to keep Harry.

Dr. Meng, who has pleaded not guilty, called the charge "ridiculous." He said both Mr. Robinson and Harry's agent in New York City have the proper papers. Conviction could bring a fine of up to $250 and loss of license.

Harry was seized on Nov. 5 in one of a series of statewide raids by 33 Federal and state wildlife officers. They cited 11 licensed falconers, including Mr. Robinson, for violations of regulations governing the capture and use of raptors and Dr. Meng for improper paper work. There were no charges of mistreatment of birds.

At the time, the officers said their intention was to take Harry to a "federally licensed rehabilitator" to be trained for reintroduction to the wild. But Dr. Meng and Mr. Robinson obtained an injunction preventing the training. They said releasing Harry, a tame bird used to humans, was tantamount to a death sentence.

Harry's return today was under a court-approved agreement between Robert Abrams, the State Attorney General, and Norman Kellar, the lawyer for Dr. Meng and Mr. Robinson. Their agreement specified that Harry would be available for further proceedings if necessary.

HORSES
(July 23, 1979)

ALBANY—The first equine census of New York State shows that Westchester County leads the state in horses.

Westchester has 12,100, the census found, by far the largest number in any county of the state and almost twice as many as in the second-ranking county, Orange, which has 7,300. Suffolk County ranked third, with 6,800.

Paul Bascomb of the New York Crop Reporting Service, which made the survey, said: "In this day, within limits, horses tend to be concentrated where the people are—and that's the suburban areas around the big cities."

One reason for the census, according to Jerome A. Fisher, the statistician in charge, was to give the Legislature information so it could revise laws giving tax incentives to breeders.

The census showed that New York State had 180,000 horses, ponies, mules and donkeys. Despite what the experts say is a boom in horse ownership and breeding, racing and pleasure riding, the state remains second in the nation to Kentucky as a horse state. Two years ago a census in Kentucky put its horse population at 204,000.

The last previous indication of New York State's horse population was in a Cornell University estimate, not a census, back in 1964, when the figure was 117,074.

In a breakdown by use, the census showed that 106,500 horses were used strictly for pleasure, 24,250 for show, 16,150 for harness racing, 7,400 for flattrack racing and 16,300 for breeding.

Of all the geographic regions of the state, the area around New York City led the rest in almost every category of horse population and use. For example, in the 10-county area just north of the city, including Westchester, 28,400 horses were kept for pleasure use.

"This is a heavily populated horse area," said Pete Peterson, manager of Silver Spur Horse Farms, a boarding stable on Croton Avenue just off Route 202 in Cortlandt, in northern Westchester County. "It goes on and on here with hundreds and hundreds of horses."

Mr. Peterson attributes the rise in horse population to two factors; the growth of 4H clubs, in which children learn about horses and have frequent horse shows, and "people with a little more money than they used to have who get a horse for their kids."

Jerry H. Mulcahy, Cooperative Extension Service Agent in White Plains, said horse ownership was no longer restricted to the rich, although in many communities it remained a status symbol.

"It's a love of animals," he said. "Many people with a horse background have moved to Westchester County for new employment and will do anything to have a horse. It's recreation for the whole family. The horse is like a member of the family."

BUFFALO
(April 10, 1973)

STORMVILLE, N.Y.—Charles and Julia Tucker have a home where the buffalo roam 90 minutes from Times Square in Dutchess County.

Driving an old red pickup truck through the range on which the buffalo graze, Mr. Tucker came close to his herd of 37 animals the other day. There, in front of the truck, was Big Daddy, a tough old bull, who wouldn't budge.

"He wouldn't back up for a freight train," Mr. Tucker said a little proudly. "He's quick as lightning and unpredictable."

Mr. Tucker pointed to the one-track freight line that runs close to the border of his farm.

"See that?" he said. "Big Daddy and some of the other buffalo got on the track and stopped the trains a while ago. The railroad had to build some strong fences around the tracks."

The 52-year-old Mr. Tucker is one of the few New York members of the National Buffalo Association, which was founded in 1966 and is now booming. It has 300 members, half of whom are active in raising buffalo, owning a total of 20,000. There are about 5,000 more bison in state and national reservations around the country and 15,000 in Canada, according to the association. They are considered a national resource by many, a tourist attraction by some and a source of meat for a few.

Mr. Tucker has become a practical expert on the habits of bison since he bought his first animal in 1965, but he concedes he still has a lot to learn about them.

"If you don't bother them, they won't bother you," he said. "But don't get out and walk among them unless you can run fast. They're liable to hook you with their horns."

Mr. Tucker drove around Big Daddy and farther into the 1,000-acre farm that he owns with his two uncles, C. Tremain Jackson, 71, and Henry H. Jackson, 74. His family has owned the farm since 1743, when Thomas Storm, after whom Stormville is named, came up to the area from Tarrytown.

Mr. Tucker, who was born and raised on the farm, called Homestead Farm, came back to it in 1946 after serving in the Air Force as a pilot flying cargo planes over the Hump into China from Burma in World War II. It was a dairy farm then.

He stopped the truck in the middle of his breeder cattle. "Here's Tessie," he said, pointing to a small bison.

"Tessie associates only with cows and people, not with other buffalo," he explained.

"Kiss me," he said. Tessie licked his face.

Tessie was born four years ago in a twin birth, a rare occurrence among bison, according to Mr. Tucker. Her mother took one of the calves and went off, presumably leaving Tessie to die. Mr. Tucker fed the calf with a bottle and she flourished.

"She considers me to be her mother," Mr. Tucker said.

Mr. Tucker got involved with bison in 1965, when, troubled by a labor shortage on his dairy farm and eager to go into something else, he heard about a buffalo sale at a ranch in South Dakota. He called, asked the price and made a bid of $325 on some cows and $350 on a bull. That night he got a return phone call informing him that he was the owner of four buffalo.

Over the years Mr. Tucker bought some more and raised others with the help of a hired man, Samuel Williams.

"Last summer was great and I thought I had it made when nine calves were born," Mr. Tucker said, "But in the fall, four died."

The greatest natural enemy of the buffalo in the East is the choke cherry tree. Its wilted leaves, not the berries or the green leaves, produce acids that can kill an animal within 24 hours, the farmer said. As a result, Mr. Tucker and Mr. Williams have been cutting down weed trees in great numbers on their spread.

Sightseers are another problem. The Tuckers conduct tours for school children, but motorists sometimes clog Stormville Road and Route 216 that border their farm, looking for the buffalo.

But for all the problems, Mr. Tucker thinks that buffalo are easier to raise than milk cows and certainly more enjoyable.

"I have room for them to graze," he said. "They eat grass most of the year so I feed them hay in the winter only. You don't have to shelter them, not even in the snow, and they take care of themselves."

Mr. Tucker sells live animals to custard-stand owners, to game parks and to landowners who just like the idea of having a buffalo on their property.

Mr. Tucker believes that buffalo and its products are good for you. The meat is delicious, a little similar to beef, perhaps a bit more gamey, but more tender and low in fat and cholesterol, he said.

COYOTES
(March 8, 1987)

ALBANY—The mournful howl of the coyote is being heard more frequently in upstate New York. The population of the wild canines has grown so much that they have become a menace to sheep farmers throughout the state, according to agricultural officials here.

The solution to the growing problem, according to experts, is not killing them, but building fences to keep them away from one of their favorite foods, sheep. Taking that approach, the Federal Department of Agriculture and the State Department of Agriculture and Markets have signed an agreement for a pilot project to identify, control and abate the problem of the eastern coyote within New York State.

"We are not trying to regulate the coyote population, but to protect farms," said Robert Mungari, an official of the State Agriculture Department.

Under the new program, the two departments have allocated $70,000 to control two predators—coyotes and black bears, which attack apiaries but are a comparatively minor problem. Two seasonal employees will be hired to respond to complaints, evaluate the damage, and make recommendations for controlling the predators.

The recommendations will stress, according to the experts, protection of farm property, including the sheep, not shooting the coyotes.

The new program does not address what is usually considered the major wildlife threat to crops, deer, which cause large losses, particularly to apple orchards. Other research programs on deer control are under way near farms, also stressing fencing.

Although the word coyote conjures up an image of a western animal that preys on sheep herds in the plains and mountains, coyotes have been reported in New York since the late 1930s. They appeared in the northern Adirondack Mountains, possibly as immigrants from Canada, and have spread and flourished since.

The state population of coyotes is estimated to be about 10,000, according to the wildlife experts of the State Department of Environmental Conservation. They are in every county of the state except in New York City and Long Island.

For New York's 2,200 sheep farmers, who have about 55,000 sheep, the coyote is a major enemy. In 1985, the last year for which there are complete records, they lost 11,000 sheep, valued at $835,000, including $192,500 worth to predators alone, according to the State Crop Reporting Service here.

Of the 2,500 losses to predators, 54 percent, or 1,350, were killed by dogs, 42 percent, or 1,050, by coyotes, and 4 percent by other animals, the Crop Reporting Service said. But, according to the Department of Agriculture, the figures are skewed, with coyote damage reports lower than they actually are because farmers are reimbursed for damages suffered by dogs but not for those by coyotes.

Ben Tullar, a biologist with the Department of Environmental Conservation, said sheep farmers can take action.

"We recommended electric fencing of sheep pastures and lambing in barns rather than open spaces," he said. "Our emphasis is on an exterior education approach rather than hunting them. We point out to people who suffer damage that they don't have to put up with it. They can shoot or trap coyotes on their own property if they want to."

The first area of operations for the coyote-control program will be in the western part of the state, in Livingston, Ontario, Yates, Steuben and Allegheny Counties. Later, action will be taken closer to metropolitan New York, in Ulster, Dutchess and Columbia Counties.

NUISANCE WILDLIFE
(October 3, 1981)

DELMAR, N.Y.—New York State's populations of deer, geese, beaver, wild turkey and several other species are growing so fast that some have become nuisances, wildlife officials say. Even coyotes and moose have been spotted for the first time in many years.

The number of deer is estimated at 650,000, the highest in history, the officials say, which has led the state to take advantage of the hunting season to cut that figure back. And increasing numbers of such smaller animals as otters and raccoons have led to a renewal of the trapping industry.

Hunting regulations this season are being eased to let as many as 170,000 deer be taken, compared with about 136,000 killed legally last year. The season officially opened for hunters using bows and arrows in the northern part of the state on Sept. 27. Regular hunting starts in the northern part of the state on Oct. 24, and in the south later.

"We've let the deer population get a little out of hand," said the state's deer management specialist, Nathaniel Dickinson, who added that there were perhaps a quarter-million more deer than optimal for the supply of food.

Robert F. Flacke, the state's Commissioner of Environmental Conservation, said the number of deer in some areas of the state was "at undesirably high levels."

Officials of the department's Division of Fish and Wildlife say a depletion of wildlife began with the clearing of forests almost two centuries ago and the onset of farming.

But the gradual closing down of unprofitable farms in the northern and western parts of the state over the last 50 years, the experts said, has led to a resurgence of the brush and timberland that provide a natural habitat for wildlife, such as the pileated woodpecker, the mourning dove, and the fisher, a type of mink.

Mr. Dickinson, a supervising wildlife biologist at the Wildlife Resources Center in this village just outside Albany, said in an interview that "there is no question that urbanization and the widespread use of chemicals had an impact on wildlife populations."

"But the prophecy of gloom just hasn't come true," he said. "In fact, the increase in deer and geese in some parts of the state are really creating nuisances." Moreover, he added, the deer are "bigger and healthier than ever before."

Part of the recent increase, he and the other scientists who work here said, is due to two extremely mild winters back to back. This has provided more food and reduced the normal loss of smaller and weaker animals due to starvation.

"But the increased number has in turn led many of the animals to seek food in cultivated lands such as apple orchards," he said. There has been a sharp increase in complaints by apple growers in Columbia and Wayne Counties that deer are causing widespread damage.

Geese are the main nuisance in parts of Suffolk and other downstate counties along the East Coast "flyway" where grain is grown, according to John Moser, a wildlife specialist here.

Mr. Moser said that in the 1940s the number of migrating geese along the flyway was between 200,000 and 300,000, while now the figure approaches one million.

"We're also seeing for the first time large resident populations of geese in the state," he said. The number on Long Island has swelled from 2,000 or so a decade ago to perhaps as many as 15,000 today, while the number of resident birds in the Finger Lakes area has gone from almost none to about 30,000.

Mr. Moser attributed much of the increase to the setting aside of land for wildlife refuges along the East Coast, and other conservation measures.

The big increase in the wild turkey population in the state is due to the return of brushland which the birds need for cover, and restocking efforts by the state, according to James Glidden, the Wildlife Resources Center's turkey specialist.

"The wild turkey was extinct in New York by 1844, but they started coming back over the Pennsylvania line in the 1930s," Mr. Glidden said.

The natural migration plus a resettlement program has led to a resident turkey population in New York of 45,000, a number so high that state agencies have given turkeys away for resettlement to New Jersey, Connecticut, Vermont, Massachusetts and New Hampshire.

Mr. Glidden predicted, however, that the movement of turkeys into such areas as the Hudson Valley, where they had not been seen for 150 years, probably would not last because "the population is so high it exceeds the carrying capacity of the land."

According to Gary Parsons, a state wildlife management expert in fur bearing animals, the beaver was all but extinct in the state by the middle of the 19th century, until it was reintroduced in 1920.

In the last two seasons, he said, about 33,000 beavers have been trapped, a figure that does not compare with the hundreds of thousands a year killed yearly 150 years ago but nevertheless demonstrates the comeback of smaller animals.

The resurgence of martens, otters, and raccoons as well as beavers led to an increase in the number of trapping licenses in the state from 8,000 to 30,000 over the past 25 years.

"New York now is among the half-dozen most important states in trapping with production last year of $30 million in pelts," Mr. Glidden said.

CHAPTER 16

Apples

I probably wrote more stories about apples than any other single subject. When we moved to the Hudson Valley, I didn't know that we were entering one of the great apple-growing regions of the United States. The apple orchards of New York are centered in three major areas: the Hudson Valley, the Champlain Valley, and the lee of Lake Ontario, where the climate is conducive to fruit production. Of course, there are ups and downs, as the following stories will attest.

Today, New York is the second largest apple-growing state in the nation. For one brief moment, in 1971, it was number one because of a crop disaster in Washington, which normally leads the nation. And one year it dropped to third, behind Michigan, but it is now back in second place.

NUMBER ONE
(October 23, 1971)

ALBANY—New York is harvesting a bumper crop of apples this year and for the first time in a decade has replaced Washington as the state with the greatest apple production.

New York's crop will be more than 1 billion pounds, slightly in excess of Washington's total, according to the October report of the New York crop reporting service in Albany.

In Seattle, a spokesman for the Washington reporting service said production there was down this year because of spotty bloom in the spring and extremely hot weather from mid-July to mid-August.

"And we're still suffering from the freeze of 1969," he said in a telephone interview. "Trees were weakened then and have not yet recovered."

A statistician in Seattle said 1961 was the last previous year in which New York out-produced Washington. In that year, New York produced 1 billion pounds, and Washington only 835 million pounds.

In New York this year, the harvest has been a little late, but the crop will be about 11 percent larger than in 1970 because of favorable weather during the growing season.

Despite the poor crop this year, Washington's growers are confident that next year's apples will be back to normal if the weather is right, and that Washington will regain its lead position in apple production.

New York farmers are discouraged about the prices they are getting. Some are withholding their apples from the market.

In the Hudson Valley and the area south of Lake Ontario in western New York, farmers are filling bushel baskets, wooden crates and cellophane bags with apples—McIntosh, Delicious, Greening, Cortland and Rome Beauties. Of these, McIntosh is New York's favorite apple by far.

Production of apples in the United States for 1971 is forecast at slightly more than 6 billion pounds, 1 percent less than last year. Production increased in New England, Pennsylvania, Michigan and Virginia, as well as in New York. These increases were more than offset by declines in California and Washington.

New York's apple industry centers in the Hudson Valley, where the crop forecast for 1971 is 365 million pounds, and in western New York, where the forecast is for 640 million pounds.

The quality is the best in years, according to Edward Buckley, the fruit expert for the Columbia County Extension Service. The county is one of the state's largest apple producers, second only to Wayne in western New York.

Picking apples.
Photograph by Joan C. Barker.
Courtesy of Dutchess County Tourism Promotion Agency.

"But the price is ridiculous," one farmer said in a recent interview.

Most of the Hudson Valley apples are shipped to the New York City Terminal Market, where one day recently the price of a standard unit, consisting of 12 three-pound bags of McIntosh apples wrapped in cellophane, ranged from $2.25 to $2.75, wholesale.

"When apples are going for $2.50 a pack of three-pound bags, there's no money in it for the farmer," Mr. Buckley said. In Wayne County, according to the Albany reporting service, large processors of sauce, cider and the like are offering as little as 75 cents for a 40-pound box.

Many farmers are holding their apples off the market and storing them, in cold storage for a short time and in controlled-atmosphere warehouses for months. The market pattern is that prices tend to rise in the spring.

BIG CROP
(February 1, 1976)

ALBANY—Farmers in New York State grew more apples in 1975 than at any time in the last 50 years, but the result was a financial disaster for them, according to farm experts here and in the major fruit-growing areas of the state.

The state's apple trees produced more than a billion pounds of fruit, but almost a fifth of the apples were left on the trees to wither and die as prices received by the farmers plummeted. The farm value of the crop dropped 21 percent from $65 million in 1974 to $51 million last year.

For consumers, the drop in farm prices had little effect on retail prices, except for a slight decrease at the harvest season. But the cost of fresh apples has not risen, as many other food products have.

In New York City this week, for example, the price of a three-pound plastic-wrapped bag of McIntosh apples was at most 59 to 69 cents, exactly what it was a year ago, according to market experts of the State Department of Agriculture and Markets.

John Hotaling of Claverack N.Y., president of the New York Horticultural Society which includes most of the state's fruit growers in its membership, said, "Apples should be selling for roughly 25 percent more than they are, to give farmers back the money they spent producing them."

"But the prices didn't go up like everything else," he added, "which is really a cut in the price to the consumer."

The major impact of the bumper crop and drop in prices was recorded not in the Hudson Valley where Mr. Hotaling grows his apples, but in the western part of the state just south of Lake Ontario, where most of the apples are processed into apple sauce, juice, cider and other manufactured products.

"It's been a desperate year," said Mike Muscarella of the Farm Bureau Marketing Cooperative in Albion, N.Y. "Most of our growers barely cover the cost of picking the apples and shipping them to a processing plant, let alone the cost of growing them and other expenses. It just didn't pay to pick the smaller apples."

As a result, the prices received by farmers for their processing apples dropped to less than half of what they had been the year before, he said. He cited the price for the largest apples, those that were two and three-quarters of an inch in diameters, as $2.75 for 100 pounds in 1975 compared with $6.50 the year before.

Roger Barber, State Commissioner of Agriculture and Markets, said, "The situation with processing apples is one of the biggest problems we have in agriculture today." He has called all those connected with the apple-processing business in the state to an emergency meeting in Rochester on Thursday and Friday.

New York is the second largest apple-growing state in the country, exceeded only by Washington, and it is the country's primary producer of the crisp McIntosh apple. Apples for eating, including the Cortland, Rome and Delicious as well as the McIntosh, are grown in the Hudson and Champlain Valleys. Apples for processing, mainly the Rhode Island Greening and the McIntosh, are grown in the western part of the state.

Other major apple-producing states are, in order, Michigan, Pennsylvania, California, and Virginia. Small amounts of apples are also grown in New Jersey and Connecticut and many other Northern states.

In the country as a whole, the Red Delicious and Golden Delicious varieties, both produced in large quantities, are by far the favorite apples of all Americans, making up almost half the country's total production.

Production of all apples in the United States increased by 16 percent this year, mainly because of favorable weather conditions in almost every section. The national figures show that in Washington and Michigan, the areas where mostly eating apples were grown, almost all the crop was picked.

However, in New York, where almost all the apples were harvested in 1974, only 880 million pounds of the total crop of 1,080 million pounds were picked last year, leaving 180 million pounds unpicked.

Part of the reasons, according to the apple experts, was a heavy carry-over of processed apples left over from 1974. In addition, they said, the bumper crop and financial problems of processing plants helped create an atmosphere that curtailed demand and depressed prices.

Following is a table, based on facts supplied from the New York Crop Reporting Service, showing the leading varieties of apples grown in the United States and in New York in 1975:

Variety	United States (million lbs.)	New York (million lbs.)
Delicious	2,673	107
Golden Delicious	1,100	40
McIntosh	719	330
Rome	587	95
Rhode Island Greening	180	166
Cortland	105	100

—————•—————

FROST
(April 25, 1981)

HUDSON, N.Y.—Three nights of freezing temperatures in the last two weeks have severely damaged the apple crop in New York—the second largest producer of apples in the United States and a major supplier of apples for export.

Reports from fruit growers and experts in the state's three major apple-producing areas—the Hudson Valley, the Champlain Valley and the lee of Lake Ontario south of Rochester—all indicated that the crop this fall would be down substantially and that the price to consumers would rise accordingly. The freeze affects all the varieties of apples in the state, where the McIntosh is the major one produced.

"It's the worst freeze in the Hudson Valley since 1945," said Benjamin Bartolotta, who has 800 acres devoted to apples and other fruit in his orchards in Livingston, in southern Columbia County.

Mr. Bartolotta, who remembers the 1945 freeze in which tiny apples on the trees were killed by a late frost, estimated that he had lost at least 50 percent of his apple crop this year. Don De Laurentis, who operates Bryant Farms nearby, said "We expect a 50 percent crop unless we get another frost."

The frosts occurred Monday and Tuesday nights and a week ago Thursday, when the temperature dropped to 20 degrees. The cold followed a harsh winter in which subzero temperatures wiped out almost all of this summer's peach and cherry crop in the Hudson Valley.

At a meeting of apple growers in Hudson today, several reported that their trees in low-lying areas, where the cold collects, had been damaged the most. John Hotaling, who operates a roadside stand in Claverack, said that his trees had suffered substantial damage, but that he might yet have a reasonable crop.

Across the Hudson in Ulster County, Stanley Cohn of Stanley Orchards in Modena said, "If we get good weather in the next four weeks, we may have a fair crop."

He also said apple growers tried to protect their crops by using smudge pots, overhead irrigation sprays, wind machines and helicopters to blow warmer air on the trees. The state's Department of Environmental Conservation has said there was no rule against the use of smudge pots for such purposes.

The April frosts were especially destructive because they followed a few weeks of mild weather that caused the trees to produce leaves and flower buds about 10 days ahead of schedule, leaving them vulnerable to the colder weather.

"It looks bad for fruit growers everywhere," said Warren H. Smith, the fruit expert of the Cooperative Extension Service in Highland, N.Y.

In Peru, N.Y., Arthur B. Burell, who with his son George grows apples on 180 acres west of Lake Champlain, said, "I am guessing that we will lose more than 50 percent of the crop."

In Rochester, Richard Norton, the fruit expert of the cooperative extension service, said, "Our damage is heavy and significant and will be disastrous to the whole industry." He said farmers would be spending less for spraying materials, for labor, and less in general with suppliers, thus affecting the economy of the entire area.

Mr. Norton said it was too early to tell how much of the apple crop had been destroyed. An apple tree normally sets only one apple for each 20 to 25 blossoms, so that it could lose a high percentage of its buds and still produce a fair crop.

"Mother Nature has a tremendous capacity for recovery," Mr. Smith said.

Dr. C. G. Forshey, head of the Hudson Valley Laboratory in Highland, which investigates apple growth and disease, added: "We will not be able to tell how much of a crop we really have until we get into June when the apples begin to grow. At the moment, it's significant reduction, not a disaster."

But no matter how much the loss amounts to, it will be borne directly by the farmers, who are not covered by either private or governmental insurance, according to Mr. Hotaling.

For consumers, the experts predicted that the price of apples would rise because of the small crop in New York, which last year produced a billion pounds of apples. It was second in the nation to Washington, which produced three billion pounds. Together, the two states produced almost half of all the apples in the United States.

The smaller crop will affect mainly the supply of McIntosh apples, which is New York's premier variety. There will be less impact on the supply of Red Delicious, most of which comes from Washington. New York also normally produces large quantities of Red Delicious, Rhode Island Greening and Rome apples.

One indication of the price of New York apples this fall came from Van Ness Philip, who operates a pick-it-yourself orchard in Claverack. Last year, he charged $7 for a bushel, or 42 pounds, of apples. This year because of inflation, he had expected to raise the price to $8 a bushel, but now he foresees an even higher price.

As for the supermarket, where the price of a pound of McIntosh apples is 49 to 59 cents, one grower said he would not be surprised to see the price rise this fall to 89 to 99 cents a pound.

A RECORD CROP
(July 17, 1983)

ALBANY—New York State set two records for apple growing last year, according to a report this week by the State Crop Reporting Service here.

The state grew more apples, 1.13 billion pounds, than in any previous year, and it processed more of them, 730 million pounds, into such products as sauce and juice, the service said.

Despite the record, it was not a good year for farmers, because the large crop depressed prices. The total value of the crop to the growers fell 2 percent, from $102.3 million in 1981 to $100.5 million, the service said.

The average price paid to growers was 8.9 cents a pound, down from 12.8 in 1981, according to the service.

"It was a belt-tightening year for the growers," said Richard I. Pease, the fruit specialist of the Cooperative Extension Service in Lockport in Niagara County.

He said inflation had added to production costs, farmers were disappointed with prices, and a larger amount than usual was put into storage for delayed sale after the harvest.

"It was not a good year for the growers," said Ken Pollard, an official of the Western New York Apple Growers Association, headquartered in Fishers, south of Rochester.

He cited record imports of concentrated juice from abroad because of excellent crops in Europe and elsewhere and the strong position of the United States dollar relative to foreign currencies.

In January and February, he said, juice imports were 90 percent higher than in 1981, with large quantities coming from West Germany, France, Argentina, South Africa, India, Australia and New Zealand.

New York is second only to Washington in the production of apples in the United States. Last year's crop in New York was 41 percent more than the 800 million pounds produced in 1981, when the apples were damaged by an early freeze, and 3 percent about the previous record crop, in 1980.

About 60 percent of the crop went into processed apples. The largest amount, 337 million pounds, was converted into juice or cider, with 288 million pounds made into sauce or canned slices, 42 million pounds frozen and 63 million pounds made into vinegar, jelly, apple butter and mincemeat.

Last year, most of the apples for processing, 521 million pounds, were converted in plants in the western part of the state, with the remainder processed in the east.

The leading varieties grown in the west are McIntosh, Rhode Island Greening and Rome, all of which are good for processing. The McIntosh, which is also a good eating apple, is the leading variety in the east, where apples are largely grown for the table.

In the latest census, Wayne County, on the southern shore of Lake Ontario, between Rochester and Syracuse, is the leading apple-growing county. It has 313 apple farms covering 20,000 acres, with 1.2 million apple trees, about one-quarter of the state total.

Two other areas, the Hudson and Champlain Valleys, also produce large quantities.

BEES ON THE JOB
(May 17, 1981)

SAUGERTIES, N.Y.—A contingent of 125 million migrant workers—honey bees, that is—has left the Hudson Valley after completing its yearly job of pollinating the area's apple crop.

Despite an early spring freeze that killed many of the apple blossoms, the bees spend 10 days to two weeks from dawn to dusk in the Hudson Valley's apple orchards. Flitting among the remaining blossoms, the bees gather nectar and, in the process, carry pollen from flower to flower.

When their work was done one night last week, they were taken in the hives by truck to the Champlain Valley, where spring comes a little later, to begin pollinating fruit there.

"If it weren't for the honeybees, there would be no fruit," said Gerald Stevens, the bee expert of the State Department of Agriculture and Markets.

As essential component of the fruit industry, honeybees are raised in New York by about 8,000 beekeepers, most of them hobbyists interested in producing and selling honey. But there are only about 40 commercial beekeepers, who rent their bees to growers of apples, pears, peaches and cherries in the spring and use them for honey production in the summer.

Together, the beekeepers in New York State manage about 125,000 colonies. Each colony contains as many as 40,000 bees, for a total of about five billion. There are perhaps twice that number of wild honeybees.

Last year was a poor one for the honeybees, mostly because of bad weather, according to the state's Crop Reporting Service in Albany. The commercial beekeepers produced about five million pounds of honey in 1980, down 23 percent from 1979, the service reported.

A report issued last week by Dr. Roger A. Morse of the State College of Agriculture and Life Sciences at Cornell University gave an additional reason for the decline. He said that pesticides had killed a large number of bees.

Dr. Morse, one of the country's leading expert on bees, reported substantial losses in at least 4,454 bee colonies in 164 upstate apiaries—mostly in western New York State in the lee of Lake Ontario—from pesticides sprayed to control crop-damaging insects on sweet corn.

He based his estimates on reports from beekeepers, which he said were incomplete. "We believe we have erred on the conservative side and that the number of colonies affected by pesticides this year in New York is greater than indicated," he said.

The problem of pesticide contamination of bees and their hives in the Hudson Valley is not as serious as in the Genesee Valley, according to Roy I. Myer, who operates the largest commercial beekeeping operation in the state with his three sons. Mr. Myer, who has been a beekeeper for 55 years, reported some damage last year, mostly from sprays used to control gypsy moths, but not much damage so far this year.

"We keep the bees away from cornfields," he said. He added that his sons, Roy R., Edward and Robert, had moved their base of operation from the Hudson Valley to Granville, a small town near the Vermont border where very little sweet corn is grown.

The Myer operation, with 3,000 commercial hives, is the major pollinator in the eastern part of the state, although there are other commercial beekeepers in the area.

The Myers bring their bees to the Hudson Valley every spring, from 10 days to two weeks in late April and early May, renting the hives to fruit growers for about $22 each, before returning to the Champlain Valley. One grower, the Moriello Orchards in New Paltz, for example, rented 100 colonies to pollinate apples and pears this year.

Each colony or hive consists of two boxes, each 10 inches high, placed one atop the other. Inside are a queen bee, many drones, and thousands of workers, all female. The total hive population reaches about 40,000 in the spring and as many as 100,000 in the summer.

Mr. Myer, who is 79 years old and semi-retired, said bees work in the orchards in April and May and then retire to "yards" where they are kept for the summer and fall, producing honey. It is there that they winter.

"The apple blossom honey is bitter, not fit to eat," he said. "We leave that for the bees."

But the honey the bees collect in the summer and fall, gathered from clover, basswood and goldenrod, is saved, collected from the hives and sold. Each hive, he said, can produce between 80 and 100 pounds of honey in a good year.

MIGRANT LABOR
(September 6, 1984)

CLINTONDALE, N.Y.—Israel Stewart reached into an apple tree not much higher than his head and gently twisted a ripe, red McIntosh from the branch and put it into a cloth bag hanging from his shoulders.

Mr. Stewart is one of 1,550 legal aliens from Jamaica who came to the Hudson Valley this year to harvest apples under an international program involving the United States, New York State, Jamaica and the apple growers.

"Without them there's no possible way of harvesting the crop," said Warren Smith, the fruit expert of the Ulster County Cooperative Extension Service. "There is absolutely no local labor available to pick apples."

The Jamaican apple-picking force in the Hudson Valley, which works from August through October, is augmented, however, by about 300 migrant workers from the South, recruited by the state employment service.

The importation of foreign workers to pick apples in New York dates to 1943, when there was a shortage of farm help because of World War II. It has continued because of the desire of the Jamaican workers to come north to earn better wages and the reluctance of Americans to work in farm fields.

"It's a highly successful program," said Donald Irwin, a regional labor specialist of the State Department of Labor, based in Kingston, N.Y.

It is also important for the economy of New York State, the second largest apple-growing state in the nation behind Washington, with an annual crop in excess of a billion pounds.

Today, on the opening day of the McIntosh harvest, Mr. Stewart and 31 colleagues from Jamaica worked in the bright sun on the 250-acre family fruit farm operated by Phillips Hurd here in Ulster County, halfway between the Hudson River and the Shawangunk Mountains.

Picking slowly and methodically with both hands along a row of dwarf apple trees, Mr. Stewart filled his bag in less than two minutes. He walked a few steps and dumped the apples into a huge wooden bin that held 850 pounds of fruit.

"It looks like a good crop, not a bumper crop, but pretty good," said Mr. Hurd, inspecting the apples in the bin. "It's much better than last year, when we lost half our apples to hail."

Mr. Smith picked up an apple. "These are magnificent apples," he said. "They'll grade out as extra fancy, the best."

As he continued to pick apples, Mr. Stewart explained why he left his own farm in Trelawny in Jamaica, where he grows bananas, yams and oranges, to come north to pick apples.

"I come to earn better money," he said.

Under a complicated agreement negotiated between the apple growers and the Jamaican Government, Mr. Stewart and the other foreign pickers are paid 60 cents for each bushel of apples they pick, with a guarantee of $5.03 an hour, set by the Federal Department of Labor. "They can double that minimum on a good day," said Mr. Hurd.

In addition, according to the State Labor Department, the alien workers receive free housing and transportation to and from Jamaica, if they work through the end of the harvest season, usually Nov. 1.

"They can go home with a net of at least $1,800 to $2,500," said Joseph Russo, an officer of the Valley Growers Cooperative, which negotiates with the Jamaican Government each year for the workers.

A representative of the Jamaican Government, Henry McGhie, who maintains an office in Milton, in the heart of Ulster County apple country, said the system worked well.

"We're happy with it and I think the Americans are happy with it," he said. "It's been going on so long that there must be something good about it."

Unlike the uncertainty caused by a new Federal immigration law on migrant farm labor in New Jersey and the West, there has been no impact on the Jamaican program in New York, according to those involved. About the only change will be that Mr. Hurd and other apple growers will have to file new forms, listing their legal alien workers.

Each year, before the United States Government permits the entrance of the alien workers, a complicated procedure is followed to insure that they are not taking jobs away from Americans.

"We spent $3,000 in advertising for six weeks to recruit local workers and didn't get even one," Mr. Russo said.

With a certification from the state that local labor was not available, Mr. Russo's cooperative then got approval from the Immigration and Naturalization Service to import foreign workers, before negotiating with Jamaica for them.

In addition to working in the Hudson Valley, some Jamaicans are also working in New York's two other apple regions, the Lake Champlain area and south of Lake Ontario in the western part of the state.

Despite the apparent success of the program, two Federally-financed organizations have lawsuits pending challenging the minimum wages, which are set by the Federal Department of Labor.

The Farm Workers Legal Services of New York Inc., based in New Paltz, sued the growers on the grounds that the workers were underpaid in previous years because the minimum wage set by the Federal Government was artificially depressed.

In addition, the Migrant Legal Action Program, based in Washington, has sued the Federal Labor Department, contesting its method of setting the minimum wage for the apple pickers.

The suits are in various stages of litigation, with no final determination reached.

CHAPTER 17

Other Crops

Many people are surprised to learn that New York is a major agricultural state. But it is, averaging a farm income of about three billion dollars a year, with milk from dairy cows accounting for more than half that. Look at this tabulation, attested to by the State Agricultural Statistics Service in Albany, ranking New York in farm produce:

First: McIntosh apples
          Cabbage for fresh market sale
          Creamed cottage cheese
          Low-fat cottage cheese
Second:Cabbage for sauerkraut (behind Wisconsin)
          Apples (behind Washington)
          Sour cherries (behind Michigan)
          Corn for silage (behind Wisconsin)
          Water ices (behind California)
Third: Italian cheese (behind Wisconsin and California)
          Milk (behind California and Wisconsin)
          Sweet corn (behind Florida and California)
Fourth: Cauliflower (behind California, Arizona, and Oregon)
          Cheese (behind Wisconsin, California, and Minnesota)
          Pears (behind Wisconsin, California, and Oregon)
          Snap beans (behind Florida, Georgia and California)
Fifth: Green peas for processing (behind Wisconsin, Minnesota, Washington, and Oregon)

MELONS
(August 7, 1976)

GREENWICH, N.Y.—Like the Persian king of fable who waited for the right second of the right minute of the right hour of the right day to pick his melons at the peak of perfection, Aaron Allen Hand has been going out to his melon fields for days now, testing for the moment when his famous Hand melons are ready for market.

Shortly after 7 o'clock this morning, Mr. Hand made another trip to one field of his farm here and again began to look for the telltale sign of a mature melon—a light yellowing of the green-tinted skin peeking through the bright green leaves of the vines.

He spotted a few and then used what his wife, Carol, called the thumb-pressure test: If the stem breaks off with a flick of the thumb, the melon is ready to be picked.

Four melons met that test. Then Mr. Hand applied his ultimate test—taste. He took out a pocket knife, cut wedges into each and tasted his samples. Three of them qualified for his No. 1 rating—the sweet, juicy, luscious muskmelons that most people call cantaloupes and which some gourmets consider to be the finest melon they have ever eaten.

But Mr. Hand was only relatively happily. His melons were finally coming in, but the crop is at least 10 days late, missing the opening of the racing season at Saratoga, only 15 miles to the west, where his melons for breakfast are almost as famous as the horses. A year ago today, he and his farm workers picked 524 bushels, 13 melons to a bushel.

"It's usually a six-week picking season, but it won't be this year," he said, pointing out that the yield always ended in early September. "Each year is different: I think the last good year we had was 1971."

If the yield is small, a lot of people will be disappointed in the roadside stand down the road. There are clippings on the wall of Red Smith columns noting that the Saratoga Race Course is famous for two things—horses and Hand melons for breakfast in the clubhouse.

Last year, the *County Journal* had a long article on the melons under the headline, "Is This the World's Best Melon?" with the answer in several thousand words getting down to one word, "Yes."

In his home, Mr. Hand has a framed letter from Dwight D. Eisenhower congratulating him for the superb melon the President had for breakfast on Sept. 6, 1956.

By next week, it is hoped, Hand melons will be coming in by the thousands and going out to impatient consumers throughout the Northeast who have been calling and writing to order the melons, which normally grace the tables of famous restaurants, corporate dining rooms and private clubs at this time of year.

About a third of the crop is sold locally or at a roadside stand here in Greenwich, which unlike its namesake in England and Connecticut, is pronounced "Green-witch," a third to wholesalers and the remaining third by mail order.

The mature melons, which usually weigh about three and a half pounds, will sell for 38 cents a pound at the roadside stand here on Route 29, up 5 cents from last year because of a short supply and higher costs. By mail, a box of nine melons will cost $20 plus shipping charges.

Only No. 1 melons get the white label with the red hand on it, that guarantees them to be authentic Hand melons. The No. 2 melons, which will sell for 26 cents a pound, are not as sweet and are not labeled, he said.

One interesting aspect of Hand melons is that they are varieties that anybody can buy and grow from seeds—Gold Stars and Saticoy—both available from the Joseph Harris Seed Company in Rochester.

Mr. and Mrs. Hand sat around the table on their porch here and tried to explain what made the difference between their melons and the ones that most people grow at home or buy at a supermarket.

The key difference, they said, is that their melons are picked at maturity. "If a fruit is picked before maturity, it can never develop its full potential of sweetness," Mr. Hand said.

The melon operation started with his father, Allen Furan Hand, who started with dairy cows but devoted one acre to melons in 1925 and sold them for $500.

After two years at Dartmouth, one year at the Agricultural School at Cornell, and three years in the Army, the younger Mr. Hand joined his father as a farmer after World War II.

The farm now consists of 342 acres with 100 acres more rented. On it, Mr. Hand grows sweet corn for people, field corn for cows, alfalfa for hay and soybeans for processing, in addition to melons.

"The soil is sand and relatively dry," he said. "It's ideally suited for melons and strawberries."

This afternoon Mr. Hand went back into the fields. He found one more mature melon, cut a wedge and offered it to a visitor.

"How does it taste?" he asked.

"That is good," she replied, emphasizing each word.

"That's what most people say," he said.

CHERRIES
(July 6, 1993)

LIVINGSTON, N.Y.—Kneeling on the ground, Norma Saddlewire picked ripe, dark-red cherries as fast as she could from branches just pruned from heavily laden sweet cherry trees.

Nearby, her friend Joyce Nethaway stood plucking cherries from a dwarf tree not more than 10 feet high.

Here in the orchards of the 300-acre Fix Brothers farm in western Columbia County, Robert and William Fix have made it possible for customers to pick cherries without leaving the ground.

"It makes it easy for everybody," said Robert Fix's wife, Joan, who noted that eliminating ladders also reduced the possibility of accidents and lawsuits.

One of her three sons, Robert Jr., walked through the orchard using a ladder and pruning saw to cut high branches and lay them before a steady stream of customers. He explained that pruning during the fruiting season did not harm the trees, nor did it eliminate the need for major pruning routinely done in the winter and spring.

The sweet cherry season started in late June, the beginning of the annual fruit harvest in the Hudson Valley and the rest of New York State, where growing, picking and processing fruit are a major economic enterprise.

"The industry is not only important because it brings in $200 million a year, but it is also responsible for a lot of jobs, both seasonal and permanent, as well as providing us with a lot of good eating," said Richard T. McGuire, the State Commissioner of Agriculture and Markets.

Russell Bartolotta Sr., who operates the Klein's Kill Fruit Farm near here, said the cherry crop was good this year. "They are coming in plentiful and sweet," he said. "The flavor is delicious."

In New York, Niagara County is the leading producer of sweet cherries; Columbia and Ulster Counties are major producers in the Hudson Valley. In Columbia County, in one small area near the Hudson River here, eight orchards attract thousands of pick-it-yourselfers during the harvest season.

"We have people coming from all over, from New York City, Long Island, New Jersey," said Mrs. Fix.

Mrs. Saddlewire and Mrs. Nethaway drove 80 miles from Schoharie, just west of Albany, to pick cherries. In less than half an hour, each filled three four-quart cartons with 20 pounds of fruit.

"I'm going to eat some and freeze the others," Mrs. Saddlemire said.

Under a spreading cherry tree, Mrs. Fix stood behind a scale weighing the cherries, which cost $1 a pound.

In supermarkets now, Bing cherries from Washington, Oregon and California are selling for 98 cents to $1.59 a pound.

None of a dozen pickers interviewed here indicated any concern about possible danger from pesticides despite the recent report this week by the National Academy of Science that chemical residues on fruit were potentially dangerous.

"I blame the news media for the scare stories on the pesticide dangers," Mrs. Saddlewire said.

William Fix, one of the partners in the farm, said few customers asked about pesticides.

"We spray with fungicides and insecticides six or seven times a year," he said. "If we didn't use pesticides, we would not have any people here because there wouldn't be any fruit. It would be eaten by worms, covered by scab, damaged by every insect you could think of."

PEACHES
(August 4, 1993)

CLAVERACK, N.Y.—For Chris Loken, a peach is not merely a peach.

It is Brighton or Collins, Canadian Harmony, Garnet Beauty, Raritan Rose or Tri-O-Gem.

Mr. Loken grows all those varieties and 18 more on 4,000 peach trees on his 100-acre farm here in the heart of Columbia County's fruit belt. He picks them from late July through early September and sells them at his farm stand and to other nearby farm markets.

"I like to have a new variety coming into maturity every five to seven days," he said, explaining that he sells only tree-ripened fruit. "I am always looking for a new variety to be ready for the appropriate time slot."

Mr. Loken's infatuation with peaches began when he bought his farm in 1969. It reminded him of Wisconsin, his native state, he said.

The farm stand is operated by his wife, Randae, a former model in New York City. She sells other fruits and vegetables, mostly received from nearby farmers in trade for peaches, and cherry, peach and apple pies that she bakes.

209

Before becoming a farmer, Mr. Loken, 61, was a football player at Arizona State University, a law student at the University of Wisconsin, which he left before graduation, an actor, a playwright, and a novelist. He said he was working on three novels.

"The reason I bought this farm is that I liked the physical work," he said. "I thought I would have the best of all possible worlds, working on the farm in the season and writing in the winter. But the farm is a jealous mistress: it runs you; you don't run it."

He named the farm Love Apple Farm, he said, after the French word for a wild tomato. In addition to peaches, he grows cherries, nectarines, plums, apples and pears.

Mr. Loken's peach harvesting season starts with Harrow Diamonds in July and ends about eight weeks later with Redskins, Cresthavens and Elbertas. His personal favorites are the various Haven peaches, including his newest plantings, Newhavens.

Standing near several bins of large ripe Redhavens, he said: "I think the tree-ripened concept is the most important aspect of the roadside stand business. That's what separates the roadside stand from the supermarket."

He picked up a peach and cut it into segments. Juice dripped from each cut. "Taste it," he said.

"People have forgotten what a real peach tastes like," he said, noting that supermarket peaches, like tomatoes, are bred for hardness in shipping, picked before they are ripe and often kept for days in commercial channels before reaching supermarket bins.

"We keep our fruit too long and it doesn't taste good," he said. "One of the worst offenders is those Red Delicious apples. They look beautiful, but they taste awful."

At the farm stand, the tree-ripened peaches sell for $2.50 a quart, or about $1 a pound, almost double the supermarket price.

"There's a lot more cost and effort in handling ripe fruit," Mr. Loken said. "We hand-thin the peaches when they are growing, we hand pick them when they are ripe, and we hand sort them for sale."

Although the national crop of fresh peaches will be bigger this year than last year, according to estimates by the United States Department of Agriculture, the New York crop will be "very light." The department put national production at 1.7 billion pounds last year.

California is the nation's leading grower of peaches, followed by South Carolina, Georgia, Pennsylvania and New Jersey. In New Jersey, the 1993 crop will be about 95 million pounds, up from 85 million in 1992, said Robert Battaglia, the state's agricultural statistician in Trenton.

But in New York, production will be down substantially, said Robert Schooley, chief of the State Agricultural Statistics Service in Albany. The New York crop was estimated at 10 million pounds, down 29 percent from last year's 14 million pounds. The problem was attributed to a wet fall combined with winter freeze damage that killed trees and damaged buds, the service said.

Mr. Loken, one of 300 peach farmers in New York, said the winter freeze killed all the buds on his apricot trees as well as many on his nectarine and peach trees. As a result, he has only two workers in the orchards picking peaches instead of the usual eight.

"I think I will have perhaps 40 percent of my peach crop," he said.

THE SWEET CORN CAPITAL
(August 6, 1980)

HURLEY, N.Y.—In the summertime, Hurley is the sweet corn capital of the world.

Its farmers grow more sweet corn for the fresh market than any town in Ulster County, which produces more than any other county in New York State. In turn, the state passes all the others in sweet corn output in the country that is the premier corn producer in the world. (Illinois and Iowa lead in producing the hardier kind of corn that is fed to livestock.)

Every day in August, about 20 trailer trucks, each carrying crates containing about 45,000 ears of corn covered with ice to keep them fresh—a total of 900,000 ears a day—leave the farm fields of Hurley for supermarket chain stores from Nova Scotia to Miami, from Chicago to San Antonio, as well as those in the metropolitan New York area.

"Sometimes we pick in the afternoon and they're ready for sale in New York City the next day," said Jack Gill, one of the two major growers in Hurley. The other is Davenport Farms, about two miles south of the Gill farm.

The emphasis is on speed in picking and transporting corn to market because sweet corn, more than any other vegetable, is at its best when eaten as close to picking as possible.

Standing in a field of sweet corn that stretched for almost a half-mile, Mr. Gill inspected a self-propelled picking machine that moved slowly down the

Picking corn at the Gill farm in Hurley.
Courtesy of Gill Corn Farms Inc.

rows, throwing ears into a tractor-pulled wagon that accompanied it and strewing discarded stalks and leaves on the ground.

From the field, the wagon went to a nearby packing shed, where the corn was dumped on a conveyor belt. Scores of workers on each side packed the ears into crates containing four and half dozen each. The crates passed through an iced-water bath and into a waiting trailer truck.

"Sometimes we can get the corn from the stalk to the truck in 40 minutes," Mr. Gill said.

Both the Gill farm, with 1,000 acres devoted to sweet corn, and the Davenport farm, with 1,500 acres in corn, are on the fertile soil of the alluvial plain of the Esopus Creek, facing the foothills of the Catskill Mountains to the west.

"It's one of the finest soils in New York State," said Harold C. Hogan, the Ulster County Cooperative Extension Service agent.

As a result, Ulster County's 3,500 acres of corn produce about 70 million ears a year, with a farm value of about $4 million. In New York State, about 21,000 acres are devoted to sweet corn for fresh market use, producing about 200 million ears worth $12 million to farmers. In addition, western New York has about the same number of acres producing sweet corn for processors of frozen and canned vegetables.

"It's a good crop for New York farmers," said Paul Bascomb of the State Crop Reporting Service in Albany.

Mr. Gill, who has been farming for 42 years, agreed with Mr. Bascomb and added that farming in the Esopus Valley was a good way of life.

The Gill farm is a family operation. Mr. Gill's wife, Charlotte, a Cornell graduate, operates a farm stand with the help of a daughter, Karen. The Gill's two sons, John and David, help in the commercial sweet corn business.

"It's tough business," Mr. Gill said. "It's competitive and we're at the mercy of the weather and the market. But if we can harvest our crop and sell it at a fair price, we should do all right."

Packing corn for shipment at the Gill farm.
Courtesy of Gill Corn Farms Inc.

CHAPTER 18

Funny Figures

If you were to ask the State Agricultural Statistics Service in Albany how many farms there are in New York, the answer would be 36,000. If you persisted and asked how many of them were real farms, that is, commercial farms operated by farmers not just weekender gentlemen or rural home owners, the number would drop to 18,400—that is, farms with sales of more than $10,000 a year.

For me, the changing definition and numbers of farms over the years made delightful stories, although I don't know how many other people are as fascinated as I by the manipulations of statistics and the people who keep them. Here is a sampling of the many stories I wrote over the years on the subject.

HOW MANY FARMS?
(August 3, 1976)

Albany, Aug. 2—How many farms are there in New York State?

      A. 57,000   B. 43,682   C. 32,198

The correct answer is any one of the above figures, according to farm statisticians here and in Washington, where a new national census of agriculture has just been published.

Even more peculiar to non-statisticians are figures showing that the number of farms in the state either declined 16 per cent or increased 7 per cent in the five years between 1969 and 1974, when the latest count was taken.

It all depends on the definition of what constitutes a farm—and they changed the definition for the new census. The results were a little like comparing apples, which are grown in New York, with oranges, which are not.

Back in 1969, according to the official count by the Census Bureau of the United States Department of Commerce, there were 51,209 farms in the state. But in 1974, the Census Bureau reported only 43,682, with a small footnote reading "not fully comparable because of change in farm definition."

In 1969, a farm was defined as "any place from which $250 or more of agricultural products a year is sold or any place of more than 10 acres from which $50 or more of agricultural products is sold." But for 1974, the criterion for the number of acres was dropped and the minimum value of products sold raised to $1,000 a year.

Using 354 pages of detailed tables and three appendices, the new census reported that 9.4 million acres in the state are devoted to farming, with a land and building value of $4.8 billion, producing $1.5 billion worth of crops and livestock products.

In its comparison of the number of farms meeting its new definition of $1,000 gross annual income, the census showed a growth from 40,095 in 1969 to 43,682 in 1974.

If, as all farm economists agree, the number of farms in the United States and New York is falling, how could the official figures show an increase?

Simple, according to Paul Bascomb, a farm statistician with the Crop Reporting Service in Albany. Because of inflation, many small farms that did not gross enough income to qualify as farms in 1969 have now broken the $1,000 minimum barrier.

But the Crop Reporting Service here does not accept the Census Bureau farm figures as accurate. Mr. Bascomb and his superior, Glenn W. Suter, the statistician in charge, are convinced, based on samples taken in various counties, that the Census Bureau undercounted the number of small farms.

The national census was conducted by mail, using lists compiled by various farm organizations. According to the Crop Reporting Service, perhaps as many as 20 percent of the farms in the state were missed. Therefore, it has its own farm figures.

"How many farms are there in the State?" Mr. Bascomb was asked.

"57,000," he answered.

Despite all that, many farm economists do not believe that even the new definition of a farm accurately reflects the true picture of agriculture in the state. They say that an annual gross income of at least $2,500 should be the cut-off for the definition of a "real farm."

Recognizing that viewpoint, the new census gives a count of farms meeting that definition. In 1974, those farms totaled 32,198, down 6.4 percent from the 1969 figure of 34,404.

If anyone thinks that the situation is confusing now, the word is to wait for the 1979 census. There's a bill in Congress to change the definition of a farm back to any place that grosses $600 a year, which is the 1969 figure of $250 adjusted for inflation. If that figure is adopted, the next census of agriculture will provide additional grist for the mills of confusion.

20% FEWER
(March 4, 1979)

ALBANY—Because of a change in the official definition of the word "farm," New York State lost about 20 percent of its farms on Jan. 1, with the number dropping from 56,000 to 45,000, according to statistics issued by the State Crop Reporting Service.

Similar decreases in New Jersey and Connecticut were reported as a result of a nationwide change in the definition by the United States Department of Agriculture. In New Jersey, the number of farms dropped from 8,300 to 7,600 and in Connecticut from 4,000 to 3,600.

Before the change, a farm was defined as "any place from which $250 or more of agricultural products is sold" yearly or "any place of 10 acres or more from which $50 or more of agricultural products is sold" yearly. Now a farm is "any place from which $1,000 or more of agricultural products is sold" in a year.

"It will give us a more realistic picture of our commercial agriculture in the state," said Roger Barber, the State Commissioner of Agriculture and Markets. Other experts said the new definition would not affect the eligibility of commercial farmers for Federal and state programs.

The new definition was opposed by some legislators because of the decrease in farm numbers and population that would result. It was first proposed for the 1974 nationwide Census of Agriculture, but it was deferred because of the objections until this year. A new census is now under way.

According to economists, there have been rapid changes in farming that could not be adequately described under the old definition.

Under the new definition, the number of farms in the United States dropped from 2.6 million last year to 2.37 million, and the number of acres farmed from 1,072 million to 1,052 million.

When the new Census of Agriculture is completed, the figures will show a drop in the farm population, but not a substantial drop in total cash receipts of all farms, because the farms that are no longer included produced less than one-half of 1 percent of all farm products sold.

It will also mean a significant increase in the new income per farm, according to Glenn Suter, chief statistician of the Crop Reporting Service here, because the remaining farms have considerably higher earnings, on the average, than those excluded by the new definition.

In 1977, the last year for which figures are complete, the cash receipts of all New York farms totaled $1.7 billion, with net farm income at $227 million. So far, the figures for 1978, which are not yet complete, show a small increase in both categories.

What has happened to the 11,000 farms that no longer exist as farms?

"They are still there," Mr. Barber said. "But I guess we'll have to count them as rural residences."

16% DROP
(September 6, 1987)

ALBANY—The number of farms in New York State declined 16 percent in the last five years, according to the State Agricultural Statistics Service.

It said there were 40,500 farms in the state this year, down from 48,000 in 1982. The figure was based on a sampling conducted in June.

Holstein cows at the Farber Farm in East Jewett.
Photograph by Betty Verhoeven.

"It reflects a long-term downtrend in farming in New York as well as the entire United States because of economic problems on the farm," said Paul Bascomb, a state statistician.

Declines were also reported in New Jersey and Connecticut. In New Jersey, the number of farms was put at 7,600, down from 8,700 in 1984, and in Connecticut at 3,700, down from 4,000 in 1984.

"I am surprised," said Bernard F. Stanton, professor of agricultural economics at the College of Agriculture and Life Sciences at Cornell University in Ithaca. He said more accurate figures would come out of the 1987 census of agriculture, which will begin Jan. 1.

For Professor Stanton and other farm experts, the most significant figure in the report was the number of commercial farms, producing crops for market sale.

According to the Statistical Service, a farm is defined as "a place that sells or could sell $1,000 worth of agricultural products during the year." But to farm experts, a commercial farm is one that sells more than $40,000 worth of products in a year.

By that definition, there are 14,000 commercial farms in New York, down from 16,000 in the early 80's. There are 19,000 farms that sell less than $10,000 worth of products a year and 7,500 that sell between $10,000 and $40,000 worth. They are considered hobby or part-time farms.

Despite that drop in commercial farming, agriculture remains one of the largest industries in the state, with annual sales exceeding $2.5 billion.

Dairy farms are by far the largest segment of New York agriculture. Last year they produced 11.7 billion pounds of milk, about 5.4 billion quarts, with a farm value of more than $1.5 billion. New York is the third leading dairy state in the nation, behind Wisconsin and California.

Although the Statistics Service gave no specific reasons for the decline, farm experts agree that a major cause is a drop in the number of dairy farms.

Last year, for example, 535 New York dairy farmers went out of business under a Federal "dairy termination" program instituted to cut the costs of supporting prices by buying surplus milk products. The farmers slaughtered or sold their cows for export in return for cash payments from the Federal Government.

In addition, rapidly rising land prices near metropolitan areas, particularly in the Hudson Valley north of New York City, have induced some farmers to sell to developers.

For farmers who remain in business however, the economic picture is improving. Although overall income is down from the early 1980's, last year their net income increased to $17,500 from $12,800 the year before, according to the statistical service.

AGRICULTURE STILL THRIVES
(December 4, 1994)

ALBANY—Despite a continuing drop in the number of farms, agriculture remains a flourishing industry in New York State, according to a new report by the Bureau of the Census in Washington.

In its latest census of agriculture, taken last year but reflecting figures from 1992, the bureau gave statistical evidence that agriculture is one of the largest businesses in the state, with gross annual sales of $2.62 billion.

The bureau conducts its agricultural census every five years, gathering information by mail and telephone.

The total of farm product sales, $2.62 billion, was up 7.4 percent from five years before. In the same period, production expenses rose to $2.14 billion, up 11 percent.

The new census counted 32,306 farms in New York, down 14 percent from the 37,743 reported in 1987. As expected, it also found that the number of acres being farmed also shrank from 8.4 million acres in 1987, to 7.5 million acres in 1992, about 25 percent of New York's 30.6 million acres.

The drop in farm numbers in New York reflects a national pattern of agricultural decline that has accelerated since the 1930s, when the number of American farms totaled 6.8 million. In the new census, the nationwide number dropped to 1.9 million.

But while the overall number of farms and acreage decreased both in the United States and New York, the remaining farms grew in size, improved their efficiency, and increased their sales of products like milk, grain, corn, hay, fruit and vegetables.

In New York, the average size of a farm grew from 223 acres in 1987 to 231 acres last year, and the average market value of crops sold per farm rose from $64,697 to $81,161, the Census Bureau reported.

Only 16,733 farms, or 52 percent of the total, reported a net cash gain, or profit, in their operations, the bureau said. The other 15,540, mostly small farms grossing sales of under $25,000 a year, reported losses.

The bureau defined a farm as a unit that produced or had the ability to produce sales of $1,000 a year of agricultural products. But agricultural economists say that definition inflates the actual number of working commercial farms.

"If you don't take in $50,000 a year in sales, you just can't make it as a commercial farm," said Dr. Bernard F. Stanton, emeritus professor of agricultural economics at the College of Agriculture and Life Sciences at Cornell University.

By Dr. Stanton's definition, there are only 11,300 commercial farms in New York, or 35 percent of the total reported by the Census Bureau, but they account for 92 percent of all agricultural sales in the State.

The farms with the lesser incomes are either part-time farms, recreational farms or rural residences, Dr. Stanton said.

The new census bureau report also gave a wide variety of agricultural information: the average value of the land and buildings on a farm is $283,546; farmers harvest crops on 3.5 million acres in New York State; the average age of a New York farmer is 53 years; and 12,732 farm owners say they have a principal occupation other than farming.

By far the largest segment of agriculture in New York is its 10,696 dairy farms, down from 13,840 in 1987, the report said. The $1.43 billion in dairy farm sales represented 55 percent of the value of all agricultural products sold in the state.

The census figures showed that nursery and greenhouse products were the fastest-growing part of the state's agriculture, with 2,069 farms and sales of $218 million in 1992, up from 1,795 farms with sales of $168 million in 1987, a 30 percent increase.

The counties with the largest amount of greenhouse space are Suffolk, Erie and Orange, the report said.

The census also reported that Chautauqua County had the largest number of farms, 1,600; that St. Lawrence County had the largest amount of crop land under cultivation, 164,000 acres; that Suffolk County, with sales of $134 million, sold more farm products than any other county; and that there were seven operations classified as farms in New York City: three greenhouses in Brooklyn, two in Queens and two in Staten Island.

CHAPTER 19

The Struggle to Survive

The saddest stories I wrote were about the demise of family dairy farms. As you may have noticed in the previous chapter, dairy farming is declining rapidly in the Hudson Valley, although it still remains the largest segment of agriculture in the state. Behind the statistics is the human story of selling the cows and going into some other type of farming or into a different occupation.

SELLING THE COWS
(November 20, 1987)

ANCRAMDALE, N.Y—Before dawn today, Robert Podris milked his cows for the last time and went out of the dairy farming business.

"It's a sad day here," said Mr. Podris, 41 years old, who has operated Crest Lane Farm in southeastern Columbia County since 1971. "I had a dream when I came back to the farm and now it is gone."

As two trailer trucks loaded with 54 cows pulled out of the barnyard, Mr. Podris turned to the man who bought them, Jake Huizinga of Appalachian, N.Y., and said, "I worked hard to put a good herd together and I hope you guys will benefit from it."

Mr. Podris's decision to sell his cows added to the dismal statistics of dairy farming in New York State, where in the last 10 years the number of dairy farms has fallen to slightly more than 13,000 from more than 18,000.

Despite that decline, New York remains the third-largest dairy state, behind Wisconsin and California, and dairying remains the most important segment of the state's agriculture.

But this year, the pressure on dairy farms has increased for reasons ranging from rising costs and the difficulty of finding hired hands, to a Federal buy-out program intended to cut the cost of dairy surpluses, and an influx of well-off New Yorkers buying farms as country homes.

Though the cows are gone, Mr. Podris and his wife Betty, and two sons, Jason, 13, and David, 12, expect to remain on the 160-acre farm, which has been in their family since 1907.

Mr. Podris plans to earn his living by growing and selling hay and corn, managing the farms of other people, going into real estate or possibly returning to accounting, in which he received a college degree.

Jason, who has worked on the farm with his father for the last few years, stayed home from school today to help load the cows onto the trucks.

"I'll miss them," he said.

His parents are keeping two cows and two calves so he can exhibit them at 4-H Club fairs.

Sitting at his kitchen table, Mr. Podris said the main reason he had sold his herd of cows was the poor economic situation of dairy farming in New York, and of his farm in particular. The final blow, he said, was the sudden, heavy snowstorm Oct. 4, which leveled his alfalfa and corn crops and so damaged a milking shed that it would have had to be replaced.

"It's almost impossible to be a dairy farmer if you have a debt load, and I have debts," he said. "I was not prepared to go further into debt to replace the building."

Mr. Podris, who declined to discuss the specifics of his finances, was bitter about recent price increases for milk at the retail level.

"The farmer is now getting a penny a quart more for his milk and they're charging up to 10 cents a quart more in the stores, and blaming the farmer," he said. "It's just not true that the farmer is getting the money."

Empty barns on back roads in the Hudson Valley testify to the decline of the working dairy farms. In the last two years in Dutchess County, the number has dropped to 104 from 128, while in Columbia County the number is 118, down from 150 in 1985.

One farm still operating here is the 350-acre Millerhurst Farm, which has been worked by members of the same family since 1770. It is believed to be one of the oldest farms in the state.

"I don't know how long we can hold out," said Harold Miller, who, with his wife, Kathy, and three of their sons milks 140 cows.

"I really don't see any future for farming in this area because of the pressure for land and the rising costs of land," he said. "Maybe the solution is to move to the western part of the state, where land is cheaper."

Mr. Miller has seen a decline in the agribusiness support system—the dealers in feed grains, fertilizer and farm equipment. "We're at the mercy of the remaining few dealers, and sometimes have to drive 30 miles or more to get a part," he said.

The major reason Mr. Miller is able to stay in business is that he has no labor problems. His sons James, Joseph and Michael—the eighth generation on the farm—are working with him and seem ready to carry on the family tradition.

In contrast, a few miles up the road, Francis LaCasse, 68, sold his cows this month and retired from dairy farming because he could not find reliable help, one of the major complaints of farmers.

Mr. LaCasse and his wife, Anne, have two sons. One is an accountant and the other suffers from hay fever. Neither is interested in operating the farm. Up to three weeks ago, he had two hired hands to help him milk 90 cows, but one suffered a heart attack and the other was arrested.

"I was so beat up working alone for two or three weeks, I just couldn't keep it up," he said.

STAYING IN BUSINESS
(July 30, 1990)

WESTTOWN, N.Y.—When Art and Phyllis Lain sell their last cows in August, their Orange County farm will be added to the statistics of former dairy farms. Unlike the others, though it will remain in agriculture, continuing as one of the oldest farms in the United States still being worked by the same family.

In 1785, William Lain and his wife, the former Keziah (pronounced kih-ZY-ah) Mather, started to farm here on the rolling fields of Orange County, building a house of stone for their 10 children. This year, the seventh generation of the Lains, still living in that stone house, is taking steps to make sure that the Kezialain Farm remains as a working family farm for perhaps another seven generations.

"The farm is the physical part of our existence as well as a social group," said Milton Arthur Lain 4th, one of the seventh-generation Lains. His family calls him Marty to distinguish him from his father, Milton Arthur Lain 3rd, called Art, and his newborn son, Milton Arthur Lain 5th, who is being called Milton.

"This farm has come down to us from our ancestors and we want to keep it to pass down to our descendants," Marty Lain, who is 37 years old, said.

That strong family feeling was underscored a weekend ago by a gathering of 350 descendants of William and Keziah Lain from around the United States at the ancestral farm.

The 170-acre farm, surrounding a knoll where the farmhouse sits with sweeping views of the Hudson Highlands to the east, is now owned by Art Lain, who is ready to retire at the age of 65, and his wife, Phyllis, a retired nurse. They plan to leave the farm to their six children.

Marty Lain, the only one of the children now living on the farm, will continue to operate it with the help of his wife Diana, who was raised in Astoria, Queens, and their five children.

To prevent the farm from being broken up as it passes on to the next generation, Marty's parents, he and his three brothers and two sisters have set up a living family trust to own the farm for two more generations, unless five-sixths of the signers agree otherwise.

"Theoretically, it will never be sold," said Timothy Lain, 30, one of Marty's younger brothers, who is working on the farm this summer and intends to return when he completes his college education.

Another brother, Jonathan, 25, also plans to return to the farm when he finishes his education to become a teacher.

By setting up the trust, the Lains have avoided one of the major problems of passing a farm from one generation to another—no son or daughter to carry on, or too many children so that one cannot afford to buy out the others to continue.

Some other farms in Orange County have not been able to solve that problem, said Larry Hull, the dairy specialist of Cornell University's Cooperative Extension Service based in Middletown.

"This year so far, three farmers have gone out of dairying here including one of our best farmers," he said.

"The problem was that he could not expand because of the high price of real estate and he had four sons who wanted to stay on the farm."

Land for agricultural purposes is valued at between $1,000 and $10,000 an acre. "But," he added, "no one is going to sell for that when you can get between $35,000 and $55,000 an acre for one- and two-acre plots for residential purposes."

As a result of the decline in farms, he said, Orange County is gradually being transformed from an agricultural base to a bedroom community.

The same process is evident in Dutchess and Columbia Counties on the east side of the Hudson River.

"I have been here since 1972 watching the decline," said David Tetor, the agricultural agent for the Cooperative Extension Service based in Dutchess County. "In 1972, we had 275 dairy farms and today we're down to somewhere around 60."

Mr. Tetor and Mr. Hull agreed that a major result was a loss in what they called the critical mass of support for farmers in terms of dealers for farm equipment, supplies and spare parts and a rise in complaints about farming practices from newcomers.

"The intangible structure of farming goes," Mr. Hull said. "The rural feeling of the community gets lost, farmers lose touch with one another, there is overcrowding on the roads, and you start to get calls from people complaining about the smell from farmers spreading manure or using sprays."

Despite these changes, the Lains intend to keep farming by converting the farm's dairy base to a diversified operation to take advantage of its proximity to New York City, about 60 miles to the southeast, and a rising population interested in food grown without pesticides and herbicides.

Their major cash crop is hay grown for the remaining dairy farms and an increasing number of horse farms in the area. They are raising registered

227

Holstein heifers as replacement cows, making maple syrup in the winter, raising sheep for wool, producing honey and planning to raise organic vegetables.

"We are strictly organic right now," Marty Lain said. "It's hard to do. We don't use any sprays, pesticides or chemical fertilizers. We see the benefits each year. Insect pests are under better control and the hay fields look good. Our production is down slightly, but our costs are also down. We are spending a lot less for chemicals."

Art Lain said he was convinced by his sons to try eliminating chemical sprays. "They're going to be the ones doing it when I am gone, so I believed in giving them the chance, he said. "It's worked out so far."

"We're called mavericks by the farms who continue to use the chemical herbicides and fertilizers," said his son Timothy.

THE QUIET MRS. ROCKEFELLER
(January 22, 1980)

LIVINGSTON, N.Y—"I've always wanted to farm," Margaret Rockefeller said, standing in her boots in the muck caught up by her herd of Simmental cattle on one of her newly bought farms.

"This is a serious business for me," said Mrs. Rockefeller, the wife of David Rockefeller, chairman of the board of the Chase Manhattan Bank.

"For a lot of people raising cattle might be a hobby, but not for me. I intend to make a go of it. I want to prove that it can be done as a business."

Mrs. Rockefeller, who has a home in New York City and in Pocantico Hills, near Tarrytown in Westchester County, has bought three farms here in western Columbia County and is closing soon on a fourth farm. The farms total about 800 acres for a combined price reported to be about $1 million.

"We've got all we need now," said Mrs. Rockefeller, who makes frequent trips to the farms, which are about an hour and a half ride from Pocantico. Her intention, she said, is to raise purebred Simmental cattle for breeding and resale to other ranchers and farm owners for eventual use as beef. Already, she owns 405 head and is buying more.

Once an exotic or rare breed in the United States, the Simmentals, which are dull red and white in color, are increasing in popularity in this country because of their ability to grow rapidly without excess fat and to produce large calves.

They originated in the Simme Valley of western Switzerland and are popular in that country, France and Germany, where they are used to produce both milk and beef. They are a little taller, wider and heavier than the Angus and Hereford, which are the major beef animals in the United States.

Mrs. Rockefeller, a quiet, soft-spoken woman, discussed the cattle operation in a rare interview. A private person, she has remained out of the Rockefeller limelight.

"That's not by accident," she said with a smile. "I've never done anything public before."

But now she is going into business, with a public sale of her cattle tentatively scheduled for October 1981. "You have to promote your breed," she said.

Her venture into the cattle-raising business is the first outward expression of a woman described in a recent history of the Rockefellers as "an intuitive rebel" with "an unadmitted hunger for independence" and "the most independent and spirited woman to marry into the Rockefeller family."

"I always loved the country, farming and animals," said Mrs. Rockefeller, the former Peggy McGrath of Mount Kisco, which was semi-rural at the time of her marriage in 1940. She and her husband reared six children. Gradually, she grew interested in preserving farmland and in farming itself, she said, reading and learning all she could about it until "little by little I was trapped."

About five years ago, she began to buy and raise cattle, first on an island in Maine near the Rockefeller summer home, then at Pocantico, and just recently, at her Columbia County farms. She employs 10 people in the operation, under the supervision of Don Homer, her farm manager. Stanley Vorhees Jr., a member of the family from which she bought her farms, manages the crops.

Mrs. Rockefeller said she was specializing in polled Simmentals, animals without horns. One of the bases for the breeding operation is Polled Power, a 2,300-pound bull that furnished semen for artificial insemination and some natural breeding.

"David and I are in this together financially, but he doesn't have the time for it," she said, making it plain that the farming was her business.

"That story about him coming up here to raise cattle that came out about the time he announced his retirement from the bank made him laugh. It's just not true. He's proud and he's pleased and he follows it with great interest."

Residents of the area are also following her activities with interest. They are pleased that the land is being kept in active farming. One neighbor, however, complained that she had driven a hard bargain in negotiating for the land.

And stories already are being spread about her. Mrs. Rockefeller was amused to hear that she came and went by helicopter. "I tried that once to see how long and how expensive it was and I can't come up that way any more," she said. Another story circulated locally is that she gets up on a tractor and operates it like a pro. "Not true," Mrs. Rockefeller said. "I have been on a tractor at Pocantico, but not here."

Mrs. Rockefeller came to Columbia County looking for good farmland, with room for expansion, not too far from Pocantico Hills.

By coincidence, she returned close to the place where the Rockefellers first settled in this country and from which they left to go to western New York State in the 1700s and finally to Ohio, where John D. Rockefeller made his fortune in the oil business.

Near Germantown, only a few miles from her farms, a state historical marker notes the place:

Rockefeller Home
Home of Simeon son of Diell Rockefeller
who landed at East Camp in 1733.

Peggy Rockefeller with some of her Simmental cattle.
Courtesy of Donald A. Homer, Hudson Pines Farm.

CHAPTER 20

A Miscellany

And now, several stories in and around the Hudson Valley that I particularly enjoyed—about subjects like telephone booths, covered bridges, barbecued chicken, historical markers, and the size of the United States.

STILL A NICKEL
(March 2, 1973)

CHATHAM, N.Y.—"Deposit 5 cents please." The operator's voice and the message have been confusing and surprising strangers who use telephone booths in this pocket of rural New York close to the Massachusetts border.

It is the last remaining area in New York State where it is possible to make a 5-cent local telephone call from a booth, a leftover of the era when hot dogs, beer and cigars were only a nickel each.

The booths are operated by the Taconic Telephone Company, one of 53 small privately owned telephone companies in upstate New York. The booths are in northeastern Columbia County and southeastern Rensselaer County.

In 11 different exchanges in New York State, the records show, it is still possible to make a local call for a nickel—in Berlin, Canaan, Chatham, Chatham Center, East Chatham, Lebanon Springs, Old Chatham, Petersburg, Spencertown, Stephentown and West Lebanon.

In addition, although the records of the Public Service Commission do not show it, the company, which also operates in a small area across the state line in Massachusetts, has one 5-cent booth in Hancock, Mass.

At a time when the cost of everything, including telephone calls from booths elsewhere, is rising, the company has maintained the nickel call. But its officers are not sure how long they can hold out.

"We may have to apply for a dime call this summer," according to John B. Ackley, president of the company. He conceded that he would be reluctant to lose the distinction of being the only company in the state, and perhaps in the country, to offer 5-cent service, but said that rising costs might make it necessary.

No application has been made as yet to the Public Service Commission for the increase, but it was pointed out that some companies in New York and other parts of the country have been applying to raise their 10-cent local calls to 15 or even 20 cents.

At present the nickel telephone booth call is alive also in Louisiana, according to a Bell System spokesman, who indicated, however, that some small independent phone companies throughout the country might have 5-cent booths.

Almost everywhere in the nation, the normal local phone fee is 10 cents, except in the state of Washington, where it was raised to 15 cents last year. In four states, North Carolina, Iowa, Oklahoma and Utah, applications to raise

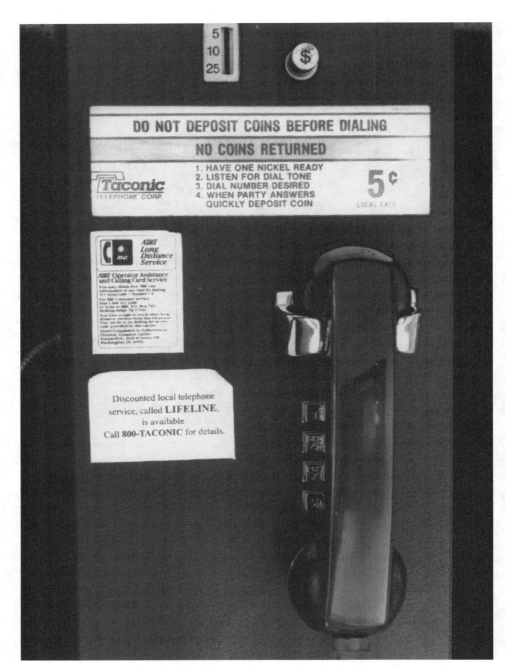

A nickel phone booth.
Photograph by B.J. Pendergast.
Courtesy of Taconic Telephone Corp.

the fee to 20 cents are pending. A similar application by the New York Telephone Company in New York was denied last year.

One of the reasons the Taconic Telephone Company has been reluctant to apply for an increase in rates is the high cost of replacing the equipment, according to William M. Barry, an official of the company. He estimated that it would cost about $575 to $600 per telephone booth, considering the main office connections, to make the switch.

Each of the 57 nickel telephone booths now in service averages 384 local calls a month, Mr. Barry said, indicating that it would be a long time for even a dime toll to pay back the capital costs of any proposed change.

If and when an increase is applied for and granted, the telephone operators in the main office here in Chatham will no longer grin when they hear an astonished voice on the other end of the line gasp, "I can't believe it."

"It happens every day," according to Mrs. Barbara McMann, one of the operators. "Somebody, usually from New York City, says, "Only a nickel? You can't get anything for a nickel any more."

If you have fond nostalgic memories of the five-cent cup of coffee and the five-cent subway fare in New York City, take heart. The five-cent telephone call still exists in the eastern reaches of Columbia and Rensselaer Counties. Almost twenty-five years after I wrote the story of the five-cent telephone booths, I called Lorinda Ackley, who succeeded her father, John B. Ackley, as president of the Taconic Telephone Company, to find out what happened to the five-cent telephone booth.

"We still have them," she replied. "And we hope to keep them."

So, if you ever are driving north on Route 22 into Canaan or Berlin, stop at a phone booth and try it. It's still a nickel for a local call.

NEW COVERED BRIDGES
(November 5, 1972)

NORTH BLENHEIM, N.Y.—Blenheim Bridge isn't exactly falling down, but it is sagging at one end.

One of the relatively few authentic covered bridges in America, it is now being restored, but it will never again return to its primary function of carrying horse-drawn traffic across Schoharie Creek.

No longer in active use, the bridge, considered to be the longest single-span, two-lane, covered wooden bridge in the world, crosses the creek just off Route 30, north of this hamlet in Schoharie County, west of Albany. A modern steel bridge, about 100 yards away, carries today's high-speed traffic across the creek.

A prime tourist attraction and a National Historic Landmark, the 232-foot Blenheim Bridge has its lovers, those who have been fighting for years to preserve it as a nostalgic reminder of the horse-and-buggy days, and more pragmatic moderns who use it as a romantic trysting grounds.

Within the last few weeks Milton S. Graton, the master bridge-builder and restorer from Ashland, N.H., has arrived on the scene, with timbers and tools, disturbing some of the trysters, but pleasing the bridge-lovers. He has an $8,600 contract to replace the rotted underpinnings and to raise the eastern end of the bridge about five inches.

Blenheim Bridge is one of the 74 covered bridges in New York, according to a current tabulation by the New York Covered Bridge Society. However, only 25 of these are historic bridges, remaining from the days when they were built for functional use. The other bridges were built in more modern times to recall the past.

Most of New York's covered bridges are privately owned. Only 17 covered bridges in the state now belong to the public and fall under the jurisdiction generally of the county in which they are situated.

In line with the current mood of nostalgia, there seems to be a country-wide trend toward building new covered bridges. In 1970, the Covered Bridge Society listed 64 covered bridges in the state; in its current listing just issued it added 10 more, all of them privately built since 1970.

According to one national tabulation, there are about 1,100 covered bridges in the United States. The newest bridge, the Henniker Bridge over the Countoocook River in Henniker, N.H., was dedicated in May. Built by Mr. Graton and his associates, it is described by bridge buffs as "the first authentic covered bridge to be built in New Hampshire in a hundred years."

Even though New England is considered by many to be the home of covered bridges, Pennsylvania has more than any other state—more, in fact that all six New England states combined. One recent survey listed nearly 300 covered bridges in Pennsylvania, with Ohio second and Indiana third.

According to Richard Sanders Allen of Round Lake, N.Y., in his book, *Covered Bridges of the Northeast*, published by the Stephen Greene Press of Brattleboro, Vt., there are about 200 covered bridges in the New England states, with more than half of them in Vermont.

The covered bridge at North Blenheim
during the January 19, 1996 flood.
Photograph copyrighted by Gross & Daley.

Moreover, Mr. Allen says, the first covered bridge in the county was built in Pennsylvania in 1805, when Timothy Palmer, a Massachusetts man, built a three-span bridge across the Schuykill River in Philadelphia and then enclosed it.

To the question of why bridges are covered, the answer, part of American folklore, has always been the same: "Why did our grandmothers wear petticoats? To protect their underpinning. Why were bridges covered? Likewise."

Although bridges were covered to protect and preserve their wooden skeletons, it was not long before Americans discovered that covered wooden bridges had another function, one that gave them the description of "kissing bridges."

The statistics on covered bridges are shifting as fire and storm destroy some of them. For example, the latest newsletter of the Covered Bridge Society reported that tropical storm Agnes washed away the Fiddlers Elbow Covered Bridge in Pennsylvania and that fire destroyed the Hurricane Shoal Covered Bridge in Georgia in June.

Delaware County, where 30 years ago there were 18 covered bridges, now has only three, all in need of repair. The Downsville bridge, built in 1854 at a cost of $1,700, now requires $250,000 for repairs, but the money is not available, according to the county.

But covered bridge restoration is a matter of priority elsewhere. The only remaining actively used covered bridge in Central and Western New York, the Newfield Bridge on Route 13, southwest of Ithaca, was restored at a cost of $42,000 and re-dedicated in July, 150 years after it was built.

The prime mover to save the Newfield Bridge was Mrs. Marie Musser of Ithaca, an officer of the Covered Bridge Society and an editor of its quarterly, the *Empire State Courier*. Mrs. Frances Withee of Rochester is president of the society and editor of the *Courier*.

The Newfield Bridge, a single-span 114 feet long, is the oldest covered bridge in New York still in active daily use. The oldest existing covered bridge in New York is the Hyde Hall or Black Bridge in Glimmerglass State Park, near Cooperstown. It was built in 1830 and is no longer in use, except as a tourist attraction.

The Blenheim Bridge, built in 1855, is being restored through the cooperation of Schoharie County and the State Historical Trust, each paying half the cost. Closed at one end with a line of bushes, it spans the creek, dry at this time of year, to a small glen with picnic tables.

Above the eastern entrance to the bridge is a sign reading "$50 fine to ride or drive this bridge faster than a walk."

Mr. Allen, the chronicler of covered-bridges lore, tells the following story of a sign that hung on the portal of a covered bridge at Hartford, Conn., differing slightly from the usual "walk your horse" sign.

A farmer's wife in a hurry to get to market on Saturday drove across the bridge too fast and was arrested. She was ready to plead guilty when her lawyer leaped to his feet.

"May it please your honor," he said, "I think the case should be thrown out of court."

"How so?" asked the judge.

"The sign on Hartford Bridge reads 'Ten dollars fine for any man to ride or drive faster than a walk on this bridge.' Your honor, the horse was a mare and my client is a woman."

In the uproar that ensued the case was dismissed.

BARBECUING CHICKEN
(August 20,1975)

ITHACA, N.Y.—Prof. Robert C. Baker is the uncrowned king of barbecued chicken in New York State and the surrounding area.

For 30 years he has been giving demonstrations of his technique in the Northeast, publishing scientific papers, conducting barbecues himself, and distributing "how to" booklets about proper barbecue procedures and his famous Cornell barbecue sauce.

More than 300,000 copies of his pamphlet "Barbecued Chicken" (price 15 cents) have been distributed, and orders come in daily to the New York State College of Agriculture and Life Sciences here, where he is Professor of Food Science and director of the Institute of Food Science and Marketing.

For 25 years, he has been the major barbecuer of chicken at the New York State Fair in Syracuse, where he and his assistants serve up to 5,000 barbecued-chicken dinners daily. He is now making plans for this year's fair, which opens on Aug. 26.

To some in the field, Professor Baker is to barbecued chicken what Colonel Sanders is to fried chicken; he did not invent it, but he has done more than any other person to popularize it.

"To say I was the first to barbecue chicken would probably be wrong," he said at a chicken barbecue here the other day. "But as far as I know, the chicken

239

barbecue as we know it today really didn't exist when I started my work at Penn State in 1946."

Professor Baker's interest in barbecued chicken arose from his attempts to develop new products and markets for the chicken industry. His investigations after World War II, first at Penn State and then at Cornell, coincided with the mass movement to the suburbs and contributed to the speedy growth of one of the major suburban cliches—the home outdoor barbecue.

When he started his inquiries, the standard method of barbecuing was the old-fashioned beef barbecue—digging a pit in the ground, starting a fire and then putting the meat on a spit or on a grill above the fire, scarcely a practical method for the amateur at home.

Professor Baker developed the first of his three major contributions to chicken barbecuing at Cornell—the above-ground method of barbecuing large numbers of chicken halves. This proved to be the key to the growth of mass commercial chicken barbecuing as it is known today.

It involved the use of portable sheets of galvanized iron, two feet high and set two feet apart, with a charcoal fire between them. The chicken halves rest on metal turning racks 22 inches above the fire, supported by the iron sides.

This method is now the standard used at fairs, church suppers and fire company dinners almost everywhere in the state. The home version involves a more permanent small outdoor fireplace or a small portable grill.

"How close should the chicken be to the fire?" he said. "It's no problem, as long as it doesn't burn. But make sure you baste the chicken each time you turn it."

He came to a more scientific conclusion in a paper, "The Effect of the Rate of Cooking on the Quality of Barbecued Chicken," published in *Poultry Science*. He found that the quality was not affected by the distance from the fire or the length of the cooking time, as long as the chicken was turned and basted frequently enough so it did not char.

"At six inches, or approximately 50 minutes of cooking time, the chicken was turned every three to five minutes to prevent burning, depending on the grill temperature," he reported. "At 22 inches, or approximately two hours of cooking, the time between turnings was 8 to 10 minutes."

"When I cook 1,000 chicken halves at one time, it's relatively easy," he said. "But when you barbecue at home, it's much more difficult because of the heat losses on home grills."

But Professor Baker's two other major contributions—the sauce and scientific findings on how far from the fire the chicken should be and how long it should be cooked—are equally applicable to the home chef as well as to commercial barbecuers.

His advice is to buy fresh broiler halves with a large amount of yellow color and some yellow fat, but he accepts the reality that most home cooks will have to buy what is available at the local supermarket. A one-pound broiler half is his ideal size for an individual serving.

For the sauce, he has one rule: Never use tomato paste or sauce as part of a chicken barbecue sauce.

"It's a sure way to burn the chicken," he said.

He also has a suggestion for those who prefer to marinate chicken in the sauce overnight before cooking: Use half as much salt as in the Cornell recipe because it penetrates so much that the chicken may become too salty.

During the cooking, Professor Baker bastes every time he turns the chicken.

His test for doneness is to pull the wing away from the body. If the meat there splits easily and there is no red color in the joint, it is done, he says.

But the time also depends on factors such as humidity, wind, wetness of soil and outdoor temperature, he said the other day, just after he had prepared 200 chicken dinners for the professionals of the trade, the New York State Poultrymen, at their annual get-together here.

He and his assistants also served cabbage salad, baked beans, rolls and a beverage, the usual country barbecued-chicken dinner.

"It was terrific," said John S. Dyson, State Commissioner of Agriculture and Markets.

"We're happy," said Mrs. Crawford Argotsinger, of Gloversville, an egg rancher. "So many times, it is red around the bones."

"The chicken was up to Bob Baker's usual fine standard," said Philip Gellert of the Pine Lane Poultry Farm in Hillsdale.

Following is Professor Baker's recipe for Cornell chicken barbecue sauce (for 10 chicken halves):

1 cup cooking oil	1 tablespoon poultry seasoning
1 pint cider vinegar	3 tablespoons salt
1 egg	1 teaspoon pepper

Professor Baker says the important thing is to use a blender to mix the egg and oil until they have an almost mayonnaise-like consistency Then add the other ingredients. The sauce should be almost white, "You can't get the same consistency with a hand beater," he says.

241

HISTORICAL MARKERS
(April 24, 1981)

BOSTON CORNERS, N.Y.—On a quiet country lane here in southeastern Columbia County near the Massachusetts state line, a blue historical marker stands out from the burgeoning green of a hayfield beyond it. In white letters, it reads:

FAMOUS PRIZE FIGHT
Won by John Morrissey over
'Yankee' Sullivan in this
area on Oct. 5, 1883, lasted
37 rounds and was witnessed
by more than 3000 persons.

Ethel Miller, the town historian of Ancram, copied the words in her notebook while her companion took the picture. A few days later she sent the data and the picture of that sign and others in the town to Florence Mossman, the county historian, who is compiling a countywide record.

Mrs. Miller is one of several hundred local historians who are cooperating in a new inventory of roadside historical markers throughout New York State. The last inventory, made in 1949, showed 3,000 markers.

"But we know that figure is not accurate," said Edmund J. Winslow, a senior historian in the State Division of Historical and Anthropological Services in Albany. "Many signs have been put up since that inventory and many have been taken down."

For example, the inventory does not list the Morrissey-Sullivan fight sign, which was erected in 1955, or another one erected in 1979 along Route 3 in Ancram marking the site of the "Grist Mill Defiance" built in 1775 by the Livingston family.

Similar finds are being made by local historians in all parts of the state. In Erie County, about 40 new signs were erected during the Bicentennial celebration in 1976, according to Walter Steesy, president of the Heart of the Lakes Publishing Company in Interlaken, N.Y., which will publish a complete record of the historical markers next year, in cooperation with the state.

But signs are disappearing. On Staten Island, where the 1949 inventory listed 10 signs, only three are still standing. One marks the burial place of Dutch settlers on Richmond Avenue; another marks Perine House on Richmond Road, and the third the Conference House near Philip Avenue

Street where Benjamin Franklin, John Adams and Edmund Rutledge met with British officers in 1776.

On Staten Island, the explanation is simply that the missing signs "disappeared." But in New York City generally, the greatest enemy of historical markers is vandalism, according to the Landmarks Preservation Commission. In upstate areas, snow plows and vehicles frequently damage the roadside markers.

The out-of-date state inventory shows 36 markers in Manhattan, 25 in the Bronx, 17 in Queens and 4 in Brooklyn, in addition to those on Staten Island, and scores in nearby Nassau, Suffolk and Westchester Counties.

At present, the new survey in the metropolitan area is being made in all the counties except New York. Eugene Bochman, the county historian, who is also the City Commissioner of Records and Information Services, said that he had not been asked to make an inventory by the state and that, in any case, he questioned a city agency doing research for a proprietary publisher.

In the city, most of the markers are in parks, with ample room for people to stop and read them. But the upstate signs, which usually are along the side of a road, sometimes pose a danger for motorists who slow down to read them.

One of the signs in New York City is in Inwood Park along the Hudson in upper Manhattan. It reads:

> HENRY HUDSON
> In the Half-Moon, anchored
> off this point, September
> 1609. Indians of Nipnichsen
> on Spuyten Duyval Hill
> attacked Hudson's crew

But perhaps the best known of markers in the city refers to a tragedy. A sign near Grant's Tomb in Riverside Park reads:

> AN AMIABLE CHILD
> Grave of St. Claire Pollock
> Killed by a fall over cliff
> 1797. Plot deeded by Uncle
> George Pollock, to Cornelia
> Verplanck to preserve

Financing for roadside historical markers started and stopped with a one-time appropriation of $10,000 by the State Legislature in 1927 as part of the

Road marker showing site of the Morrissey-Sullivan fight in Ancram.
Photograph by Harold Faber.

state's sesquicentennial celebration. Between 1927 and 1932, the state erected several thousand markers at a price between $2 and $5 each.

Although the state does not pay for markers anymore, about two dozen a year are being put up, Mr. Winslow said, either through his office or by local officials.

Applications can be made through his office, which checks the wording and historical accuracy and which reserves the right to reject any application that it deems "frivolous or of questionable historical merit," he said. The cost: $150 each, paid by the applicant.

A GROWING NATION
(December 15, 1991)

The United States is bigger today that it has ever been.

To be exact, the country is 168,655 square miles larger than it was in 1980, an addition bigger than the State of California, according to figures just published by the Census Bureau.

But the growth did not result from geographic expansion or the acquisition of new land. It came about because the Census Bureau changed its definition of what constitutes the area of each of the 50 states. Under this new definition, the United States now has a total area of 3,787,425 square miles.

In 1980, the last previous overhaul of the nation's geographic extent, the Census Bureau, using what were then the latest maps of the United States, the Geological Survey, came up with a national total of 3,618,770 square miles. That was slightly higher than its previous figure of 3,615,211 square miles, which was calculated in 1960, a year after Alaska and Hawaii were admitted to the Union.

But in the 1980 census, the Census Bureau followed the pattern of previous censuses by including ponds with fewer than 40 acres and streams less than one-eighth of a mile in width as part of the land area, while ignoring territorial waters.

Last year, in an effort to make its figures more accurate, the Census Bureau reclassified the small bodies of inland water category, re-computed some areas and corrected some errors. It also included, for the first time in a census, the oceanic, or territorial, waters abutting coastal states to the three-mile international limit.

Robert Marx, chief of the geographic division of the Census Bureau, said the territorial waters were added because the three-mile limit "made a nice seamless edge" to a new computerized map of the United States, put together by the Census Bureau and the Geological Survey.

As a result, in the 1990 census the land area of the United States dropped to 3,536,342 square miles from 3,539,289 in the previous census, but the water area increased to 251,083 square miles from 79,481.

In the new state statistics, the most striking change came in Michigan, which went from being the nation's 23rd largest state to the 11th. Its area increased more than 65 percent, from 58,527 to 96,810 square miles, because it now officially includes some of the waters of four of the Great Lakes that it abuts—Michigan, Huron, Erie and Superior.

Only Hawaii, which is surrounded by the Pacific Ocean, showed a larger percentage gain, nearly 69 percent. Hawaii's area increased to 10,932 square miles from 6,471, making it the 43rd largest state in the Union, rather then the 47th largest.

"Generally, it's interesting information of interest mainly to trivia buffs," said Don Hirschfeld, chief of the Census Bureau's geographic assistance staff in Washington.

As far as Mr. Hirschfeld and other public officials could tell, the new sizes and rankings of the states will have no effect on the allocation of Federal money to the states.

But Mr. Hirschfeld said the new numbers were important because they provided the latest information in answering many questions about geographic matters that his office receives: What is the largest state? The smallest state?

"There is a great interest out there, for whatever purpose," he said.

For trivia buffs, the new measurements show that, despite the changes, Alaska remains the nation's largest state, and Rhode Island the smallest.

Alaska grew to 656,424 square miles from 591,004 because of the addition of 65,420 square miles, mostly of territorial water along its long coastline on the Pacific Ocean, the Arctic Ocean and the Bering Sea.

Rhode Island also grew by 333 square miles, to 1,545 square miles from, 1,212, mainly because of the inclusion of the coastal waters of Block Island Sound, Rhode Island Sound and the Atlantic Ocean.

New York rose in the ranking of states, to 27th from 30th, with a 5,367 square mile increase to 54,475. This increase was attributed largely to the inclusion of some of the waters of Lake Ontario, the St. Lawrence River, Long Island Sound, and the Atlantic Ocean.

New Jersey dropped a notch, from 46th to 47th despite a gain of 935 square miles for a total of 8,722. Connecticut increased 526 square miles, to 5,544.

Texas, the nation's second largest state, showed a modest increase of 1,794 square miles, and now totals 268,601 square miles. California, the third largest state, also increased, by 5,001 square miles, making its new total 163,707.

The new computations show slight losses in overall area for three states and the District of Columbia because of recomputations and correction of errors in previous censuses. Arkansas lost five square miles, making its area now 53,182 square miles; Oklahoma lost 53 square miles, to 69,903; West Virginia one square mile, to 24,231; and the District of Columbia one square mile, to 68.

But the new figures for all the states are not engraved in stone, the Census Bureau says. It is already planning to update, correct and change them again in the census for the year 2000.

CHAPTER 21

Dining and Restaurant Guide

One of the pleasures of covering stories up and down the Hudson Valley was the opportunity to eat in restaurants from the northern suburbs of New York City up to the Albany-Troy area (and it still is, even though I am no longer on the news trail and going out to lunch is a hobby now.) In the good old days before I completed an assignment, I always asked people to name the best restaurants in the area—and my wife and I tried them.

In the preceding pages, I have deleted the dining out sections of many articles, especially those particularly devoted to travel, because we have found that prices have risen dramatically upward, some restaurants have closed, and many others have changed ownership and chefs, making them quite different from what they were when my pieces were written. Instead, I have updated the data that follow as my own culinary guide to the Hudson Valley. It has two parts: one, a report on our favorite restaurants, and, two, a compact section devoted to addresses and phone numbers.

Now a few cautionary words: Many of the restaurants serve dinner only, so call to find out if it is open if you want to go to lunch—and to get directions. Our policy is to avoid restaurants on weekends, when they are crowded, which, of course, is not possible in many cases, but reservations are a good idea on weekends.

Also, I have not included restaurants in Westchester and Rockland Counties because, in the bureaucracy of *The New York Times* they were, and are, considered suburban, and thus outside the scope of a Hudson Valley correspondent. Of course, there are many other fine restaurants in the Hudson Valley, which for one reason or another I have not yet tried, so the list includes only personal favorites that I have visited. And here they are:

Best-all-around: the Stewart House in Athens; the Paramount Grill in Hudson; and the Plumbush in Cold Spring.

Best Sunday brunch: elegant and expensive, Xaviar's in Garrison, which was $32 a person when we went; moderate, the Hotel Thayer at West Point,

$17.75; and inexpensive (and often crowded and noisy), the Rolling Rock Cafe in Rhinebeck, $6.95.

Best shepherd's pie and other English dishes like fish and chips and sherry trifles: the Dickens Pub in Poughkeepsie.

Best Chinese: the China Rose in Rhinecliff, which, unfortunately, is open for dinner only. My favorite there—the whole baked red snapper, enough for two people, and its dragon noodles. For lunch: the Mill House Panda in Poughkeepsie and in Rhinebeck.

Best wurst: profound regrets that my current anti-cholesterol diet precludes the luscious liverwurst and cheese platters at Schneller's in Kingston.

Best Italian: for an inexpensive red sauce lunch, Coppola's in Hyde Park; Lombardo's in Albany, and Mama Rosa's in Hudson.

Best French: Le Petit Bistro in Rhinebeck; La Rive, off Route 23A near Catskill, both open for dinner only; and Le Canard Enchaineé in Kingston, open for both lunch and dinner.

Best elegant lunch: the Plumbush in Cold Spring.

Best pizza: La Parmigiana in Rhinebeck, which occupies an old church.

Best Mexican: the Armadillo in Kingston for lunch. Its tortilla chips are home made and excellent.

Best cajun: Spanky's in Poughkeepsie.

Best seafood: Mariner's Harbor in Highland, nearly under the old abandoned railroad bridge across the Hudson River, more for the view than the food; and the Real Seafood Company on bustling Wolf Road in Albany.

Best hamburgers: the Raccoon Salon in Marlboro; the Paramount Grill in Hudson; and, surprisingly, the Armadillo in Kingston.

Best elegant dinner: Harrald's in Stormville, where the price fixed dinner when we went was $72, but on several midweek nights they serve a smaller version for less. By reservation only.

Best roast beef: the Stage Stop in Bangall. Its barbecued ribs are excellent, too.

Best ropa vieja (that's pot roast prepared Cuban style): Justin's in Albany.

Best diner: the Palace in Poughkeepsie; the College in New Paltz; and the Daily Planet in Lagrangeville.

Best river view: Mariner's Harbor in Highland; the Castaway in Troy.

Best mountain view: Mohonk Mountain House near New Paltz.

Best barbecued pork sandwich: Bois d'arc in Red Hook; it also has the best macaroni and cheese side dish I ever ate.

Best patisserie: the Calico in Rhinebeck; it's a small restaurant, too, and very good.

Best place to take visiting tourists: the Beekman Arms in Rhinebeck, which boasts of being the oldest continuously operating tavern in America; and the Culinary Institute of America, with four restaurants operated by students—the least pretentious is St. Andrew's Cafe.

Best picnic sites: the Clermont State Park in Germantown and Bard Rock at the Vanderbilt Mansion State Historic Site in Hyde Park, both with wonderful views of the Hudson River.

And here is a more complete list of recommended restaurants in the Hudson Valley, with addresses and telephone numbers:

Albany
Lombardo's	518 462 9180	121 Madison Street
Jack's Oyster House	518 465 8854	42 State Street
Justin's	518 462 7008	301 Lark Street
La Serre	518 463 6056	14 Green Street
Real Seafood Company	518 458 2068	195 Wolf Road
Scrimshaw	518 869 8100	660 Shaker Road

Athens
Stewart House	518 945 1357	2 North Water Street

Bangall
Stage Stop	914 868 1042	Hunns Lake Road

Catskill
La Conca D'oro	518 943 3549	440 Main Street
La Rive	518 943 4888	Old Kings Road

Cold Spring
Hudson House	914 265 9355	2 Main Street
Plumbush	914 265 3904	Route 9D
Vintage Cafe	914 265 4726	91 Main Steet

Fishkill
North Street Grill	914 896 1000	Main Street

Garrison
Bird and Bottle Inn	914 414 3000	Route 9
Xaviar's	914 424 4428	Route 9D

Greenville
The Greenville Arms   518 966 5219   Route 32

Highland
Mariner's Harbor   914 691 6011   On the river, off Route 9W

Hopewell Junction
Stockyard   914 221 3444   Route 82

Hudson
Charleston   518 828 4990   517 Warren Street
Mama Rosa's   518 828 6324   614 Warren Street
Paramount Grill   518 828 4548   225 Warren Street

Hyde Park
Coppola's   914 224 9113   Route 9
Culinary Institute   914 224 7969   Route 9

Kingston
Armadillo   914 339 1550   97 Abeel Street
Dreisen's Bakery   914 338 7503   109 West Front St.
Le Canard Enchaineé   914 339 2003   276 Fair Street
Schneller's   914 332 9800   61 John Street

Marlboro
Raccoon Saloon   914 236 7872   Route 9D

Newburgh
Chianti   914 561 3130   362 Broadway

Poughkeepsie
Caesar's   914 471 4857   2 Delafield Street
Dicken's English Pub   914 454 7322   796 Main Street
Mill House Panda   914 454 2530   289 Mill Street
Spanky's   914 485 2294   86 Main Street

Red Hook
Bois d'arc   914 758 5992   29 West Market Street

Rhinebeck

Beekman Arms	914 876 7077	Route 9
Calico Restaurant	914 876 2749	9 Mill Street
La Parmigiana	914 876 3228	Route 9
Le Petit Bistro	914 876 7400	8 East Market Street
Mill House Panda	914 876 2399	19 West Market Street
Rolling Rock Cafe	914 766 7655	Route 9 North

Rhinecliff

| China Rose | 914 876 7442 | 100 Schatzel Avenue |

Saugerties

| Cafe Tamayo | 914 246 9371 | 89 Partition Street |

Stormville

| Harrald's | 914 878 6545 | Route 52 |

Tivoli

Cafe Pongo	914 457 4403	69 Broadway
Santa Fe	914 757 4100	52 Broadway
Stoney Creek	914 754 4117	76 Broadway

Troy

Old Daley Inn	518 235 2656	499 Second Avenue
Lo Porto	518 273 8846	85 Fourth Street
Castaway	518 273 2244	377 River Street

West Point

| Hotel Thayer | 914 446 4731 | Academy Grounds |

INDEX